UP ALL NIGHT

Also by Lisa Napoli

*Radio Shangri-La: What I Discovered on My Accidental Journey
to the Happiest Kingdom on Earth*

*Ray & Joan: The Man Who Made the McDonald's Fortune
and the Woman Who Gave It All Away*

UP ALL NIGHT

TED TURNER, CNN, AND THE BIRTH OF 24-HOUR NEWS

LISA NAPOLI

ABRAMS PRESS, NEW YORK

Library of Congress Control Number: 2019939895

ISBN: 978-1-4197-4306-1
eISBN: 978-1-68335-826-8

Printed and bound in the United States
10 9 8 7 6 5 4 3 2 1

Abrams books are available at special discounts when purchased
in quantity for premiums and promotions as well as fundraising
or educational use. Special editions can also be created to
specification. For details, contact specialsales@abramsbooks.com
or the address below.

Abrams Press® is a registered trademark of Harry N. Abrams, Inc.

ABRAMS The Art of Books
195 Broadway, New York, NY 10007
abramsbooks.com

In memory of my father, Vincent,
a news junkie before anyone called it that

and

For "the other" Ted, my one and only,
who voluntarily gave up the sets

Someday, I'm going to be the first person in the history of the world to talk to everyone. I'll be able to talk to all the world's leaders and bring peace to the world through television.

—Ted Turner

Contents

March 2001   1

CHAPTER ONE: The Little Girl in the Well, 1949   5
CHAPTER TWO: The Lunatic Fringe   13
CHAPTER THREE: Girdle 'Round the Earth   36
CHAPTER FOUR: Watch This Channel Grow!   61
CHAPTER FIVE: Captain Outrageous   85
CHAPTER SIX: "No News Is Good News"   109
CHAPTER SEVEN: Every Drop of Blood   136
CHAPTER EIGHT: Reese's Pieces   162
CHAPTER NINE: Until the End of the World   193
CHAPTER TEN: Duck Hunting with Fidel   207
CHAPTER ELEVEN: The Little Girl in the Well, 1987   231

AFTERWORD: June 2000   241
APPENDIX: Timeline   247
NOTES   251
BIBLIOGRAPHY   283
ACKNOWLEDGMENTS   291
INDEX   295

March 2001

His handsome face tired, his silver hair and mustache now fully white—his speech as bombastic as when reporters first anointed him the "Mouth of the South," a nickname he despised—Ted Turner grabbed the Goldsmith Career Award for Excellence in Journalism as he ascended the stage at the Forum of Public Affairs at Harvard University.

He found the honor amusing. Before him, it had been bestowed on luminary broadcast journalists like Ted Koppel, Mike Wallace, Barbara Walters, and Lesley Stahl—venerable practitioners whose networks Ted had charged after with nuclear force, changing the very nature of TV. Though he'd never reported a story in his life—though he'd long ago derided news as "evil"—he supposed he had been a journalist of sorts. After all, he still drew a paycheck from a media company, Time Warner, which had acquired his Turner Broadcasting years earlier, including the service for which he was being feted that night—CNN, a source of news to two billion people around the globe. Heck, way back in grade school, he'd hawked newspapers at a streetcar stop for a penny a pop. Didn't that count as journalism?

Even as a kid, he'd been a salesman above all else, shouting, "EXTRA!" to the passersby to suggest that the latest issue promised big, breaking news.

"It wasn't an extra," he confessed to the audience, who lapped up his irreverence, "but I was trying to sell these goddamned papers."

After a few too many drinks at the pre-event dinner party, he propped up the framed commendation on the seat of a chair next to the podium. The citation proceeded to fall to the floor. He left it there.

"It won't stand up," he said, "and I'm having trouble doing the same myself."

As much as the cocktails, the dismal facts of life since the dawn of the new millennium had knocked him off-kilter.

When clocks ticked into the year 2000, the world had not imploded, as many had expected it might, but Ted's universe had.

Days into the new year, his third wife, the actress Jane Fonda, had moved out. He'd honored her wish that he not run for president of the United States, a job he wanted if only to promote his passion for environmental preservation. Fonda had said she'd leave him if he ran, so he didn't—she went ahead and split anyway. He loved her still.

"The best lay I ever had," he'd lamented to the dean's wife earlier that evening—the ultimate compliment by this inveterate ladies' man.

Just a few days after that personal loss, a different life-altering bombshell exploded, this one dropped by Time Warner chairman Gerald Levin. Levin had altered the course of Ted's life before. In 1975, he'd sparked a media revolution when he catapulted a faltering pay-cable service called HBO into space—then a brand-new frontier. When Ted learned about this pioneering use of a satellite to transmit a television signal, he was inspired to make the copycat move for his little independent station in Atlanta. This changed everything for him, and for the station, and, ultimately, for all of television.

Swept up in this new century by the "irrational exuberance" of the World Wide Web, Levin, now Ted's boss, had negotiated the sale of their company to a preposterous suitor, the red-hot America Online. Ted had his doubts, but he no longer had any say. Wall Street so disapproved of this merger that Time Warner's stock tanked. In the past months alone, his personal fortune had shrunk by $3 billion.

Just a week earlier, he'd suffered another incalculable loss—of power. He'd been shunted aside into an emeritus role. The networks he'd created, including CNN, would no longer fall under his control.

Absent his job, his wife, or a healthy slice of his fortune, now he had to stand tall here in Cambridge at the august university that had, decades earlier, rejected his application for admission.*

"If I had come to college here, God knows what I would have accomplished," he mused, as the audience erupted in laughter. Because, aside from the recent tumult, no one could argue that his achievements had been anything but formidable.

In introducing Ted, his Harvard host extolled him as a "visionary" in the spirit of the savior of the venerable *New York Times*, Adolph Ochs, or, better yet, Elvis. Elvis Presley changed *music*. But Ted had done one better. He'd changed *America*.

Yet few in that audience remembered—if they ever knew at all—the improbable empire-building that had emboldened Ted to believe he could start the very first all-news channel in 1980. Hardly anyone thought the idea could work, much less last—much less that a rogue like him could pull it off. Then, there was the parade of obstacles that had threatened to derail him every step of the way.

That evening, the audience at Harvard wasn't concerned with history, especially history they didn't even know. They were worried about CNN's future and what would become of the news network they relied on now that Ted would no longer be a part of it. Layoffs had just been announced, and the accelerating power of the Internet loomed large. How would *that* change CNN? a student asked. It already had, Ted responded, his voice tinged with regret. But, he added, he had no crystal ball. All he could do was hope for the best.

---

* After his rejection from Harvard, Ted attended Brown, a school to which he reminded the audience he'd just gifted $100 million—the same sum he'd given Jane Fonda after she'd left. She turned around and pledged $12.5 million of that to fund a gender studies program at Harvard's Graduate School of Education. (The award was later rescinded for various reasons, most notably the collapse of the stock.) "Goddamn it," Ted groused. "I want you to know it's my money. I love her still."

Before the digital revolution unleashed a never-ending tsunami of information; back before videotape and portable camera gear and time-code editing and live shots allowed television news to rev more quickly and vividly than ever; way back when the world was a slower, quieter place and television's crackling black-and-white glow began to muscle radio for mindshare, Ted had been a little boy with a ferocious disciplinary problem about to be shipped off to military school, selling newspapers to commuters on their way home from work—fretting, as he voraciously memorized the stories of kings and battles and explorers, that there were no new worlds left for him to conquer. It was as if the medium of television was waiting for him to come along to upend it.

"I was like Columbus when he left Spain for the new world," Ted told the amused audience, wistful for that strange and wonderful and faraway moment in time. "He didn't know where he was going when he started, he didn't know where he was when he got there, and he didn't know where he'd been when he got back."

CHAPTER ONE

The Little Girl in the Well, 1949

That late Friday afternoon in April, before the world shook for one family and shrank for everyone else, the sun beamed clear over an open field in San Marino, California, a perfect day for carefree outdoor play. Two sets of cousins frolicked in a footrace with a fox terrier named Jeepers, while their mothers prepared dinner, keeping an eye on the kids out the kitchen window.

At a quarter after four, the day turned instantly dark, as the kids stomped inside—only three of them.

"Where's Kathy?" asked the girl's mother, Alice, about her three-and-a-half-year-old daughter. Neither Kathy's sister, Barbara, age nine, nor her cousins Stanley, ten, and Gus, five, had an answer.

Alice jumped in her car and rode up the street, assuming the little girl had strayed toward the nearby school and a swing set she loved. Not a trace of the blond-haired, blue-eyed Kathy Fiscus. The family frantically fanned out across the field, calling her name. As they approached an uncapped well, fourteen inches wide, circled by weeds, they could hear her cries beneath the earth.

"She's here!" Gus shouted.

Police and fire crews were summoned. Awaiting their arrival, the frantic mother dropped a telephone cord into the narrow hole, amazed that her daughter could fit down there and certain she could hoist her out. No luck.

"Can you hear me, Kathy?" her mother pleaded. "Are you standing up?"

"Yes, Momma," the child responded, crying.

"Are you lying down?"

"Yes, Momma."

Suddenly, as if conjured from the heavens, half a million dollars of equipment arrived with a host of skilled workmen who began tearing into the earth in pursuit of this child they didn't know and had never seen.

Law enforcement issued a call to the nearby Santa Anita racetrack in search of a brave jockey willing to burrow down to bring the girl to the surface. Central Casting's files were scoured for diminutive actors who might volunteer. No one who answered the call was small enough. With dusk about to fall, film studio 20th Century Fox dispatched fifty towering klieg lights so would-be rescuers could work into the night.

The fracas intensified with the arrival of the press corps—reporters and photographers from each of Los Angeles's five dailies and more than a dozen other newspapers from the nearby communities that dotted the Southern California landscape. Film crews from the newsreels and radio reporters added to the pack. They knocked on the neighbors' doors, hoping to use their phones to dictate dispatches back to their editors. Couriers stood poised to ferry exposed film to area newsrooms so that images of this drama could be developed and transmitted around the globe over the wire.

As word spread about the trapped little girl, hundreds, and soon thousands, of curious onlookers began to gather. So, too, did opportunistic vendors, who arrived to peddle coffee and ice cream to the public, turning the usually quiet street into a circus. To keep the volunteer rescue crew hydrated and nourished, a Red Cross canteen mushroomed near the excavation site—a reminder that this nail-gripping drama was not theater or frivolity; it was a real-life, fraught scene of distress.

Miles away, over on Loma Linda Avenue in Hollywood, the phone rang at the home of KTLA station manager Klaus Landsberg. Since his childhood in Germany, he'd displayed a passion for electronics, building his first radio set at just six years old and later earning two degrees in engineering. Though he had been marginalized because of his Jewish heritage, so great was his knowledge of technology that he was permitted, at age twenty, to work on the pioneering crew assembled to televise the 1936 Olympic Games in Berlin. Adolf Hitler believed that this new medium of television was a "cultural development that promises to be of unsuspected importance to mankind."

Landsberg escaped the Third Reich thanks to his invention of an aircraft navigation system, which earned him a coveted visa to emigrate. After arriving in New York Harbor, he scored an invitation to work in the laboratory of Philo T. Farnsworth, one of the inventors of television, who was racing to bring this radio-with-sound creation to a mass audience. Mere invention was one sort of achievement; popularizing it and commercializing it for the marketplace was quite another.

Next came the command to assist with TV's dazzling public debut at the 1939 World's Fair. Millions of Americans who visited the grand pavilions erected in the New York City borough of Queens were enthralled by their first glimpse at this new medium about which they'd only read.

When the film studio Paramount Pictures decided it needed to experiment with television on its brand-new soundstages in Hollywood, Landsberg had been the natural choice. In 1941, carrying two suitcases stuffed mostly with electronic gear, he hopped a train west.

The blank canvas before him was thrilling, from building the station to inventing and producing all manner of new programs that would fill the brief programming day—debates, discussions of community issues, musical variety shows. Among his talent discoveries was the bandleader Lawrence Welk.

The West Coast was still an island sequestered from the television production revving up in New York. The almighty phone company AT&T had agreed to drop out of the business of producing TV in exchange for the exclusive right to build out an essential "golden web" of high-speed lines necessary to transport it from city to city. It would be several years, at least, before California was connected.

Landsberg's air, then, was entirely his own. Each day presented a fresh petri dish for experimentation in this new frontier. He relished start-up mode; no technological obstacle seemed insurmountable. If a tool didn't exist, he'd set about inventing it. "The word 'cannot' simply did not exist in his vocabulary," said his adoring and tolerant wife,

Evelyn, who quipped that she found herself in a ménage à trois with her husband's mistress—television. So addicted was Landsberg to TV that he'd proposed to her from high atop Mount Wilson on a visit to the station's transmitter. On their wedding day, after a celebratory lunch, he'd popped into the studio to attend to an equipment malfunction.

Then came that Friday, when collective eyes and concern focused on the plight of young Kathy Fiscus. Callers who'd heard the radio bulletin jammed KTLA's switchboard, pleading for the station to cover the rescue. The growing attachment to radio had primed the public to rely on it for up-to-the-minute news. But this was a story they wanted to see as well as hear.

Most of the nation's television stations—in 1949, there were fewer than a hundred—didn't carry much in the way of news. What there was of it on TV consisted of a man sitting behind a desk reading headlines from the local paper. The scant visual might be a still photograph, held up for the camera, or two-day-old newsreel footage. The technology didn't allow for much more than that. Conveying commercial messages, though, was a cinch. In the midst of his fifteen-minute report, the newsreader might pause for a word from the sponsor, picking up a soup bowl handed to him by a stagehand and enjoying a few slurps.

The tone had been set nationally. Those in the east who were able to tune into NBC's nightly fifteen-minute national news couldn't miss the ubiquitous logo of cigarette maker Camel, which sponsored the broadcast, allowing the suave host, John Cameron Swayze, to "hopscotch the world for headlines" from the comfort of his news set.

Journalists and executives alike agreed that news was something better covered by the papers, radio, and newsreels. Besides, the best of them didn't wish to be bothered or demeaned by this nascent medium.

Like most of his colleagues, Landsberg was certain viewers who'd heard a story on TV would surely clamor to read more, leading to a boom in newspaper readership. Television's true raison d'être, many believed, was as an extension of movies—a medium for entertainment and escapism. Not that so many people could tune in. Though each day a thousand new sets were sold across America, still only 1 percent of the country owned a TV. Fewer than twenty thousand of them could be found in the metro area's four million homes. A basic television cost $385—a tenth of the average annual salary, and a third of the price of the far more utilitarian purchase of a new car.

Still, the arrival of television was so wildly anticipated that in some towns without a station yet to service it, eager consumers bought and installed the clunky consoles just so they'd be ready.

The size of the audience wasn't the point to Landsberg, especially at this moment, with an urgent matter unfolding. The rescue of a little girl seemed tailor-made for the medium he loved and was helping to invent. As it became clear that it would take more time than expected to release her from her prison, he rerouted his experimental mobile unit from a wrestling match in downtown Los Angeles to the drama a dozen miles away in San Marino, and headed out there himself. Police attempted to keep back the crew, but Landsberg persisted. Beaming out pictures on television, he explained, would keep away more looky-loos than a physical barricade.

The field where men labored to save Kathy's life now served as his living television laboratory. Positioning his mobile truck for a perfect line of sight toward the mountaintop transmitter, he then begged a worker from the electric company to let him hitch up to a power line. No such thing as a portable television camera existed, so the men hoisted studio cameras that weighed hundreds of pounds onto tripods, then jury-rigged some gear in order to transmit pictures and sound simultaneously—no simple feat. By the time they were ready to go live, rival station KTTV, co-owned by the Times Mirror Company (owners of the *Los Angeles Times*) and CBS, pulled onto the scene.

Absent a news staff, Landsberg pressed veteran sports announcer Bill Welsh and an eager young staffer named Stan Chambers into service. But what was there to say? No one had ever broadcast live from the scene of a developing story. The rescue operation was slow and repetitive, and there wasn't much to see above the ground. The two men asked their boss how to fill the time.

"Pretend it's a sporting event and give them the play-by-play," he advised. Landsberg helped by observing the crowd and feeding human interest bits to his newly anointed field reporters. They, in turn, sought out interviews with bystanders, conversations which provided more emotion than fact. But the emotion was precisely what made this compelling television.

Four miles east, in Temple City, a twenty-five-year-old man named Clyde Harp found himself captivated by the images flickering on his brand-new $450 RCA receiver. With alarm, Harp noticed that the workers were digging in a way that could cause the trapped girl harm. A father himself, he rushed out to his car, drove over to the scene, and jumped the fence to join the rescue team. Within moments, another of the crew was admonishing Harp to quit swearing—the viewing audience could hear his foul language.

Suddenly, a TV didn't seem such a frivolous luxury; rather, it was a crucial lifeline to the community. People dragged mattresses into their living rooms so they could stay up all night for what they hoped would be the happy conclusion of the ordeal. Television stations usually ceased broadcasting by midnight or so, but given these circumstances, they couldn't possibly. Curious onlookers gathering in front of appliance store windows begged shop owners to please stay open, or at least leave the set on, so they could watch till the story's end. Even Kathy's anguished parents sat in front of the television at a neighbor's house before their terror overwhelmed their desire to peer in on the operation. Then, they retreated to the cocoon of safety in a police car to wait for word in silence.

During this aching interlude, they were hardly alone. Anxious citizens jammed the switchboards of the nation's newspapers and radio stations—some back-seat driving the rescue crews, others, mostly, expressing plaintive concern. "I hope you don't mind if I keep calling you through the night," one man told the operator at the *Pittsburgh Post-Gazette*. "I'm the father of three little ones, you know, and this story about poor Kathy really hit me." The *Dallas News* received a million calls; the *Albuquerque Journal* said it hadn't had such reader interest since the first atom bomb had been exploded in the state four years earlier. Wire service reports trumpeted the girl's plight around the world, elevating this private tragedy to international concern.

Not everyone found this media frenzy enthralling. A journalism professor from the University of California declared the marathon of coverage "in bad taste." The state news agency of Czechoslovakia refused to run the story, deriding it as "purely sensational" and "without educational value." "Czech Press Cold to Kathy's Fate," scolded the headline in the *Baltimore Sun*. Those communists had no heart.

The collective eyes and worries of the planet weren't enough to save the poor little girl. Forty hours after she'd disappeared, and twenty-seven hours after live television coverage began, the aching wait yielded a terrible conclusion. At six p.m. on Palm Sunday night, the crew determined Kathy was dead, and likely had been for some time.

To convey this crushing discovery to the family, police turned to KTLA's Welsh. They were certain that his was a voice they'd find comforting. Then, the Fiscus family doctor—the same man who'd delivered Kathy into the world a few years earlier—delivered the tragic news to a world of onlookers. The crowd gasped. Grown men wept. Stan Chambers signed off shortly after nine p.m., apologizing to viewers for his failure to have delivered a better outcome.

Stunned crowds were advised to disperse immediately, out of respect for the devastated family. Telegrams of condolence streamed into the Fiscus home from all over. Local florists ran out of stock. The family implored the public to please route the money spent on such well-intentioned expressions of grief to charitable causes or a fund to pay the volunteer workmen for their time. One of the crew presented his reward money to a home for girls, whose residents in turn purchased a television. They named it "Kathy."

Landsberg explained to his wife that the saga of Kathy Fiscus was far more than a sad accident. It was television history. Never before had it been possible to watch an event unfold, live, without physically being present.

"Until that night, the television set was no more a threat to serenity than any other bit of furniture in the living room," wrote one viewer. "Now you have utterly destroyed this safety forever." That people who had no connection to the family or the area had become so consumed by the drama was a jolting indicator that a mass medium had been born.

Sales of televisions tripled in the immediate aftermath. No one wanted to miss out on whatever one might bring them next. Still, it was impossible to imagine that one day, that box would serve as an open spigot out of which news would pour, endlessly, twenty-four hours a day.

Not far from the well, another little girl died that same weekend after falling into a fishpond at her home. But no one talked about that. It hadn't been broadcast.

CHAPTER TWO

The Lunatic Fringe

You couldn't miss the eleven-hundred-foot red-and-white lattice steel tower as you steered into the bleakness of midtown Atlanta. It was nearly twice the height of the city's tallest skyscraper, the First National Bank building, puny by comparison at just 566 feet. Soaring over the spaghetti junction of highways that tangled the city center, the tower had been erected in 1967 on the tallest permissible spot in the neighborhood, behind the tired old brick building it served on West Peachtree Street. The only loftier nearby perch was a few blocks west across the highway, a now-protected historical site at the corner of Fourteenth Street and Techwood Drive. There, long ago, General Sherman and his Union Army stationed cannons in the months-long battle of Atlanta, ultimately burning the city to the ground before marching in triumph to the sea.

Bill Tush didn't know any of this local history as he passed by the imposing structure in 1974. Never could he have predicted the role he would play in the revolution that tower would spark. All this twenty-five-year-old radio announcer could see from the perilous curves of the highway convergence called the Downtown Connector was the mighty obelisk, a beacon of broadcasting. And all he wanted was to be a star.

Since acquiring his first record player as a nine-year-old in 1957, Tush* had dreamed of riding the airwaves away from life in his native Pittsburgh. He'd devour episodes of *The Little Rascals* and bathe in the sonorous voice of game show host Bob Barker—the smoothest man on television, as far as he was concerned. The characters he followed on screen and radio came alive for him. He was so much more comfortable with them than with the people in his real life.

* Rhymes with "crush."

His father, a truck driver, later sold caskets; his mother considered her job in a factory that made plastic binders a grand improvement over her previous one as a short-order cook. Tush's destiny in the Rust Belt working-class seemed sealed.

Still, his parents indulged his aspirations, patiently listening to their son as he read the day's paper out loud, practicing his announcer voice. Each evening, he'd retreat to the privacy of the attic to sign on to his very own low-powered radio station, WJTC—audible to a grand audience of one square block—introducing records with cool enthusiasm, as if the artists themselves were about to jam the number right there in front of him. Down in the basement, he rigged a makeshift TV station out of cardboard. Lucky neighborhood kids were invited over to "broadcast" from the studio.

At bedtime, he'd tuck his transistor radio next to his ear and fall asleep to the distant signal of WABC in New York, reflecting over the nighttime airwaves. His spine shivered at the scene in the film *Midnight Cowboy*, where a bus soars over the George Washington Bridge carrying Joe Buck, clutching a radio himself, into the majestic city. Fade down the soundtrack as the star deejay with the silky drawl, Ron Lundy, chimes in with the station ID, "This is WABC New York."

That, Tush thought, *that* could be me.

His school friends laughed at his invented fantasy, especially when he'd gaze longingly in the window of his favorite local station, KQV. "Hey, deejay," they'd tease, their voices laced with sarcasm, as if appearing on the radio was an outrageously unattainable ambition, like winning an Oscar or flying to the moon. People in Lawrenceville, his predominantly Polish neighborhood, didn't venture into fancy-pants creative professions. They graduated from vocational high schools and reported for work at the steel mill.

But Billy Tush was resolute. As a high school junior, he landed a job as a jack-of-all-trades utility player—announcer/newsman/deejay/engineer—at a dinky low-power station in nearby Latrobe. The man he replaced had been deployed to Vietnam. Tush reveled in his laundry list of responsibilities; he admitted years later to an interviewer that he didn't know what he was doing, but that didn't matter. He was *on the radio*. So dazzled was he by the work that he declared he was finished with his formal education. His mother put the kibosh on that. College might not be in his future, but that didn't mean he could ditch high school.

Her interference proved wise. Though Tush fared well as host of the daily polka show, he got axed for wreaking havoc on the local agricultural community by miscuing the taped farm report one time too many. This experience hammered home the immense power of broadcasting. People *did* tune in to even the smallest stations, and they responded to what they heard. There was, it turned out, more to this medium than the thrill of broadcasting your own voice. There was power attached to this job, and responsibility.

After he graduated, Tush landed a coveted job at WEDO, but his plans were derailed that very afternoon, when he returned home and discovered a draft notice on the mail table in the hallway. His affinity for communications saved him from the front lines. Instead, he was dispatched to learn Morse code from the safety of an office. Once his mandated military service was complete, Tush resumed course and marched right back to the station to claim his slot. Adding an additional gig over at KQV, he chose the plain-vanilla on-air name "Bill Williams" to appease his employers, each of whom wanted to claim him as their own.

When the union representing talent called a strike in the dead of winter, Tush joined the picket line. Marching in the freezing cold inspired his dream of a balmier climate. A woman he'd been dating declared that Atlanta was "happening," so he ditched the protest, hopped into his '72 Fiat Spider convertible with his roommate, and headed south across the Mason-Dixon line.

As they pulled into town, the first thing that caught his eye wasn't the city skyline but that soaring television tower. The first thing to catch his ear was the oldies music, his favorite, playing on the car radio. Just as the announcer read out the station call letters, Tush's gaze veered across the highway. As if by magic, there were those letters, emblazoned on the side of a building: W-G-S-T. Emboldened by the coincidence,

Tush drove in that direction, marched in the front door, demo tape in hand, and declared to the front-desk attendant, "I want a job."

Luck was on his side. A deejay spot had just opened up on the afternoon shift. Dazzled by how the stars were aligning, he got back in the car and pointed north, collected his belongings from the family row house on Willow Street, and said goodbye to Pittsburgh. In the rearview mirror, he spotted tears in his father's eyes.

* * *

One sleepy Atlanta Sunday about a month after his arrival, a co-worker invited the newcomer deejay, with his sly sense of humor and mop of straight hair, for dinner. As she prepared the meal, an old black-and-white movie crackled on the television. The fuzzy picture didn't deter Tush. He loved old movies as much as he loved oldie music. Each time a commercial break interrupted the scratchy film, he thought to himself that this station was so low-rent, even he, with zero television experience, might be able to land work there. Channel 17, WTCG, it was called, said his hostess—that station attached to the soaring tower. Tush's larger fantasies fluttered. Didn't everybody on radio long to graduate to TV? Having a recognizable voice didn't stroke the ego nearly as much as the fame attached to a recognizable face.

His awareness of the location emboldened him. The next day, armed with his résumé and reel-to-reel demo tape, Tush stopped off at the old brick building straddled by the tower on West Peachtree. Up close, the soaring labyrinth of steel seemed even more foreboding. And yet, it was anything but majestic. A tired, sorry pall was cast over the property, which was in as awful shape as the on-air product. Old tires were layered atop the building, giving it the look of an auto junkyard. A decaying carton that once held videotape propped open the back door from the parking lot. A sign warned visitors, "NO BARE FEET ALLOWED." A funeral home behind the property, and a cluster of mature oak trees up front, added an eerie element of foreboding.

Tush waltzed into the station. He had nothing to lose.

"I'd like to apply for a job as an announcer," he said.

"I'm temporary," answered the receptionist lazily. "I don't know who you need to see."

After some goading, she picked up the phone and made a call, and soon a guy emerged to escort Tush back through a crowded warren of hallways to another man, who squired him over to the production manager, R. T. Williams, the almighty Oz of channel 17.

In the corner of Williams's tiny office sat evidence of his own ambition—a director's chair, its back adorned with the words "Brilliance Is a Heavy Burden." Tush shifted about as he waited for this person who held his fate to listen to his reel. His timing, once again, turned out to be fortuitous. The staff announcer had just walked out the door, and Williams needed someone to record station IDs and announcements. Come in for an hour once a week, he said. We'll pay you fifty bucks.

Tush couldn't believe his good fortune. First the radio gig, now a foot in the door in the vaunted medium of television. He started to believe some unseen power had guided him to Atlanta—he didn't usually buy all that mystical hippie stuff, but how else could you explain landing two jobs so effortlessly in a place where he knew no one? It all felt destined, surreal.

And that was even before the young man from Pittsburgh had officially come to know the scrappy, unpolished, unprofessional world of WTCG; before the space-age innovation that would elevate it, and him, into a national sensation while, in the process, disrupting the entire business of television.

* * *

The flea-riddled bunker that housed the television playground Tush found himself invited into had served an earlier bit of Atlanta television history. Built in 1949 at the dawn of commercial television, it had first been home to Atlanta's second-ever station, WAGA, an affiliate of the CBS network.

By 1966, the neighborhood around it deteriorated into a sketchy, southern-style Haight-Ashbury known as the "Tight Squeeze," and WAGA abandoned the building for larger, fancier quarters north of the city. The old location didn't deter local coal impresario Jack M. Rice Jr., who found 1018 West Peachtree Street ready-made for his newly licensed plaything, a TV station he anointed with his initials, W-J-R-J. On channel 17, the independent station inhabited a virtual address on what wags called "the lunatic fringe."

All television was not created equal. By the sixties, the plum broadcast real estate, stations numbered two to thirteen on the powerful VHF, or "very high frequency," of the airwaves, had been doled out. Dials on most older televisions—that is, most televisions in operation—stopped at the number thirteen. Stations issued licenses later rested on the UHF (ultra high-frequency) band and had been assigned higher numbers—closer to God, quipped FCC commissioner Robert E. Lee, a major proponent of the technology. On newer sets, those high numbers were segregated to a separate dial that had to be precisely tuned in order to catch the signal. Depending on where you lived, even a loop antenna positioned just so on top of the set might not help reception.

So financially risky and "predestined to failure" a venture was UHF that another insider called it a "plot to bankrupt Jewish dentists," for it seemed well-to-do non-broadcasters were the only fools willing and able to plunge into that slice of the airwaves.

Besides their more powerful signals and desirable locations, those VHF stations possessed another advantage. Most had aligned as affiliates with one of the three mighty networks: ABC, CBS, and NBC, which had evolved from their stranglehold over radio to dominate the newer medium of television. Network affiliation equaled access to star-studded programs with higher production values than stations could produce on their own—including a nightly national newscast to complement the local headlines. It also meant adhering to the network's schedule—a worthy trade-off, for the audiences these shows commanded translated into bountiful ad sales for all.

Nonplussed, Rice was primed for his independent corner of the exotic business of entertainment. To give his weaker television signal a boost, he erected that mighty eleven-hundred-foot tower out back, one of the tallest in the nation, a phallic reinforcement of his might. At four p.m. on September 1, 1967, WJRJ debuted. A photo in the next day's paper captured the moment—Rice and his executive team grinning like Cheshire cats at the dedication ceremonies, flanked by their honored celebrity guest, Lisa Baker, the latest *Playboy* Playmate of the Year. The film chosen for the honors of the station's debut? A 1964 Joan Crawford picture, *Della*. The programming day would run from four in the afternoon till around midnight or so, at which point channel 17—and the rest of television—signed off till dawn.

Though the proud new owner declared the Atlanta airwaves ripe for an indie, the TV critic for the *Atlanta Constitution* dismissed the station's schedule as lackluster—a hodgepodge of discards from the networks, like the crime drama *Target: The Corruptors!*, mixed with gems from long-ago, like *I Was a Male War Bride* and *Come to the Stable*.

But Rice, the newbie broadcaster, had a grander scheme in mind. Like a handful of hopeful businessmen around the nation, he believed that Americans obsessed with television would soon be willing to fork over small sums of money to watch premium programming—newer movies, sporting events, and filmed versions of Broadway shows.

Consider the math. Only six hundred thousand people had seen the smash musical *My Fair Lady* during its three-year, sold-out Broadway run. If every one of the 107 million households that had tuned in for the live production of *Cinderella* when it was staged for TV in 1957 had paid just a quarter, the take would total close to $27 million.

Pay television seemed a sure bet—and an obvious cash cow. As an experiment, the masterminds behind this service had been installing coin-operated set-top boxes on select televisions hooked up to special channels in test markets. So enticing was its buzz and promise that an investment banker managed to sell stock in Rice Broadcasting without a shred of evidence that channel 17 could turn a profit. Once this new service rolled out nationally, the money was sure to flow.

Theater owners and the networks decried as absurd this concept of charging viewers for what had long been free, like expecting them to pay for air. Their rancor was a shield for their terror; surely such a service would crush their control of entertainment. A fierce lobbying campaign was mobilized against this potential menace. The Joint Committee Against Toll TV derided Rice and his ilk as parasites and vampires aiming to "gouge the American people." But their concerns were far less about the viewers than about their bottom line. The committee prevailed, and strict limits were placed on the development of pay TV.

Left now with only subpar programming and fuzzy reception, channel 17 failed to attract either viewers or advertisers. Rice's folly began bleeding $50,000 a month.

The would-be media man waged a last-ditch effort to rally an audience for his faltering venture. He purchased space on a lone billboard on the Lakewood Freeway, which ribboned south of the city toward the airport, in the service of convincing passing motorists that WJRJ was Atlanta's "number one independent station." This wasn't a false claim. Channel 17 *was* the number one indie. There were no others in operation.

The sign caught the eye of at least one person—the handsome young man who owned it.

* * *

Roadside advertising had been integral to the life of Robert E. Turner III since practically the moment of his birth on November 19, 1938. Ted watched his namesake father, Robert Edward Turner Jr., construct an empire, piece by piece, escaping his own heritage as the son of a struggling sharecropper in Mississippi who'd lost his farm during the Great Depression.

Unable to pay tuition at Duke University, the elder Turner, known as Ed, broke into the ad business as a human car counter, helping advertisers determine the number of eyeballs their boards received on the emerging matrix of America's roads. To help cobble together enough money to launch his own "outdoor advertising" company, he sold Chevrolets in Cincinnati. There he met and wooed Florence Rooney, a tall beauty who delivered him a son fifteen months after they married. Ted was the first Turner born north of the Mason-Dixon line, but he took his rightful place as a southerner when his father's work moved the family to Savannah, Georgia. There, over time, through might and acquisition, Ed built Turner Outdoor into the largest such concern in the southeast.

A charmer with a natty sense of style, he was determined that Ted not become soft or spoiled. While Florence begged him to stop, he walloped the child with a razor strap. "A few fleas are good for a dog," he'd say as justification for the beatings. "Insecurity breeds greatness." The lashes were a form of discipline, he explained to his son, "to try to make you do the right thing and grow up to be someone we are proud of."

Besides, Ed said, it hurt more to strike than to be hit himself. To prove it, he once insisted that Ted turn the strap on him. The kid couldn't do it. He collapsed in tears.

Believing that boys who spent too much time with their mothers turned out to be too much like girls, Ed sent his son to boarding school starting at the age of four. There, Ted endured crushing loneliness. After stints at various other schools, he was enrolled at McCallie, a prestigious military academy in Tennessee, where he became a hell-raising "show-off" and "smart-ass," leading his dorm mates to beat him mercilessly, screaming of the native Ohioan, "Kill the Yankee!" Slapped with a pile of demerits for insubordination and disruption, young Ted walked holes in his shoes fulfilling the mandated punishment laps around the track.

As a self-described "skinny little shrimp," Ted discovered that his true mettle was his wit. At bedtime, when the dorm supervisor asked who was responsible for a lingering light, Ted piped up, "Edison, T., sir." Better to be a quick thinker, he decided, than a high school quarterback. In just two places did he excel—on the debate team and on the water, where he fearlessly, recklessly sailed Penguin dinghies. His drive to win at anything he undertook was fierce. "When basic characteristics were doled out," he observed, "I got more than my share of competitiveness."

On summer vacations starting at age twelve, Ted was expected to work full-time in the family business. Being the boss's son didn't exempt him from scut work. For a salary of fifty dollars a month, he dug holes for the poles that held up billboards, mowed the grass around them, and delivered water to crews in the field. Lest his son become an entitled brat, Ed charged the kid half of what he earned for room and board.

The virtues and merits of outdoor advertising were baked into Ted's very being. Though he'd hawked papers at a streetcar stop during second and third grades, he adopted his father's mistrust of newspapers for the editorials they ran decrying billboard "blight." Fiercely loyal, Ed admonished Florence that she should purchase only products made by his advertisers.

A womanizer who bragged to his son about his conquests and believed men were naturally polygamous, Ed disappeared every few months on a bender that involved his other extracurricular passion: alcohol. He'd drink so much that he'd brawl in the bar, and, then, when he hit bottom, check into Silver Hill, a leafy resort-style rehab facility up north in New Canaan, Connecticut. Once the staff helped him sober up, he'd return home and get back to work, eventually resuming the cycle of destruction.

Ed's innate tumult was amplified by the diagnosis of his beloved only daughter, Mary Jean, with lupus, a cruel, degenerative disease. As her brain swelled with encephalitis and her health spiraled downward, the girl would scream with pain, banging her head against the wall, begging the good Lord to have mercy and take her life. In a rare instance of defiance against her husband, Florence refused to relinquish the girl's care to an institution. Unable to face the crushing travails of his dying daughter, Ed filed for divorce. Freed from the domestic trauma, he intensified his immersion in work. This also gave him more time to micromanage his son.

Mary Jean's illness destroyed more than the Turner family unit. It shattered her brother's faith. Before her decline, Ted professed to be deeply religious, saved four times in Christian crusades. A career as a missionary held appeal. He felt sorry for souls in those parts of the world who didn't have access to Christianity. He believed they would burn in hell, and he intended to help them find salvation.

But the God that would allow his beautiful, innocent sister to fall so cruelly into the "dark shadows" of a horrific disease was not one the young man decided he could abide. When his daily prayers for her improved health continued to go unanswered, he swore off religion.

In its place, he became devout about the classics. Obsessed with ancient warriors and kings like Alexander the Great, Ted would spontaneously launch into passages from Homer's *Iliad*, or Babington's *Horatius at the Bridge*. From Edward FitzGerald's *The Rubaiyat of Omar Khayyam*, he developed a seize-the-day, live-life-to-the-fullest philosophy:

> *Ah make the most of what we yet may spend*
> *Before we too into the Dust descend.*
> *Dust into dust and under dust to lie*
> *Sans wine, sans song, sans singer—sans end.*

When it came time for college, Ed forbade Ted from attending the Naval Academy, his first choice of school. "It probably wouldn't have been much fun without a war on," Ted rationalized about his father's decision, "without being able to push destroyers around and shoot each other." Rejected by Harvard but admitted to two other Ivy-League schools, he opted out of the urban campus of the University of Pennsylvania and headed instead to Brown University in Rhode Island, perfectly situated to allow him to indulge his love of water sports.

The tweedy New Englanders couldn't make sense of this redneck southern sailor with a dimpled chin and wild personality. In defiance of the school's blue-blood decorum, he'd erupt into rebel yells on the fire escape of his dorm and shoot his gun into the sky, sing Nazi songs outside the Jewish fraternity, and "prank" black students with menacing notes on their doors that read, "WARNINGS FROM THE KKK." Delighting in the shock it inspired among the northeastern liberals abundant on

Brown's campus, Ted would drone on about Hitler, whom he considered the "most powerful man of all time." One classmate observed with incredulity that despite "his basic racist tendencies, his chauvinistic approach to women, his elitist view of society, and his fascist political ideology," Ted was likable, even enjoyable. Said another classmate, "He's an asshole, but a glorious, totally mad, larger-than-life asshole."

Ted couldn't blame booze for his behavior—yet. Ed had made him a bet: If the young man reached twenty-one without touching alcohol or tobacco, he'd be rewarded the princely sum of $5,000.

But when his father refused to let him take a summer job at a yacht club, Ted plunged into the substances he'd pledged to avoid before winning the award. Those habits were, if not exactly congenital, deeply ingrained in the Turner being.

A month into his new drunken lifestyle, he was caught partying and throwing chairs out the windows at Wheaton, the nearby women's college. For this act of defiance, he was rewarded with a suspension. He rode out the lost semester by enlisting in the Coast Guard and, after returning to school, chose the classics as his major. This impractical course of study outraged Ed, who, in a five-page screed, declared his belief that Ted was "rapidly becoming a jackass."

> I can see you drifting into a bar, belting down a few, turning around to the guy on the stool next to you—a contemporary billboard baron from Podunk, Iowa, saying, "Well, what do you think about old Leonidas?" Your friend, the billboard baron, will turn to you and say, "Leonidas, who?"

Ted's riposte? He turned the letter over to the school newspaper, which published it in its entirety. Then, he obediently switched majors, to economics.

But the familial damage was done. Ed refused to continue underwriting his foolish progeny. Left to struggle with his own tuition bill, Ted saw his troubles mount. Instead of dismantling his fraternity's homecoming display, he torched it. When he ratted out a woman's extracurricular love life to her steady beau, the cuckolded man retaliated by calling the campus cops and turning Ted in for the worst possible infraction at his all-men's university: harboring a woman in his room. Suspension—again.

And with it, the end of Ted's college career. Off he ran with a friend to sunny Florida, the perfect locale in which to indulge his love of sailing. Unable to find steady work and eager to stretch what little money they had, they resorted to living in Ted's car in a poor Cuban neighborhood, using the phone book for toilet paper and eating peanut butter and jelly sandwiches on a single paper plate they'd reuse again and again. It was the first time in his life that Ted had ever been hungry.

Experiencing poverty convinced him that "being a bum was not for me." Desperate to head in any direction that didn't involve working for his dad, he leapt when the Coast Guard sought him out to complete his service. His shipboard assignment on the USS *Travis* involved scrubbing wretched, rat-infested latrines, which seemed a picnic compared to starvation. Though the captain found his dedication worthy of admission to the Naval Academy, Ted capitulated to his fate, returning to work for his father. Ed relegated him to an outpost of Turner Outdoor in Macon, Georgia.

Along the way, as if to prove himself emancipated, he impetuously married Judy Gale Nye, the daughter of a famous sail maker, herself a skilled skipper. Nascent women's lib had hardly caught up with Ted. Judy was expected to dress as her husband wished, to iron his socks and provide three square meals each day—comprised only of products purveyed by his billboard customers. Ted, meanwhile, worked almost constantly—unless there was a race in which he could sail or a woman he could seduce. In case it wasn't apparent to his bride, he boorishly declared his priorities: business first, *then* sailing, *then* family.

When his sister's tortured existence came to an end at age seventeen, Ted, like his father, subsumed his grief and ratcheted up the intensity of his drinking, smoking, and carousing. The only major difference between the two men was their haberdashery. The elder Turner favored

Ted Turner made no secret to his family that
sailing was his priority. In 1966, when this photo
was taken, he'd only just begun to amass the honors.
*(Floyd Edwin Jilson/*Atlanta Journal-Constitution *via AP)*

silk robes, Panama hats, and white linen suits, and he impressed guests
with his private-label whiskey. His perpetually rumpled offspring, on
the other hand, took pride in cutting his own hair and didn't seem to
care that his jackets and pants didn't fit quite right.

Together, they lived and breathed their business, talking about it
to the exclusion of all else, exasperating everyone around them. What
better form of advertising, they asked, than a billboard? The profit mar-
gins were unbeatable and surefire. Billboards required minimal upkeep,
performed on location by unskilled laborers. Unlike ads in newspapers,
which got trashed or redeployed as birdcage liners or fish wrap, outdoor
advertising endured.

The tenacity and strategic sensibility that helped become Ted a formidable sailor helped propel him in the business world, too. Working
fifteen hours a day, six and a half days a week, he doubled sales in his
territory. At long last, he felt he'd won approval from the man he feared
and admired and considered his best friend.

One day, he boldly asked his father for a moment alone. He'd figured something out, and he wished to discuss it.

"You've always said you're leaving your business to me," he told Ed Turner. "It hit me. That's not it. You're going to leave *me* to your business."

The elder Turner took a deep breath, sat back, and acknowledged his son's observation, as Ted continued with his emancipation proclamation.

"I'm not Ed Turner," he told his father. "I'm Ted Turner. I'm your son and proud and happy to be so. But I've got to have a little room to be my own person and not just your idea of what I should be."

Ed nodded in understanding, though it seemed unlikely that a man with such a strong personality had the capacity to allow Ted more space. Besides, he'd become fixated on the boldest business move of his life. In 1962, he teamed up with Bob Naegele, a friend and associate up north, to purchase the assets of a competitor, General Outdoor. Ed's slice of the company would render Turner Outdoor the largest billboard concern in the south. The deal involved taking on several million dollars in debt, which, carefully navigated, he'd have no problem repaying over the five years stipulated in the deal's terms. The expanded business would establish a Turner Outdoor presence in Atlanta and Richmond—the big leagues, compared with the smaller cities the company had conquered thus far.

Ed invited Ted to join him in Atlanta, the big-time, to oversee the leasing side of the operation. This proved an exciting but enormously stressful development. With Judy having delivered a baby in the nest back in Macon, Ted's weight plunged under the pressure of shuttling eighty miles back and forth between home and his new assignment. Meanwhile, Ed's girth ballooned as he smoked three packs of cigarettes and downed a fifth of liquor each day.

On his typical cycle, the elder Turner headed back to rehab in Connecticut. This time he unwittingly swapped his addiction to alcohol for one to pills. With his tortured state of mind unabated, he retreated to his thousand-acre plantation in South Carolina for a weeklong vacation. A few nights later, he called his son, jabbering, his talk tinged with mania. Ted was mystified by his father's state of mind—perplexed by the words and tone of voice beaming out of the receiver. The salient points in his rambling included his certainty that buying General Outdoor had been a colossal mistake. His life was a failure, he wailed. This business deal would ruin him. He couldn't hack these extended responsibilities.

And because of this, he informed his heir, he'd decided to sell out his share of the business to Naegele. There was to be no arguing or debate. The deal was already done.

Over his short lifetime, Ted had experienced his father's wide range of moods, but he'd never heard the fierce and focused fighter Ed Turner in a state like this. Quitting had never been an option before. Why was he giving up now? There was no indication of any problem, no sense of anything but upward momentum for Turner Outdoor, as long as he kept his usual pace. Was his father having a nervous breakdown? Was it the pills? Ted had no clue, but he was reconciled to the fact that he was helpless to intercede.

On March 5, 1963, as he did each day, Jimmy Brown, a trusted family employee, served Ed breakfast. Brown noticed that his boss seemed more content than he had in a long time. After the meal, Ed retreated to his upstairs bathroom, picked up a gun, and shot himself in the head. When Brown heard the blast, he rushed to Ed's side but quickly discovered that his beloved boss could not be saved. He was fifty-two.

This incalculable loss pierced the heart of twenty-four-year-old Ted. As he had after his sister's demise, rather than grieve, he jolted into action. He soon discovered that his father had, indeed, signed a deal to sell to Naegele the day before his suicide. Ted blamed it on temporary insanity.

Take what he's left you, counseled the elder man's advisor, and do what you love—go sail.

Yes, he loved the water and stole off for races every chance he got, but sailing his life away was not how he wished to avenge the hard work and death of Robert E. Turner Jr. He was a fighter, not a dilettante who lived off the fat of the land. Like his hero, Alexander the Great, who'd been twenty when his father, the Macedonian king, was assassinated, Ted was determined to forge ahead. Rescuing the business his father had struggled to build, and making it larger, was the best memorial he could imagine.

Ted hopped a plane to meet with Naegele and implored him unsuccessfully to rip up the deal. When that failed, he laid on the guilt. "How can you take your best friend's business away from him?" Next, he tried dirty tricks, orchestrating an elaborate sabotage. Finally, Naegele responded with steep terms. If the young man could deliver an eye-popping $200,000 cash in the next ninety days, he could buy back what Ed had sold him. With little capital and no prospect of raising any, Ted counteroffered the counter. Aware that the tax gains a rich man like Naegele would have to pay on such a sum would be steep, he offered company stock instead. This time, Naegele bit.

Ted's advisors were incensed. This kid simply didn't have the maturity or the finesse to handle the management of the company. They were sure he'd crap out with this roll of the dice.

That the family industry was in the crosshairs of a growing movement to regulate billboards didn't help Ted's odds of success. The state of Georgia intended to clamp down on what President Lyndon Johnson disparaged as "unsightly man-made obstructions" that had transformed the nation's thoroughfares into "junkyards." The "stop billboard blight" movement sparked by the national highway beautification bill could very well destroy the entire industry. He took this as a clue to diversify.

Advertisers eager for a mass audience had already begun to route more of their dollars to broadcasting. To stake a claim in the medium of radio, he overbid on a jalopy of a station in Chattanooga, simply because he owned a billboard company there. First, he converted the station to the wildly popular Top 40 format. Then, he deployed his unsold inventory to promote it. The tactic worked. In short order, Turner swapped cash and stock to purchase three more radio stations across the south.

All the while, he found comfort in the only place on earth he felt wasn't spoiled—the water. The vast, limitless potential of the seas was the only kind of "field" expansive enough to match his dreams. The stifling confines of a stadium, where other sports were played, was too restrictive. He began collecting accolades, shocking the world of sailing by pushing boats to the limits, from St. Petersburg to Fort Lauderdale, Sydney to Hobart, Cape Hatteras to Montego Bay, spending tens of thousands of dollars on racing and less and less time at home. Which was just as well. Acrimony ruled the roost.

Judy filed for divorce, but when she immediately discovered she was pregnant again, Ted implored her to stick around, though even with a new baby on the way (Robert Edward Turner IV), the renewed relationship never mellowed. The sport that had brought them together ultimately did them in. When he rammed Judy's boat during a race in order to win, she decided she'd had it, once and for all. She packed up the kids and returned to her hometown, Chicago.

He hated being alone. "F. Scott Fitzturner," as he called himself, had no shortage of female companions. He wasn't single for long. At a fundraiser for the 1964 Republican presidential nominee, Senator Barry Goldwater, the politics weren't as much the draw as the chance to meet women. There, he'd been introduced by a friend to Janie, a home economics major and flight attendant. Initially, this belle bristled at the divorced man with children. "My impulse was to run as fast as I could the other way. And he came on so strong," she said. The gap in his teeth and his bright blue eyes trumped that he seemed crazy and ferocious and was forever bragging. Her father's intense admiration of this paramour provided the final push of her doubts. After marrying less than a year later, a new baby was born, a son Ted insisted on naming Rhett—after the lead character in his favorite movie, the epic Civil War drama *Gone with the Wind*. By now, Ted had grown a mustache, emphasizing his resemblance to the character as brought to life in the film by Clark Gable.

As his family continued to expand, he wavered about his future. Radio didn't turn him on as much as he'd hoped. In fact, Ted found it to be more hassle than it was worth. Too much competition in each market meant commercial airtime sold too cheap. Personnel hassles with what he described as "drugged-out deejays" proved tedious. The impractical reality of geography—all the stations were scattered around the southeast—made managing them all the more complex.

In search of new capital, Ted paid a visit to banker Lee McClurkin of the august Atlanta investment firm Robinson Humphrey. Maybe if he could buy a radio station in Atlanta or infuse his business with cash by taking his company public, that might ignite his passion for broadcasting.

McClurkin, for his part, had a problem on his hands, and the visit from young, enthusiastic Ted sparked an idea about how to solve it. Just like the owners of the other 145 independent stations around the country, his client over at channel 17, Jack Rice, was bleeding money to the tune of $600,000 a year. Indies just couldn't compete with the networks, and now that the great promise of pay television had proven to be a bust, so had Rice's interest in continuing on the "lunatic fringe." Perhaps McClurkin could solve both men's problems by merging the businesses together.

Ted confessed to the banker that he didn't watch much television. He was too busy and too hyperactive to sit down and engage in such a passive indulgence. He also wasn't ashamed to admit that he had no idea what "UHF" was. Still, he was smitten—television, even a low-power independent station high on the dial, seemed far sexier than radio. He figured TV commercials were just like billboards, except that the visuals moved, right? They'd be fun to sell. Besides, the losses incurred by channel 17 would offset the profit he was reaping in the outdoor advertising business, which were sure to soar when a new rule banning tobacco advertising on television soon went into effect. Plus, he could deploy the same tactic he had in Chattanooga, putting fallow boards around Atlanta to work promoting his new station.

When Ted announced his plans to merge with Rice, his advisors erupted yet again. The $2.5 million stock swap was bad enough. That this channel 17 came saddled with hundreds of thousands in losses underscored the deal as an unmitigated dog. But Ted was unrelenting. Ownership of a broadcast license seemed, to him, the equivalent of a winning lottery ticket. A new media playground awaited!

A garbled proxy vote submitted by a member of Ted's board of directors unintentionally green-lit his plan. By the time it was discovered that the ballot had actually been cast as a no, it was too late. The merger squeaked through.

Even before he officially took over, channel 17 sank from fourth of four stations to fifth of five. A well-funded UHF competitor with the catchy call letters WATL announced it would debut on channel 36, hardly vanquishing the skepticism of Ted's advisors. No way could a market the size of Atlanta sustain *two* independent stations. Right out of the gate, WATL possessed an advantage: a psychedelic, twenty-eight-hour-long weekend music marathon hosted by two local rock deejays called *The Now Explosion*, which promised "TV so turned on you can't turn it off." The tube had never seen anything like it before—gyrating go-go girls in miniskirts dancing to music of the day, embellished by wild, pulsating special effects made possible by state-of-the-art television equipment that allowed for fancy zooms and color bursts and fades in time with the music, an acid trip without the windowpane.*

Another setback: the call letters Ted wished to name his new acquisition—WTBS, for "Turner Broadcasting System," an aural cousin of the mighty CBS—were already in use up north at a radio station on the campus of the Massachusetts Institute of Technology. Instead, Ted settled on the letters WTCG, for "Turner Communications Group," as the name for his baby.

And so, on the first day of January 1970, channel 17 began broadcasting in its reincarnated state. There seemed to be just one person in town who believed it could be a winner.

This proud new owner quickly discovered that his new plaything was rife with problems beyond its physical decor, pathetic finances, location on the television dial, and cellar-dwelling ratings. The general manager had the temerity to lounge around all day with his feet propped up on the desk, lazily leafing through the newspaper as if it were a Sunday morning. Personnel, who routinely reported to work stoned,

---

* For an archive of *The Now Explosion*, please see http://www.thenowexplosion.com /3segmaster1.html.

often loaded what few commercials had been sold upside down in the film projector. Not that anyone was watching or noticing besides Ted.

In search of bargain-rate equipment that would enable channel 17 to broadcast in color, Ted trekked north to call on another struggling UHF channel, this one in Charlotte, North Carolina. WCTU had been launched by an overambitious dentist named Harold Twisdale and had been bleeding money from the start. (Fortunately, said Dr. Twisdale, he'd never given up his thriving dental practice.) The plug on the station was about to be pulled, freeing up the one tangible asset he possessed: gear. By the end of the meeting, Ted wasn't just buying that. He was buying the whole damned station in a fire sale.

Once again, his board erupted in anger and disbelief. Several members expressed such exasperation with Ted's latest show of fiscal irresponsibility that they resigned.

One associate wasn't surprised by this latest impetuous twist. Jim Roddey, an executive now in charge of Turner Outdoor, had concluded that his boss, while "very, very bright," was also "wacko, semi-loco." What kind of person admired Hitler for his organizational skills? Who else likened billboard painters to Michelangelo and allowed his staff to paint an anatomically correct fifty-foot sign of the Coppertone girl? During sales calls to potential clients, Roddey had personally witnessed Ted writhing on the floor to show his desperation. "I'm a dead man if you don't buy," he'd plead. At station meetings, he'd whine to his team that business must be conducted like the Frank Sinatra song: "*My Way.*" A man who'd chosen *Black Cat* and *Pariah* as the names of two of his boats was hardly trying to convey the straight and narrow.

And yet, as unorthodox a businessman as Ted was, Roddey knew how masterful he could be at creating the illusion of success. He dwelled in a perennially positive fantasyland the staff referred to as Planet Hope, refusing to buckle to fear or prudence. Yes, Ted was a motor-mouthed egomaniac who dominated every conversation—for his continuous, impenetrable monologue, even people who liked him called him "Radio." But he plunged into this new business of television with his characteristic manic zeal, devouring the trade magazines and studying the demographics by fifteen-minute segments so intently he could recite them like poetry. And he crafted an ingenious spin on the station's biggest liability—its location on the dial.

"UHF viewers are more intelligent than the people who watch the *other* stations," he explained. "Only an *extremely smart* person could figure out how to work that antenna in order to tune in a UHF station like ours." This ballsy, circuitous logic impressed Roddey, even if it had yet to yield much fruit. The general managers at the other stations in town felt such pity for this Turner kid for buying into such a pathetic part of broadcasting that they paternalistically agreed to meet this TV newbie for lunch. As they witnessed how he deployed his arsenal of billboards in the service of promoting channel 17 and started snapping up movies and programs to air, they recognized that this newbie to their business might sound like he fell off a turnip truck, but, in reality, he was dumb as a fox.

The more people said something couldn't be done—or that Ted Turner couldn't do it—the deeper he plunged in. A wild risk taker was the perfect fit, perhaps the only fit, for a station on the lunatic fringe.

One night, after strategizing channel 17's future over drinks at the local watering hole, Ted and Roddey made their way back to the station parking lot. The soaring tower loomed. By its mere existence, it teased an intrepid onlooker to ascend. Frat boys from Georgia Tech, located just across the highway, routinely scaled the steel giant as part of a hazing ritual. Ted himself couldn't resist. He proposed a challenge: "Let's do it."

Before Roddey could say a word, Ted was on his way, climbing higher and higher, one rung after the other, as if the tower were the mast of a ship. Up and up he ascended, until he was out of sight, shrouded by the darkness of night and cloud.* Never mind the uncertainties he was facing; never mind the doubters and the challenges

---

* Production manager R. T. Williams told writer Christian Williams that he climbed the tower while Ted stayed on the ground. It took nine hours to get down from the top.

and the improbabilities. In that instant, the journey before him didn't seem one bit daunting. Though he had no idea what the next day would bring, right that instant, he could see clear ahead to the future. "Hang on to my coattails," he shouted. "We're going to the stars or the moon."

CHAPTER THREE
Girdle 'Round the Earth

Since he arrived on earth on November 5, 1931, Maurice Wolfe Schonfeld had been adjacent to greatness, this close to the A-list. To be born in Newark, New Jersey, in the shadow of New York City, the indisputable center of the universe, was to perennially feel kicked around—an also-ran.

The neighbors on the Schonfelds' block included Newark's power elite: the police chief, a prominent rabbi, and a gangster. Reese's father, meanwhile, dutifully worked as an executive at a glass manufacturer. He was successful enough that he made his wife stop working, lest the neighbors perceive that meant he wasn't able to support the family.

Early on, Reese—his baby sister, unable to pronounce "Maurice," unwittingly gifted him his nickname—had shown himself to be a daring ringleader. Unlike other kids his age, he didn't *play* football— he ran the football pool, which yielded his other nickname, Big Mo, a nod to his towering frame. He was constantly stirring up trouble, cutting school, lashing out at teachers, and pulling pranks, such as stealing the rabbi's daughter's diary, which mortified his father, who was devout.

As Jews during the precipitous march into World War II, the Schonfeld family closely monitored Hitler's ominous rise. It felt a matter of life and death to devour the news conveyed in the latest issues of *Time*, *Life*, and *The New Yorker*—to gather around the radio, as most of the nation anxiously did, for the latest dispatches from the likes of H. V. Kaltenborn and Edward R. Murrow, who, one columnist explained, had "more influence on America's reaction to foreign news than a shipful of newspapermen." Together, the Schonfelds listened hopefully to Gabriel Heatter's daily show, which promised, "There's good news tonight," though good news seemed in short supply. From all of this, Reese discovered a wide world beyond Newark's borders. He yearned to inhabit it, to be part of the conversation—to jump across the river to the big time.

Though his grades were mediocre, he tested well on the college boards, landing him admission to Dartmouth in 1949, just as TV was beginning to roll out on a wider scale. The postwar era was liberal, but Reese, the eternal contrarian, considered himself archconservative. It wasn't politics so much. If he could, he was always going to take the other side.

At school in rural New Hampshire, his strategic mind and fiercely competitive nature allowed him to excel at cards. The money he raked in from winning at bridge boosted his meager allowance.

After graduation, he earned a spot at the most prestigious of law schools: Harvard. Months into his studies, a fellow student ratted him out for drinking, cutting class, and running a poker game in his dorm room. He was summarily expelled. Though his heart wasn't in the legal profession, filial duty compelled him to continue his course of study. His father had abandoned his own dream of becoming a lawyer when he dropped out of school at age fourteen to help with the household expenses. While Reese was certain he hadn't inherited the elder man's ambition, he wasn't quite sure what else to do with his life. He'd sold subscriptions to the *Newark Evening News* and worked as a clerk there, but the idea that this could be a career for a grown man hadn't crossed his mind.

For his second try, he enrolled closer to home, at Columbia University in New York. In 1956, a campus employment office placed him in a summer job as a copyboy at the news service United Press–Movietone News. The thirty-five dollars a week he'd receive would turn out to be the least consequential part of the experience.

His employer was a fusion of two companies at the forefront of a growing appetite for visually presented news. The table had been set in movie theaters in the 1920s, back when commercial television was but a glint in its inventors' eyes. While the very notion of moving pictures was pure magic, a live keyboard player provided the only soundtrack possible. To make the evening at the cinema more of an event, Movietone and a handful of competitors began providing newsreels, appetizer-length briefs that ran before and in between the feature films.

These weekly dispatches transported the audience to the scene of current headlines far more dramatically than the static text and photographs available in print. Brief captions on title cards punctuated dramatic images of politicians and celebrities, war and natural disasters. Even without sound, they opened a window to the world most people could only dream of peering through—and made them feel, if but for a moment, a tiny part of it.

The arrival of the talkies in the late twenties intensified America's love affair with the cinema. Movietone's newsreels evolved, too. Now, a booming narrator's voice accompanied the fifteen-minute presentation of film clips gathered from points around the globe, a powerful voice of God updating entertainment-seekers on the week's current events.

As Americans settled into a postwar boom—babies, suburbs, houses, commutes—television, consumed from their plush living rooms, commandeered their leisure time. Library use plummeted, the take at jukeboxes fell, and theaters, suffering from plunging attendance, began to close at an alarming rate. Who needed to go to the movies when the entire family—plus envious neighbors who'd not yet purchased their own sets—could be entertained at home with the likes of *I Love Lucy*, *The Adventures of Ozzie and Harriet*, *The Honeymooners*, and *Lassie* for free? The networks continued to expand their broadcast hours, offering a wider array of programs, from kids' fare, game shows, Westerns, variety programs, and soap operas. Though newscasts were but a tiny piece of nightly network programming, just fifteen minutes in length each night, 90 percent of the nation consumed their dinners while watching the headlines.

Grasping at staying relevant, Movietone partnered with the wire service United Press. In addition to supplying newsreels to theaters, the service offered news footage to the television networks as well as to local stations. Few could afford the manpower and film equipment necessary to maintain their own crews. A subscription to United Press–Movietone News allowed them to embellish their rudimentary newscasts—typically comprised of a man behind a desk, reading wire copy to the camera, occasionally punctuating a headline by holding up a photograph from the wire service.

When Reese stepped onto the blisteringly hot movie-soundstage-turned-news-factory at the corner of Tenth Avenue and Fifty-Fourth Street for his first day as a copyboy, he found himself instantly captivated by the sizzling electricity of the newsroom. The frenetic motion matched the speed at which he spoke—the words tumbling out so quickly it was as if he was inhaling the thoughts that followed.

Movietone's cameramen shot on the fly out in the field, true craftsmen racking deftly through their lenses in an age before built-in zoom, recording images on hundred-foot reels of film that yielded a minute and ten seconds of footage. "Can carriers" spirited the exposed film to a processing lab a few blocks away, which in turn handed the footage to wizened editors, who screened and spliced the images into news clips. Grizzled veterans groused about the newfangled but cheaper and easier-to-process sixteen-millimeter film—spaghetti, they called it—quickly replacing the sturdier old standard, thirty-five millimeter. And they'd complain about stringers who didn't precisely choose their shots by editing "in-camera" as they filmed. Inefficiency meant more footage to process and wade through, which in turn slowed down the works. Reese absorbed it all.

After pictures came the words to vivify them. The best writers, he observed, crafted the stories on a dime, with ease, carpenters of language: "Two and a half words a second, making sure to identify each face, each action, as it pops on the screen." If you couldn't write—if you couldn't write *fast*—you couldn't survive.

In watching stories take shape on this assembly line of production, piece by piece, Reese experienced the eye-opening notion that the news, every step of the way, was formed by humans—from the choice of stories to cover, to the choice of pictures and words that conveyed them.

The otherwise menial task of mimeographing scripts provided the young copyboy with a crash course in the bigger picture. He studied the pages curiously, carefully, as he cataloged the day's material for the company archives. On index cards, he'd meticulously type out the specific shots used in each one, cribbing the unique language of film he'd gleaned, like "close-up" or "medium shot."

Another of his daily duties involved monitoring the nightly network newscasts and keeping a handwritten log of each story. He'd not watched much television before, mostly the fights on a Friday night over at a neighbor's house in Newark. Now that it was Reese's job to hawk it closely, he observed and absorbed the pace and flow that made for a compelling program. Breaking news to start, softer news and features at the end. The utter homogeneity of the three shows surprised Reese. Not only was what they reported on virtually the same, but the men who delivered the newscasts all resembled one another in tone and demeanor. They spoke as if theirs was the voice of God. Their staffs, he learned, had all attended the best East Coast schools and eagerly mimicked the front pages of the *New York Times* and *Washington Post* with their story selections.

"They were all first-rate," he observed, "but they saw things through the same set of eyes. It was as if you were running the same raw materials through the same strainer and expecting different results. No matter how many times you ran it through, the product was always pretty much the same." A man delivering a scripted report, the occasional filmed piece from a reporter in the field.

Underscoring the sameness, the networks all aired their newscasts at the exact same time, with the end result for the viewer being, he observed: "You will watch the news when we tell you to watch the news, or you will not watch news at all."

Continuing the dominance they'd created in radio, the three networks formed a mighty TV troika. And they all managed to get stories on the air faster than Movietone could rush them out the door. A carrier pigeon would have been more efficient than their system, which relied on motorcycle couriers who whisked the little green boxes of film, scripts carefully tucked inside, out to the airport. By the time the footage arrived at stations the next day—or later—the news was as stale as day-old bread. Even newspapers, reliant on the printing press and delivery trucks, published more timely information in the multiple editions they updated throughout each day.

Reese was shocked to learn the networks collectively possessed an advantage his employer did not. Their secret? Each paid $25 million annually to the phone company for the use of its speedy information superhighway, zigzagging their programs and footage over a complex matrix comprised of thousands of miles of high-speed copper coaxial lines and two-hundred-foot-tall microwave towers strategically placed around the nation. The system wasn't explicitly unavailable to others, but the high cost of using it made it prohibitive to all but the mighty three. Even still, there were limits. Remote and mountainous swaths of the nation were still unreachable, and, most limiting of all, there was no way to transmit a TV signal across the ocean.

Reese began to see that a news organization didn't rise to the top because it had the best stories. The key to success was size and how much you had to pay to transmit your stories. Competing with the triopoly of ABC, CBS, and NBC seemed an impossible task, an unattainable dream—never mind the ability to beat them.

After just a month in the hallowed, bustling halls of the news factory, Reese knew for certain he'd discovered his life's passion. He couldn't imagine leaving this mighty ringside seat to history in which he'd inadvertently found himself. When an Italian ship, the SS *Andrea Doria*, capsized en route to New York City from Nantucket, the young newsman watched as film crews pressed into action, rushing to the West Side docks in search of reaction. Here was the access he'd longed for to a world far beyond his block in Newark. When the fall semester arrived, his bosses allowed him to juggle his work schedule around his studies. While earning master's and law degrees, he rose up the ranks in the newsroom. On the assignment desk, he grew skilled at negotiating with stringers. The higher-ups admired his thrifty nature. The flush networks could afford to spend money in pursuit of a story, even waste it, but his second-string employer required and exalted in parsimony.

Out in the field, he had no compunction about muscling his way to the front of the press pack to land comment from newsmakers of the day. Big Mo, the fearless gambler from Newark, face-to-face with one of the world's biggest movie stars, Marilyn Monroe, whispering a reply to *his* query about how she was feeling after being released from the hospital. Big Mo, scuffling with a rival crew that obstructed his cameraman's shot as he interviewed the American Nazi Party's George Lincoln Rockwell. Big Mo, with his toothy grin and mile-a-minute speech, roaming the halls of the 1960 political conventions. The bar exam? Why bother? He was a journalist—a broadcast journalist.

Time and again, though, his triumphs were tempered by technological hindrances. When an air force bomber accidentally dropped an unassembled A-bomb on Mars Bluff, South Carolina, Reese scrambled to find a local cameraman. The footage he commissioned didn't arrive in New York until the next day, delaying its arrival to subscribers until the day after *that*. By then, the story was too old. It never aired.

The unstoppable rise of television ultimately rendered newsreels as obsolete as the horse and buggy. Slowly and steadily, as they vanished, so did United Press–Movietone News.

And yet, television needed that filmed news footage more than ever. Reese and some of his colleagues found themselves scooped up by a reincarnation of the wire service's television arm, UPI Newsfilm. But with no newscast of its own and a delivery system as slow as a tortoise, it was, out of the gate, an also-ran. With annoyance, Reese began to see why the mighty networks could boast that "news was what they said it was." If they didn't cover a story, it didn't make it into the public eye.

When would fresh viewpoints and other voices be heard? Reese wondered. When would the delivery speed of news accelerate? When would the umbilical cord to the phone company's superhighway get cut? He held on to his quixotic hope that one day, stories might flow at the speed of light—with no jag or delay or reliance on rich corporations. Long before modern connectors like airplanes and telephones had been created, William Shakespeare's character Puck in *A Midsummer*

Night's Dream had expressed his desire to lasso a "girdle 'round the earth," to cinch the enormous planet tight in order to traverse it in just forty minutes.

What if not a person but the *news* could travel the earth in an instant?

* * *

Great minds had been working on collapsing space and time for as long as people had communicated. From the tom-tom drum and smoke signal to the carrier pigeon and the Pony Express; from speeding trains to the telephone. As each domino of discovery fell, the girdle 'round the earth cinched a bit tighter—ratcheting up the desire for greater speed and connection.

The first time a message had been transmitted over transatlantic telegraph lines, in 1858, it was cause for celebration that merited a parade and a hundred-gun salute. The eighteen hours it took to deliver the hundred-word message seemed like lightning compared to the ten days it typically took a steamer ship to squire a letter across the ocean.

While the ability to beam moving images into the nation's living rooms had seemed a miraculous step forward, as ubiquitous as television had become by the early 1960s, it was still an imperfect technology. If you lived in an area where trees and mountains obstructed the clear lines of sight, you might not be able to tune in at all. And that was assuming you lived near enough to a city that could support a television station with enough ads to keep it afloat, much less two or three.

In 1945, the futurist Arthur C. Clarke imagined a fantastical solution, "a true broadcast service, giving constant field strength at all times over the whole globe." Instead of beaming phone calls and television programs over AT&T's terrestrial superhighway, why not shoot the signal up into the heavens? A constellation of orbiting rockets, deployed 22,300 miles over the equator, rotating at the same speed as the earth, could receive the data and then shower it back down to an interconnected planet.

If only such a system had existed for the historic June 2, 1953, coronation of Queen Elizabeth II. Even once the shy young Elizabeth buckled to public demand and agreed to allow television to document her installation, it was only a fantasy, utterly inconceivable, that the ceremony might be seen around the world as it happened.

To maintain decorum in the hallowed halls of Westminster Abbey, only British Broadcasting Corporation cameras would be allowed. Copies of the three-hour ceremony would be provided to international broadcasters by the BBC. Vexing technological hurdles remained. Duplicating film required darkened labs, chemicals, and time. Transmitting the three-hour ceremony across the pond using existing cables under the sea was impossible. A CBS executive calculated it would take ninety-nine years and seven months. American network executives and engineers schemed elaborate work-arounds to ensure their viewers could see Queen Elizabeth wearing her crown as soon as possible after it was placed on her head. This included renting airport hangers in England where they would record the historic broadcast right off the television with their own cameras (a process known as "kinescoping"), then spiriting away that film onto a waiting chartered jet—one of only a handful of planes then capable of making the transatlantic journey—that had been retrofit with a processing lab and edit bay; arriving in Boston, which put them on American soil an hour earlier than if they'd gone directly to headquarters in New York; then feeding out film from Logan Airport over the speedy phone company system.* While Elizabeth was rousing from her first official night of queenly

* The morning of this special day, the only regularly scheduled, nationally televised morning television show, NBC's *Today*, took to the airwaves an hour earlier than usual as the event unfolded live in London. Host Dave Garroway treated viewers to the only images available: still photos of the queen ticked off a state-of-the-art Mufax wire machine at nine minutes' transmission time each. Occasionally, he'd cut away to radio coverage from the scene or chat up experts on the royal family who joined him in-studio. Wide shots of Garroway's "co-host," the chimpanzee J. Fred Muggs, gazing at images of the queen on a monitor proved a matter of wicked irreverence later decried in the House of Commons—as was CBS's sale of coronation coverage to a car company sponsor that declared its vehicle "Queen of the Road."

slumber, an American television audience finally got to see the pomp and ceremony.

A more efficient system was in the works.

Four hundred scientists had been toiling away on an invention that would ultimately enact Clarke's dream and link the corners of the world in real time, instantly. Years and $50 million in the making, the very first active communications satellite was a wonder called Telstar, and by 1962, it was ready for a dazzling debut. At 170 pounds, a tad under three feet in diameter, and framed in magnesium, the sparkling curiosity was covered with 3,600 sapphire-encrusted solar cells mounted in platinum and filled at the core with ten thousand electronic components. It hardly looked as if it possessed the power to connect the globe.

On a clear day in June, a square white air-conditioned truck pulled out of a nondescript warehouse in Whippany, New Jersey, with this odd-looking masterpiece in tow. As it embarked on the thousand-mile journey to Cape Canaveral, Florida, final preparations were under way there for its ascent. After a battery of tweaks and tests, the engineers strapped the precious cargo onto the back of a Thor-Delta rocket and, at 3:35 a.m. on July 9, blasted it into space.

From its orbit in the heavens, the miraculous Telstar could, just as Arthur C. Clarke had imagined, receive phone calls and television pictures beamed up from Earth, then shower these data bits back down to receiving stations where they'd be relayed instantaneously—far faster, more widely, and at a fraction of the cost of the flawed information superhighway on the ground.

As Telstar orbited the earth at eighteen thousand miles an hour, a team of broadcasters from the three rival American networks worked together in unprecedented fashion with their counterparts in Europe on a grand show to illustrate the power of a satellite to revolutionize communications.

From the dimly lit Studio 4J at the RCA Building in midtown Manhattan, an anxious production team oversaw the American side of the extravaganza. A startling split screen of images welcomed viewers: simultaneous live transmissions of French masterpieces separated by an ocean. On the left, Alexandre-Gustave's majestic Eiffel Tower in Paris, on the right, Bartholdi's Statue of Liberty, standing watch in New York Harbor. BBC broadcaster Richard Dimbleby shouted an enthusiastic hello to the hundred million viewers across the United States, crying, "Go, America, go!"

And go America did. The voice of the man installed just months earlier as anchor of the CBS nightly news became the first televised American voice to be heard in real time across the ocean in sixteen nations.

"Good evening, Europe," Walter Cronkite intoned in his trademark warm timbre. This simple juxtaposition of two relatively static live shots awed even the most wizened of the broadcast team. In his voice viewers could hear the utter sense of "primal wonder and amazement" he felt as technology allowed them to collapse time and space.

"This is the North American continent live via Telstar, July 23, 1962, three p.m. Eastern Daylight Time in the east, the New York skyline on the Atlantic Ocean," he declared, as live pictures punctuated his words. "On the west, three thousand miles away, San Francisco, twelve noon at the Golden Gate Bridge. Between these two oceans, 180 million Americans have begun another week."

There was nothing remarkable about the average week in America except that humans across these great United States and on another continent could see these images live, in real time.

Thus began a glorious skip-hop of a travelogue across the continent, a wild, expansive tour from sea to shining sea that most Americans had not taken and likely never would, made possible in a matter of minutes thanks to a series of well-positioned cameras and the magical communications power of a multimillion-dollar girdle. The armchair traveler was guided from Niagara Falls down to the southern border at El Paso, Texas, so close to Mexico one could sneak a peek across, back up north to the bustle of the World's Fair in Seattle, and over again to a serene meditation room at United Nations headquarters in New York. A team of translators converted Cronkite's words into a dozen languages, but it was the live pictures that were indisputably the star of this show.

From the control room, director Sid Smith called his crew to punch up the image of a live baseball game at Wrigley Field in Chicago, where the Philadelphia Phillies were playing the Cubs—another milestone, as this now counted as the first international transmission of a sporting event. The game's announcer rallied the fans assembled in the stadium to, "Give all the baseball fans in Europe a big hello from Chicago. We know this doesn't make sense to people in Europe. Our colleagues are going crazy trying to say 'runs,' 'hits,' and 'errors' in Swedish and Italian."

Next, the 312-member Mormon Tabernacle Choir, imported to South Dakota for this special occasion and positioned in front of the majestic Mount Rushmore, launched into a rendition of "A Mighty Fortress Is Our God" as director Smith commanded his crew, from seventeen hundred miles away, to "cue the buffalo." A local cowboy fired a gunshot, mobilizing a gigantic herd that stampeded across the screen like a scene out of a Western. Locals laughed at the big-city folk staging the wild, but around the world, the shot provoked awe, offering a glimpse at a frontier most people had never seen. It was, observed NBC anchor David Brinkley, "not so much what they saw but that anything was seen at all." The images were not just real, they were live. They were *television*.

The cascading power of Telstar immediately became apparent. Curious citizens flocked to the tiny town in Maine that housed the powerful receiving antenna, and newspaper columnists waxed rhapsodic about its potential to transform worldwide communications. By the year 2000, they predicted, communicating via space would become a billion-dollar business. This possibility, however, also unleashed concerns. Responding to reports that negotiations were already under way to transmit the Miss America beauty pageant via satellite, columnist Dick Shippy of the *Akron Beacon-Journal* fretted about the vacuous image of the nation that would be presented to the rest of the world.

At least on this maiden Telstar voyage, Europe got a glimpse of a shining exemplar of America, the charismatic president of the United States. Though he was personally committed to sending a man to the moon, Kennedy was well aware that much of the nation remained skeptical, even wary, of space exploration. As the action of the demonstration broadcast moved to the White House, the international audience was allowed to peer into his regularly scheduled presidential press briefing—something no one outside the press corps, much less the United States, ever got to see. The president acknowledged his virtual visitors—several hundred million people in sixteen countries—as well as the gravity of this achievement.

"This is another indication of the extraordinary world in which we live," he said. Carrying messages from both sides of the planet "is of course a very essential requirement for peace, and I think this understanding, which will inevitably come from the speedier communications, is bound to increase the well-being and security of all people here and . . . across the ocean."

Could live TV erase the world's divisions? Would wars cease when we could speak across borders in real-time? Would individual cultures begin to erode? As the technology was refined and governments hashed out the details of which companies would be allowed to commercialize the skies, it would be years before we could know, years before this kind of broadcast was possible on a regular basis. The ultimate ramifications of instant global communications were, for now, only imagined.

There was, however, one clue in the aftermath of that milestone Telstar broadcast. Though he'd been quoted in the papers saying for weeks that he wouldn't devalue the dollar in order to stem the tide of gold, once the whole world heard the same words uttered directly by the president, live, on television, the dollar rose, and the price of the precious metal dropped. Of all the firsts Telstar could claim, this was perhaps the most powerful. Thanks to this potent technological marvel of satellite and television, a politician had swayed the markets.

* * *

Fourteen months later, on a Friday in November 1963, a limo carrying four journalists rode five cars behind President Kennedy, who was en route to deliver a speech at the Trade Mart in Dallas. The press corps was on high alert. Extreme right-wing protestors who despised the president had been issuing bomb threats before his other appearances. His United Nations ambassador, Adlai Stevenson, had been struck in the head by a protestor a few weeks before. There had been talk that the president should not make the trip.

Ever grateful for the press's lucrative business, the phone company had outfitted this car with a futuristic luxury, a two-way device called a radiotelephone, which allowed a caller to reach an operator who'd then patch him through over the phone lines. As one of the reporters allowed to travel in this well-placed vehicle, UPI White House corre-spondent Merriman Smith muscled his way to the front, even though it was technically the turn of his rival Jack Bell of the Associated Press to sit in that plum seat.

In one devastating instant, three loud cracks shattered the pomp and circumstance of the parade. Smith, a collector of weapons, instantly identified the sound as gunfire. Grabbing hold of the radiotelephone, he asked the operator to patch him through to the regional newsroom, then dictated what he'd just witnessed to the rookie reporter who answered the call. Reporters, especially those who worked for the wire services, had to be skilled at spouting off-the-cuff dispatches; in a breaking-news situation, there was no time to write. Bell pounded Smith on the back, demanding his turn on the phone, and only after Smith was certain this urgent news had been received did he surrender it.

Four minutes later, his bulletin crossed the wire, cinching his place in history as the first to transmit the terrible news.

"Dallas, Nov. 22 (UPI): Three shots were fired at President Kennedy's motorcade today in downtown Dallas."

An instant later, at subscriber newspapers and stations around the world, wire machines beeped, five times, indicating that urgent news was about to cross and required immediate attention. Over at the assignment desk at UPI Newsfilm on West Fifty-Sixth Street in New York, Reese Schonfeld marveled that a president had paraded openly in an uncovered car. At his Dartmouth graduation years before, com-mencement speaker President Eisenhower had arrived on campus accompanied by a veritable army of guards, who immediately fanned out to protect him. He blurted to a colleague with the bravado of a wizened newsman his concern about the second-string cameraman on duty in Dallas that day, "If that fucking Lawrence missed the shot, I'll fire the bastard."

Over at CBS News headquarters at Grand Central Terminal, Walter Cronkite put aside his brown-bag lunch of cottage cheese and pineapple and rushed into action. Only weeks earlier, news executives had prevailed on their higher-ups to allow them to expand the nightly newscast to a half hour—debuting the lengthier program with filmed reports from as far away as Saigon and Tokyo, and a one-on-one interview with the president at his home in Hyannisport. Critics had wondered if there would be enough material to fill each night's broadcast, and local affiliates balked at having to generate a longer newscast of their own—until they realized a longer broadcast would plunk more advertising revenue into their coffers. To fill the time, the news now included commentaries and features and quirky news bits and Cronkite's new signature sign-off, "That's the way it is." At midday, with the nightly newscast still hours away, the searing studio lights were powered off. The state-of-the-art cameras would take at least ten minutes to warm up.

Presented with this earth-shattering news in the middle of the day, Cronkite knew he needed to urgently convey what he'd learned to the American people, even without pictures. Ten minutes into the live performance of the soap opera *As the World Turns*, up popped a slide, interrupting the action: BULLETIN. And then the voice of the man who would one day be called the most trusted in America calmly, sternly informed the audience that, "In Dallas, Texas, three shots were fired at President Kennedy's motorcade." The soap opera resumed, and a few minutes later came the BULLETIN slide again, as Cronkite's voice delivered a tiny dribble of more detail. Back to the soap opera again, and ten minutes more elapsed before the newsman appeared visible on-camera, seated at a desk in the newsroom, as his colleagues rushed frantically around. NBC and ABC followed with their own, similar bulletins. An hour later, all three networks dutifully, solemnly, announced the cataclysmic update: President John Fitzgerald Kennedy was dead.

As they witnessed this procession of events, the staff at UPI Newsfilm felt like warriors without a battlefield. Reese had scant footage to offer subscribers and no airtime of his own to fill. He ached to have even a toe in the coverage of this monumental story.

Salesmen for the service frantically worked the phones, calling stations to peddle two biographical documentaries they'd produced about the president during the 1960 election cycle—which now served as instant obituaries. When Reese learned that Harry Truman happened to be in New York, he rushed over to the Carlyle hotel with a crew, hoping to extract some sort of comment from the former president. So did all other press in the city. The dazed man faced the assembled pack of reporters.

"Are you going to Washington?" Reese shouted, desperate for a crumb of news.

"I'm going upstairs, I'm going to bed," the former president said—clearly stunned.

Meanwhile, Reese's boss, Burt Reinhardt, hopped a flight to Dallas in search of amateur footage. Before becoming a deskbound news administrator, Reinhardt had done time in the field. As a still photographer for the military during World War II, he'd been present for General MacArthur's amphibious landing on the island of Leyte in 1944—although modesty kept him from discussing the details. He'd joined Movietone as a cameraman after the war, and as he'd moved up the ranks in management, he had helped indoctrinate Reese into the business.

Word was that a garment maker named Abraham Zapruder had, much to his own surprise, inadvertently captured the gruesome assassination on his eight-millimeter home movie camera. That world-class news photographers didn't have better pictures astonished him. Reinhardt was authorized to bid high, but by the time he arrived, Zapruder had accepted *Life* magazine's offer of $50,000. (Days later, they paid $100,000 more for expanded rights.) Licensing these precious twenty-six seconds of footage allowed *Life* to print thirty chilling still images of the assassination. Screening the complete film on television would have seemed disrespectful.*

The enterprising Reinhardt, reasoning that other amateur cine-matographers might have captured the gruesome moment, visited all the eight-millimeter processing labs in the city, leaving his business card behind.

"If any film of the JFK shooting shows up," he told them, "let me know and I'll give you a hundred dollars."

The next day, the Dallas bureau chief of United Press rang him up at his hotel. "Burt, we got a lady here, Marie Muchmore, she says she's got a piece of film showing the Kennedy assassination. What should we do?"

"Lock the door," Reinhardt shouted, rushing over to the bureau to learn more. Miss Muchmore, he discovered, had taken a lunch break with co-workers at a nearby dress factory, hoping to catch a glimpse of the visiting president in Dealey Plaza. She hadn't used her camera before, and she had no idea how much, if any, of the tragedy she'd cap-tured on film.

Reinhardt possessed a particular talent for haggling. Calmly, he explained that he could pay Miss Muchmore a thousand bucks now and assume the risk there wasn't anything usable in her footage. Or, he could get the film processed first and see if she'd captured the brutal act, in which case he would pay much more.

Devastated by what she had witnessed and feeling guilty about cashing in on the tragedy, the amateur filmmaker accepted the immedi-ate offer. But by the time the transaction was complete and the film had been processed, it didn't matter that her footage unmistakably showed the president slumping in the car after the gunfire. By now, the story had taken another startling turn. Live, on television, before a riveted nation, a man named Jack Ruby had shot and killed Kennedy's alleged

* In fact, the Zapruder film did not air on local television *in Chicago* until 1970, and then on national television in 1975.

assassin, Lee Harvey Oswald. (Viewers of CBS missed this drama. The network had briefly cut away from Dallas for a tribute to the president read by newsman Harry Reasoner.) The Muchmore film could have been earth-shattering. Now, it seemed not just tasteless but old. It ran on only one station.*

The fatal shooting of the leader of the free world was one kind of monumental. The ability to watch each distressing moment of the aftermath on television was another. From the comfort of their living rooms, Americans witnessed, alongside distant newscasters, the ultimate unscripted drama as it continued to unfold: The parade of world leaders following the First Lady as she walked behind her husband's caisson; the sea of mourners; daughter, Caroline, bowing to kiss the coffin; the president's namesake son, barely four years old, and his poignant salute.

November 22, 1963, had coincidentally been predetermined as the maiden voyage of the very first satellite hookup with Japan. This grand communications exchange was to have kicked off with a taped message from the president. Instead, the first televised pictures transmitted to the Pacific conveyed his senseless assassination.

A million people lined the streets of the nation's capital to participate in the funeral procession on that cold, clear Monday. But a better view could be had from one's own living room. More than fifty cameras positioned around the city allowed an audience that spanned more than twenty-three nations to witness the somber procession in exquisite detail more clearly than had they been on the scene, while basking in the warmth and comfort of home. Except for the instant the casket was lowered into the grave. The man in charge of Arlington National Cemetery cut off power to the cameras then. He felt it disrespectful to broadcast such a sacred image.

---

* A month later, Reinhardt bought another film from an amateur cameraman named Orville Nix. The cost: $5,000 and a fedora requested by Mr. Nix. The film became the centerpiece of conspiracy theorists who believed another gunman had sniped at the president from street level. For more see Schonfeld's essay "The Shadow of a Gunman," *Columbia Journalism Review*, July/August 1975.

* * *

It wasn't fair, Reese believed, that the networks dominated broadcast journalism. For them, news was just a sideline—a by-product of their immensely lucrative mainstay operations, which he dismissed as "mindless entertainment." Detractors had begun to eye the hundreds of millions each network earned using the airwaves, fretting about the social impact of violent programs, creeping commercialism— particularly on children—and what would become of a passive, screen-addicted citizenry.

To mint goodwill and stave off the critics, the networks allowed their staffs of journalists to experiment with documentaries, news specials, and talk shows, funding them with lavish budgets that demonstrated their investment in the public welfare. Executives continued to sputter over how more serious fare should be presented. When a live, two-hour morning show on NBC called *Today* proved to be a dud, a chimpanzee was enlisted as co-host, and ratings soared. (The program's newsreader, a serious journalist, quit in disgust.) Ed Murrow knew in 1955 that his well-regarded, issue-oriented, prime-time magazine show, *See It Now*, was not long for the airwaves the minute he laid eyes on the first episode of the quiz show *The $64,000 Question*. There was little doubt in his mind that America would prefer this more populist fare— which, unlike his program, would surely rake in abundant commercial dollars for the network.

Reese loved and respected news so much, he felt it deserved a place at center stage. But how? And where? UPI's filmed news service—*any* news service—could never possibly compete with the resources and audience of the powerful triopoly.

In 1966, a new competitor emerged in the person of Daniel Overmyer, who'd made his fortune in the unglamorous but lucrative fields of shipping and warehousing. Now, he had designs on the media. After purchasing a weekly newspaper in his native Toledo, Ohio, he'd also picked up a UHF station there, along with the rights to operate four others around the country, each to be assigned call letters reflecting the initials of his wife and children. With these and several dozen other independents he'd signed up as affiliates, he planned to start a fourth network. Through his rose-tinted glasses, he overlooked the experience of a man named DuMont, an early pioneer who'd been more focused on making technology and TV sets than on programming. His attempt at creating a network had failed, in large part, because it couldn't keep up with those AT&T transmission costs.

With an evangelist's zeal, Overmyer pledged to infuse $10 million to make this new network a success. Television critic Lawrence Laurent of the *Washington Post* syndicate observed that while the sum might seem lofty to the average Joe, it was, in reality, "but one blue chip in the poker game played by the TV networks."

"The time has come for independent television," Overmyer declared as he announced the creation of a fourth network, O.N. To bolster this claim, he cited several crucial developments:

One: The Federal Communications Commission had passed the All-Channel Receiver Bill, meaning new television sets had to be equipped to receive UHF channels high on the dial.

Two: Color television was booming, meaning people were likely to upgrade to new sets soon.

Three: Technological improvements were allowing independent signals to beam more powerfully, meaning another boost of potential audience.

The flagship of the O.N. was to be a nightly two-hour variety show transmitted live from different Las Vegas casinos—ambitiously programmed against NBC's blockbuster *The Tonight Show with Johnny Carson*. Well-known comedians Bob Newhart, Alan King, and Bob Crane had been signed to rotate as hosts.

Another slice of Overmyer's cash was earmarked for United Press Newsfilm, enlisted to create a two-hour daily package of news materials. The would-be media mogul was tired of the "Casper Milquetoast news reporters" who proliferated on television. The opportunity to distribute

UPI Newsfilm's stories each day to the thirty-five Overmyer Network affiliates meant even more exposure for their work—even if the audience could never match that of the networks.

Optimistic though the would-be mogul might be, the majority of the nation was still reliant on television provided by the three networks, with a hundred million people a night tuned in to primetime. Three-quarters of the viewing public still couldn't catch a UHF signal. Despite Overmyer's ambition and investment, his stab at penetrating the holy trinity of broadcasting went belly-up after just a month. What ultimately squelched Overmyer's grand intentions wasn't the cost of talent, or paying for news, or the lack of audience and advertisers. It was the $6 million transmission bill from the phone company.

* * *

By June 1974, United Press Newsfilm had succumbed to defeat, too— and its assets, including Reese, were absorbed by another rich, wildly idealistic would-be media mogul, Joseph Coors, the Denver-based heir to a beer fortune and his generically named news service, Television News, or TVN. Seventy-two stations had signed up in the United States and Canada to receive an hour-long package of daily reports late each afternoon. Coors was rich enough that paying the exorbitant phone company transmission costs wouldn't be an issue. Though the service was losing money, Coors optimistically hoped to expand what was now the only non-network source of national news film into an all-news channel.

Like Reese, Coors believed greater competition in the news business would yield more stories and more points of view, which could only translate into good news for democracy. But to Coors, that involved promoting a conservative agenda to offset what he felt was the left-leaning slant of the networks. In service of that goal, he hired a young Republican political operative and wily public relations man named Roger Ailes as his news director. Ailes boasted that while he'd never before run a newsroom, he'd been around them and surely had the common sense to learn.

The purist Reese was offended by this cocky man's very presence, especially after he made it clear that he intended to keep running his public relations business (and using TVN to promote his clients). Reese and the majority of his TVN colleagues staunchly believed that journalism wasn't supposed to come with a point of view. At the same time, he had a family to feed and considered himself lucky to be employed, especially by a deep-pocketed organization.

Early in the year, Reese had spotted a page-one story in the *New York Times* that ignited the flames of hope inside him. At long last, the first private, domestic communications satellite in the United States had been launched. Only a technology aficionado and news-hawk like him could completely understand the implications of this development.

Since Telstar had soared into the heavens over a decade before, a number of companies had been experimenting with the ground-breaking tool. After years of regulatory deliberation and pushback from the networks and AT&T, satellites were finally ready for business. Not only would they radically reduce the cost of transmitting information, they would prove more reliable, too. This was sure to drive down costs and, finally, encourage competition. Never before had it been possible to reach a national audience without the gateway of the networks and the phone company.

Reese rushed to share the news of this "chance to break the AT&T leash" with the deep-pocketed ideologue for whom he worked. Sending TVN's daily feed via satellite would ultimately save millions of dollars and give Coors bragging rights as the first television outfit to deliver news in this revolutionary new way.

The beer mogul signed on to the plan. But this was only a piece of the equation. To pull down the news segments TVN fed up, TVN members would need special equipment. That meant installing a thirty-foot-wide government-approved satellite dish whose price matched its gigantic footprint: $100,000. Recognizing that most local television stations were unlikely to invest in such unwieldy technology, Coors agreed to subsidize the cost.

Eager to plunge in, Reese hopped a ride south to visit Scientific Atlanta, the only company in the nation to be constructing these strange-looking, clam-shaped "earth stations" at that time.

Sid Topol, the firm's president, knew the networks were right to fear the democratization of television that satellites would allow. After spending his entire engineering career on the development of radar and microwave systems, he was certain that this new technology offered an elegant solution to the complex, invisible limitation of terrestrial TV— that satellites were the future of broadcasting. So sure was he about their impending success that he'd redirected his entire business to making receiver dishes necessary for cable operators to pull down the signals.

He was tantalized by the prospect of an infusion of $12 million of Coors "beer money" and eager to do business with Reese, who needed no hard sell of the technology he was peddling. The industry was otherwise filled with skeptics who didn't believe satellites could possibly be reliable or who were simply afraid to or unable to make the first move.

To date, only one firm commitment had been made to link cable to satellites. Gerald Levin, the president of an upstart subscription cable entertainment channel in the northeast called Home Box Office, planned to distribute his fledgling service via satellite as soon as the FCC signed off on his plans. Along with the financial might of his parent company, Time, Inc., he had the backing of two of the nation's largest cable operators. The entire industry had lit up at this announcement and eagerly waited for the debut.

Perhaps Reese would be Topol's next taker. Topol fetched him from the airport, asking if he'd mind stopping off along the way to visit another of his potential customers. Ted Turner, he explained, the owner of Atlanta's UHF channel 17, had also inquired about pricing. After reading in the trades and hearing from his allies in cable about this HBO development, Ted had some questions.

Reese knew all about Ted. His channel 17 was becoming industry legend. Reese had been trying to convince him to subscribe to his news service, to no avail. There was no room on the station for news, he'd been told.

For his part, Topol knew Reese had been wading through the ever-changing rules and regulations governing the emerging technology. Anyone interested in fighting the networks needed to stick together. The more media people who signed on to satellites, the better.

Now the two men found themselves climbing the stairs of the tired-looking channel 17 building, laboring to pull open the heavy fire door to Ted's receiving area. His secretary buzzed them into a wood-paneled office, filled floor to ceiling with bookcases jammed with nautical paraphernalia. The place looked more like a suburban den than the enclave of a broadcaster. Running this business clearly hadn't prevented Ted from continuing to sail competitively, and judging by the dozens of silver trophies that gleamed on the shelves of his bookcases, this was no idle pursuit.

The proprietor himself matched his decor. The filthy railroad conductor's cap perched on his head—his good luck totem for sailing—made him look like an insolent frat boy after a night of partying, not the innovative impresario he fancied himself to be. The carpet was stained, and the blinds were yellowed with age. An ornately framed plaque on his messy desk declared outsize confidence for such shabbiness: EITHER LEAD, FOLLOW OR GET OUT OF THE WAY.

The mess repelled Reese, an urbane sophisticate who proudly worked in an office high above Columbus Circle. Having elevated himself from Newark to Manhattan, he felt he'd made it to the center of the media universe—even if, in truth, the media universe in which he dwelled was adjacent to the true power of television. He certainly was more plugged in than this yahoo cracker. What kind of money could Ted really have? And what could he possibly want, or do, with access to a satellite?

"How much does space on one of those satellites cost?" Ted asked his visitors, as if such a purchase was as inconsequential as a bag of chewing tobacco.

Reese explained that buying time on a transponder, satellite-speak for "channel," would cost roughly a million dollars a year.

Turner sniffed dismissively. "Is that all?"

As they made their way out back to the parking lot, Reese sniffed back. Nobody in the media world would take this guy—nor his joke of a station, in a joke of a city—seriously. Even conservative brewer Joseph Coors had the sense not to have located his news service in his home base of Colorado.

"Can you imagine that asshole Turner," he said to Topol as the men made their way back to the parking lot, "thinking he's going to put his rinky-dink channel on satellite?"

CHAPTER FOUR

Watch This Channel Grow!

New Antenna Improves 17 SIGNAL

OUR NEW ANTENNA IS DESIGNED FOR BETTER RECEPTION IN METROPOLITAN ATLANTA. IT'S EASY TO TUNE US IN NOW, SO JOIN US FOR OUR GREAT NEW LINE-UP OF YOUR FAVORITE TV SHOWS

FOOTBALL HIGHLIGHTS
MILLER-HARPER SPORTS REPORT
IT TAKES A THIEF
WILD WILD WEST
TWILIGHT ZONE
BANANA SPLITS
WRESTLING
GET SMART
RIFLEMAN
ULTRAMAN
CARTOONS
DRAGNET
BOXING

17 WTCG Atlanta

Ted's intrigue with the satellite was the capstone of an unprecedented ride. By force of will, a spirit of invention, well-placed geography, and extremely fortunate timing, he had managed to transform channel 17 from "shit to shinola," as he described it, in just a few short years.

Even before he'd coaxed the station out of the graveyard for which it had been headed, Ted had been determined to imbue the place with the guiding positive spirit of Planet Hope. A catchy slogan invented by some gal in promotions helped jazz up the station's on-air image.

"Super 17!"

The phone typically rang at the front desk of channel 17 a couple of dozen times before anyone answered it, but when a caller finally got through, they'd find themselves greeted by a cheerful, almost seductive voice.

"Super 17!"

To compete with the more powerful and better funded network affiliates in Atlanta, "lunatic fringe" dwelling WTCG had to boost its signal and aggressively counter-program. This ad from the *Atlanta Constitution* in 1971 was just one prong of Ted's strategy to infiltrate the market.

WTCG, Ted now claimed, stood for a Herculean dare: Watch This Channel Grow. Though its fortunes began to change, the place was still a ragtag dump. Even the rented television on display in the front lobby, a visitor's first impression of the place, screamed poor. Ted refused to toss out a three-legged chair, hoping, in looking downtrodden, people would give him a better deal.

Once, the grand antenna out back blew up, all but knocking the station off the air for three weeks. After its repair, it continued to conk out on a regular basis, setting off an alarm bell inside that alerted the engineer, who'd taken to sleeping in his office in order to attend the signal. Just getting safely into the building in the winter required an act of heroism—or, at least, a helmet. Used tires layered on the roof cushioned the chunks of ice that would plunge down from the tower precipitously after a storm. The padding did nothing to protect the cars parked in the lot, much less anyone trying to cross it. To date, miraculously, there had been no human casualties.

The first rung in the climb toward "super" occurred when the owner of WATL, the hastily launched rival UHF station, got tired of bleeding cash and unceremoniously pulled its own plug. It was a year after Ted had arrived in local television. Had the competition lasted just two more weeks, he said, he would have been the one closing down.

So thrilled was he to see channel 17 suddenly move from fifth of five in the market to fourth of four that he'd taken to the airwaves after a rerun of *The Man from U.N.C.L.E.* with a live on-air "Thank you, Atlanta" party. Thank you for *what?* his employees wondered. The competition had been a killer, but Ted, in all his egomaniacal, hyper-competitive splendor, converted its sudden demise into a personal victory. Such brass, said his production chief. After thanking everyone out there in "television land," he roved around the tiny studio he'd had filled with balloons, putting each of his employees on the spot. "Tell me about your family. How long have you been working for WTCG?" They cringed. The only thing that helped them all get through the two-hour ordeal was getting high.

Then came word that "victory" might be short-lived—that a prospective buyer for WATL, a movie theater chain, had expressed interest in resuscitating it. Irate about this possible incursion, Ted grabbed a flight up to the would-be competition's corporate headquarters in Boston and threatened that if they dared to enter the market, they'd never get their hands on his billboards for promotion. To ratchet up the drama, he writhed on the floor like a man in his death throes. Perhaps scared off by this crazy southerner, the company pulled out of the deal, leaving him where he wanted to be—the sole UHF station in the market.

That mighty arsenal of billboards, 15 percent of which sat unused at any given time, proved to be a powerful asset worth keeping to himself. Papering the fallow boards with ads for "Super 17" displayed to everyone in town that he meant business.

Wasted space—wasted anything—drove Ted crazy. It made zero sense why television stations ceased transmission each night, culminating the broadcast day with film of a fluttering American flag as the national anthem played. After that? Nothing but a test pattern—darkness until the sunrise harkened the start of the next broadcast day.

The response he got to the question "Why do we go off the air overnight?" was the kind of lazy explanation that drove him bonkers: "*Because that's how it's always been done.*" What about nurses, pipe fitters, milkmen, pharmacists—*him*? The world didn't revolve around a nine-to-five workday. Why should *television*? And what about insomniacs, him among them, who could be soothed by a middle-of-the-night viewing of a forgotten film? To this salesman, sacrificing one-third of the clock was like throwing dollar bills out the window.

"We can't afford to do things like everybody else!" he shouted in response. "We've got to do things differently. We've gotta be like a cleaners that's opened seven days a week, twenty-four hours a day. You've got to be open all the time."*

Staying on all night might not yield an immediate financial return, but it made no sense to continue keeping the lights off overnight. In

---

* The station began broadcasting twenty-four hours a day, six days a week, on August 19, 1974.

search of every scrap of audience possible, channel 17 became the first television station in the country to embark on a round-the-clock broadcasting schedule.

Up in Charlotte at Ted's other station, WRET—bleeding $50,000 a month—the projections were even bleaker. Commercials barely commanded $25 each, versus $800 for a spot over at the competition—and they *still* were a tough sell. Management was found to be swindling from the station, and the producers of a religious show that bought airtime were stealing equipment. If the place didn't turn around, it could very well capsize the entire Turnerverse. (Should the whole thing go belly-up, Ted consoled himself with inventive exit fantasies: working as a boat hand in Annapolis, or packing his family up and heading to Australia, where he could open a McDonald's.)

The prayer break held by the station manager at ten a.m. daily didn't seem to improve matters. WRET needed to snap to life, like Dead Ernest, the campy, drawling vampire who rose from a coffin to introduce the weekly horror flick, *Friday Night Frights.** Absent intervention by the divine or supernatural, a desperate Ted seized the crazy suggestion from his channel 17 station manager, Sid Pike, to reach directly to the viewers in a "beg-a-thon." Over and over for a week, the owner himself appealed to viewers to please donate the price of two movie tickets. By keeping WRET on the air, he told them, they'd be guaranteed sixteen hundred free movies a year:

> I pledge to you that every dollar will be used to pay the bills we incur to bring you these programs. If there is a surplus, we will enlarge our film library to bring you more and better movies and other programs not shown on the other stations. I wanted to give you shares of stock in the station, but it is illegal to sell stock on TV. I would like for you to consider this a loan.

---

* Some believed Dead Ernest was played by Ted Turner himself, but this was not the case. See *E-gor's Chamber of TV Horror Show Hosts* for a lively discussion: https://egors chamber.com/tvhorrorhosts/hostsd.html.

Please include your name and address with your contributions because, if we are ever able to, I promise to pay you back with interest. A check would be best for your records and ours.

Disarmed by this Rhett Butler–esque character unafraid to confess his dire straits, and eager for the stream of old movies and reruns WRET offered, the dutiful audience obediently answered the command. Donations arrived, from a quarter to eighty bucks. Some fans even hand-delivered the loot directly to the studios, which took some work, for the station was situated far from the center of Charlotte, across from a cow pasture. The $26,000 collected in the beg-a-thon was just enough for WRET to get over the hump. The pleading brought in almost as much in new ad revenue and attracted the attention of religious broadcaster Pat Robertson, who wished to buy time for his programs.

Back in Atlanta, Ted scored other programming coups. Picking up reruns of the popular mainstay about a small-town southern sheriff, *The Andy Griffith Show*, helped put Super 17 on the map. Wresting away the rights to produce and air *Georgia Championship Wrestling* was another major score. The suits at the other stations in town might laugh at the down-market theatrics of the faux sport, but it sure was a crowd-pleaser—the highest-rated program produced in Atlanta, Ted pointed out, beating the number one local newscast by 50 percent. Every week for the taping, the tiny studios jammed up with fans.

The ultimate "get" came when Ted swooped in and stole the rights from market leader WSB, an NBC affiliate, to a more respectable sport—baseball. The executives there, he declared, had been "asleep at the switch" when he made an offer that the owners of the Atlanta Braves couldn't resist—to air three times as many games. As an unaffiliated independent, channel 17's airtime was his blank slate to do with as he pleased. For Ted, this sport about which he knew next to nothing was the perfect time-filler. Now he could also brag about being the first UHF station to carry Major League Baseball.

Add to the mix: Roller Derby. Boxing. Deals to broadcast the Atlanta Hawks (basketball) and Flames (hockey). Regional college football.

Off-network reruns like *I Love Lucy* (twice a day) and *Hogan's Heroes*. And a continuous flow of old films movie companies practically gave away—dogs most viewers hadn't seen in the theaters—*Deep Valley, The Bride Wore Boots, Seven Days Leave, Dr. Ehrlich's Magic Bullet, Gold Diggers of 1933, The Silver Chalice*. While Ted dashed off to sail, which kept him away for weeks and sometimes months at a time, station manager Pike sat before a calendar and strategized how to use these building blocks to counterprogram the competition. On Monday nights during fall football season, for instance, he'd run a romance or a drama to appeal to non–football fans. When the other stations aired something serious, he'd play the Marx Brothers.

Now, none of these tiny glimmers of promise had yielded much financial fruit—yet. Sales staff scraped and fought for every commercial they sold and resigned themselves to bottom-of-the-barrel advertisers who couldn't afford time on better stations. A sales call from Ted proved entertainment in itself. He'd jump on desks like "Jerry Lewis's Wacky Professor," as one of his sales guys called it, in order to seal the deal. In the rare case when the buyer was a woman, he'd get down on his knee and woo.

And when they *still* didn't want to buy time on channel 17, Ted's team schemed other ways to fill it. There was always someone out there willing to buy time to put themselves on television. On WTCG, the godfather of soul, James Brown, revived his flagging career with a weekly on-air dance party called *Future Shock*. On WRET in Charlotte, evangelists Jim and Tammy Faye Bakker launched themselves into megachurch stardom. Praise the Lord!

No decision he made struck life-saving gold like the decision to accept a type of ad most network affiliates around the country refused—unintentionally kitschy commercials hawking products not available in stores that viewers could buy from the comfort of their couches by sending in a check or calling a special number. The "Miracle Painter" that allowed painting so drip-free you could wear a tux while freshening up the ceiling inspired its purveyors to create another product—an indispensable set of knives called Ginsu that could slice aluminum cans and pineapples like butter (purported to be Japanese, but its provenance, in reality, was Ohio). In exchange for the airtime, channel 17 got a cut of each product sold.

Inspired by the success of merchandisers on his airwaves, Ted ventured into the direct marketing business himself. He hired a buyer from the local department store, Rich's, who sought out unique gizmos and gadgets, and deployed his crew to craft commercials the local paper declared "masterpieces of bad taste." But wait, there's more! Just send $9.95 to PO Box 7500, Atlanta.

Sometimes, it took a couple of tries to find the right approach. The first commercial created for a ring with interchangeable "stones"—a "beautiful work of gold-plated art"—featured a blond southern debutante and hardly moved much merchandise. With a production budget of a hundred bucks, Greg Gunn, the director assigned to spruce up the spot, bought a mirrored disco ball to hang from the studio rafters. Then he hired a local deejay from the soul scene. As Dr. Feelgood sashayed up to an attractive woman in a halter top at a staged dance party, he posed the question:

"Hey, where'd you get that ring?"

"This is a Party Ring," she responded.

"Sure is bad! Hey! You got a Party Ring, too!"

"Yeah!"

"And with a different stone!"

"Everybody's got a Party Ring."

The simulated stones in the "Super-Bad" Party Ring were interchangeable not just with your outfits but with your moves—all for only $5.95.

The new spot was so awful, observed Ted, it was almost funny—and while it attracted attention, some of it was unwelcome. A racist crank, unnerved by the vision of an interracial couple on the dance floor, called in a bomb threat. That bit was edited out to avoid further conflagration.

Apart from that sobering reminder that hateful tension still loomed in the post–civil rights era, the commercial achieved its goal. So many orders streamed in for merchandise that a special area had to be set up at the station to answer phones and process the mail. People, it seemed, loved the convenience of shopping from their living rooms. Ted delighted in the deluge. The cash filled the station's coffers, and the response proved that viewers were, in fact, tuning in.

* * *

There were, it seemed, two types of people: Those who walked into channel 17 and quickly ran screaming out the door, fleeing from this glorified low-budget college television station and the crazy man who owned it. And those who instantly fell in love with Ted and his trickle-down enthusiasm, the free-form, let's-put-on-a-show, kumbaya camaraderie that wafted through the tired hallways. You never knew when you turned the corner at work if you'd stumble upon a wrestler's pair of underwear—or maybe even two people getting it on. The hallways were as unpredictable as Ted's moods.

Chief among the cheerleaders was radio deejay Bill Tush, who remained undaunted even after a chunk of ice plunged onto his parked Fiat convertible, slicing open the roof. The unpredictable nature of the workplace was so exciting that he'd started stopping by the station even on the days he didn't need to voice promos and commercials, determined to learn everything he could about television—performing tasks others might consider menial, like picking up the mail from the post office and pulling cables on those unwieldy, tank-like studio cameras, which were finally upgraded to allow the station to broadcast in color. Eventually, he found himself ditching the job at the radio station and joining the staff full-time.

In short order, he'd been enlisted as host of *Academy Award Theater*, the show created to counterprogram the Sunday morning religious fare on the other stations. (Ted himself had performed hosting duties for a time, which solved a personal dilemma: When he was off sailing on the other side of the world at Christmas, his kids could tune in and get a gander of their daddy on television, introducing a movie.)

One day, somebody realized the eager young Tush was the perfect sacrificial lamb for the task of drudgery they despised: doing the news.

At the end of every workday, he dutifully grabbed the newspaper and headed into the announce booth to read twenty minutes' worth of stories, their only visual a simple slide that alerted the audience in plain type that they were watching "WTCG News." An engineer cut out any stories that mentioned Atlanta and fed out the "newscast" to WRET in Charlotte so their skeletal staff didn't have to do their own.

They wouldn't have bothered if they didn't have to. Like all local television stations, Ted's were obligated to comply with governmental rules mandating that broadcasters, in exchange for profiting off these public airwaves, had to serve their communities with news and public affairs programming. Ted had zero interest in starting a full-fledged news department. Such an undertaking required an investment in equipment and staff—cameramen, film processors, editors, reporters, and producers. That would be far more costly than rerunning old shows and movies.

The bigger issue, as far as he was concerned, was that news was a bummer—an endless stream of stories about the dark side of life: rapes and murders and tragic accidents. Why was there never any good news on television? he lamented. No one ever covered the Boy Scouts! The 1 percent of the population engaged in bad behavior got all the airtime, he complained, not the people who were making positive contributions to the world.

He shouldered particular contempt for the growing trend by news anchors to infuse their opinions into their nightly reports—especially since he found those opinions to be far more liberal than his own. As a proud patriot, he felt TV news had poisoned the populace against the military by portraying the war in Vietnam as an unnecessary disgrace, depicting soldiers as "a bunch of pothead bums." As for draft dodgers or conscientious objectors, he fervently believed every citizen was obligated to serve their nation, and anyone who didn't want to shouldn't live there. He shuddered to imagine if television had been a force during World War II; likely the images of destruction would have led to a push from the citizenry for the United States to surrender! As if the power to sway public opinion using the airwaves wasn't great enough, that New York cabal of broadcasters was cashing in big profits, too.

In short, he believed that Vice President Spiro Agnew got it right in 1972 when he declared the networks a "tiny and closed fraternity of privileged men, elected by no one, and enjoying a monopoly sanctioned and licensed by the government."

In the twenty years since television had emerged as a force, Americans had become addicted to, obsessed with, worshipful of television, but that didn't mean even in their trance-like states that they loved every second of what got pumped out over it. Many viewers felt the same way Ted did, for example, about broadcast journalism.

Still, at dinner, the networks offered nothing else. They'd all tacitly conspired to air their sonorous reports from the front lines of the world's ills at the same unappetizing time. Audiences might prefer the escapist deep-dish pizza of entertainment, but for supper, they were handed that serving of broccoli—news.

To most in the audience, one network news anchor was virtually indistinguishable from the other.

Though some viewers believed the anchors and newscasts on all three networks looked exactly the same, Walter Cronkite of CBS became a trusted source as he conveyed news of the major events of the mid-century. This also made him ripe for lampooning by Bill Tush. *(Thomas J. O'Halloran)*

"I don't think it makes much difference which one you watch," said a respondent to a survey on television viewing habits that showed an overwhelming majority of Americans were tired of the nightly news. "I don't think there is much choice between them. Truthfully, after a while, it is all boring."

Very occasionally, the news rivaled the dramas. The lunar landing inspired awe and captivated nearly 100 percent of the viewing audience for hours. The Watergate hearings interrupted regular daytime network programming for weeks. The resignation of President Nixon kept two of the three networks up all night, broadcasting with the kind of analysis the disgraced leader had decried throughout his tenure.

Only occasionally, though, did television offer "breaking" news outside of its regularly scheduled programming. Doing so required technology that was just in development. Like in May 1974, when Los Angeles station KNXT learned of an impending police raid of a house in Compton. It was believed the radical Symbionese Liberation Army might be harboring kidnapped heiress Patty Hearst. The station had been working with a Japanese firm on a prototype of a portable video minicam—the Handy-Looky—that would make possible the reliable capture on tape of news stories out in the field. The camera proved indispensable during the deadly raid as it unfolded in a hail of bullets and fire, allowing images to be broadcast live. "Portable," though, was relative. The cameras alone weighed fifty pounds.

Eager to differentiate the news and to make the local version more compelling—and thus more lucrative—and under mounting pressure to balance the books and make news pay, television executives began enlisting consultants. Their recommendation? Amp up the entertainment factor in the news. Thumbs-down on long-winded governmental and policy stories, which offered boring visuals. Thumbs-up to crime and "news you can use."

These outside advisors also encouraged inclusion of a force long missing from the news: women. Till now, female broadcasters had typically been relegated to reporting the weather or consumer affairs.

Increasingly at the local level, women were being invited to sit side by side with the male anchors—a made-up, blow-dried, better-looking and nattily dressed facsimile of an American household. The presence of a woman, or the "family concept," as some consultants called it, had the capacity to "brighten up the bad news" as long as she did not seem overtly feminist or controlling. Merely assigning a woman to read a script wasn't enough. Newscasters had to leap through the screen, chatting amiably in between stories, a phenomenon more serious journalists disparaged as "happy talk." Those network guys talked down to the viewer. Local newscasters needed to seem to be just like the "average Joe" who watched them—only better-looking.

Along came the sensation of Barbara Walters, who transcended the "women's beat" at NBC to command the highest salary then paid to a journalist, a whopping $5 million contract from ABC—including chauffeur and hairstylist. Said former CBS executive Fred Friendly in scolding the exorbitant salary, "I don't think people will accept news from millionaires." Better to invest that money in more reporters and camera crews, he said.

In Atlanta, the number one station, WSB, had done its part by stealing away a star reporter from Louisville, Monica Kaufman, who also happened to be black—another rarity in TV news. She'd been so good on the air in her native Kentucky that a rival station worked to get her out of the market by sending out tapes of her newscasts. With her smooth blend of professionalism and her winning good looks, she immediately rose to local stardom at WSB.

For Ted, the news hour was when his location on the lunatic fringe came with a distinct advantage. Channel 17, he gloated, got its best ratings then, by offering alternatives like reruns of *Hogan's Heroes* or *Star Trek*. The news was just one big rerun of bad stuff, he declared. Actual reruns of entertainment shows were far more palatable to consume with the nighttime meal.

And so, having opened up a whole new slice of airtime by deciding to broadcast on the overnights, he foisted his own obligatory newscast safely onto the graveyard shift, whenever the late-night movie finished. Since it would repeat again at five a.m., Tush created an all-purpose sign-off: "Have a nice night or morning, whatever the case may be."

One night, insomniac Ted had been among those in the after-hour viewing audience. The next day at work, he ran into Tush in the hallway and wondered out loud, "Why don't we have someone on-camera doing the news? You're the announcer. Why don't *you* do it?"

If he was going to play anchor, Tush decided, he'd need a coat and tie—except that he didn't own either. After borrowing the getup, he sat for an audition in a candidate pool of one. He was a shoo-in. The station couldn't afford to hire anyone else.

Next came the issue of where to tape the program. Channel 17's only studio was the size of a two-car garage—just 1,500 square feet— the nerve center of the station, in use all day producing income-yielding local commercials or wrestling matches. Taking it offline for anything else was a drain on company resources. An anchor desk was hastily fashioned out of cardboard, not unlike Tush's childhood set in Pittsburgh, and tucked off into what staff anointed the "News Closet," to be opened after the lucrative work was done.

The already boring chore Tush faced each evening was one none of his co-workers relished either. By the end of the day, they just wanted to go out and grab a beer down at Harry's, the nearby watering hole that was practically an extension of 1018 W. Peachtree.

Nonetheless, duty called. Tush felt a bit guilty cribbing from the work he'd imagined some "poor schlub" over at the wire services had typed up so seriously. He avoided stories about murders or plane crashes, preferring quirky bits about UFOs or a CB radio funeral procession or more personally relevant items, like an impending price hike in beer and wine. Any time pot was in the news rated a mention. Weren't most people watching at that hour likely to be stoned—just like the crew?

Not long after his stint as on-air newsreader began, Ted stopped him in the hallway again.

"You're doing a good job," the boss said. "Smile more."

Tush already felt like an idiot. His impulse was to laugh and joke around, more comic than Cronkite, but this was the *news*. Wasn't being serious a requirement? He was grateful for this opportunity to appear on camera so that he might crawl his way out of the place he most feared he'd wind up—"anonymity-ville." Already, he'd started to see results. At least a few people must have been watching, because now when he was out in public, strangers called to him, "Hey, channel 17."

One fateful day, the proverbial fourth wall came figuratively crashing down. When a lock of hair fell into Tush's face as he read his copy, the director piped in over the PA system from behind the plate glass windows of the control room and, audible to all, made a request: "Hey, Tush, move the hair from your eyes." The anchorman dutifully complied and kept on reading.

The next night, as Tush recorded the headlines, the cameraman energetically swept the studio around him—the better to expedite their visit to the bar—and, out of nowhere, lobbed a piece of paper at him. Tush cracked up and kept on reading.

Slapstick had invaded the headlines. Every chance he got, Tush mocked the self-serious delivery of real broadcast journalists—and laughed at himself.

"Here I am," he announced cheerily as he looked around the frame, "sitting inside your TV set with all the news."

Or, at least, Tush's lampoon of it. One night, he told his audience about a speech Walter Cronkite had made at a journalism conference decrying the creeping "show business" approach to the news, and the chirpy, cheery trend of anchor "happy talk." Then, Tush turned to the crew, who streamed from the wings onto the tiny set, making chirpy, cheery small talk. "I have to tell you, I agree with Walter Cronkite, happy talk is not in its place in the news." "I don't like informality in a program, do you?" "I don't like the kidding around." "How's your girl doing? Stop by the house Sunday night."

When rival channel 11 began promoting its hard-charging, stylized, and self-serious "Pro-News" format, Tush took to the air with an introduction.

"THIS IS DULL NEWS," he reported. "No matter how good you feel, we'll bum you out with DULL NEWS. *Murderraperobberytaxes.* Those are the headlines. And now the weather."

The next day, Ted stopped him in the hall again. They had never talked about it, but it seemed they shared the same low opinion of broadcast journalism.

"Hey, I saw that 'Dull News' last night, that's pretty funny," Ted said.

If Ted Turner told you he liked something, you could be certain it was genuine praise. Everyone knew the man was not capable of sugarcoating. He had no filter—about anything. He'd parade through the station with ladies who weren't his wife, or lasciviously grope attractive women he'd just met, without retribution—to the shock and admiration of friends. When asked by a reporter about his reputation for chasing women, he replied, "What's wrong with that?" He prided himself on his no-bullshit seduction technique. "I tell them to look at me like a nice restaurant," he said of his conquests. "You wouldn't want to be there all the time. You just enjoy it, then leave." His frank, explosive personality was legendary, especially among his inner circle, who warily tiptoed around his ever-changing mood. Was he up, or was he down? He'd return from sailing expeditions clutching laundry lists of ideas they'd have to drop everything to pursue, only to find days later that he'd changed his mind. Once, he subjected his most trusted employees to a polygraph test.

He was like a hyperactive kid, exploding into work in the morning—if he hadn't slept on the pullout couch in his office the night before—spouting poetry, singing song lyrics off-key, roaming the halls to pump up the staff.

Indeed, despite or perhaps because of his unorthodox behavior, his very presence seemed to inspire his troops to commit to a higher cause—like, said one of them, military leaders who convince their young troops to walk into lines of fire. Even the people he routinely pissed off or berated somehow managed to get caught up in this infectious spirit.

Crew member Ron Kirk was waiting for a bus outside the station at the end of his shift when Ted pulled up in his everyman blue Toyota—a car he drove to show he was just a low-profile, regular guy—and offered him a ride.

"Ted," the grateful employee said, "you strike me as someone who's living life on his own terms. What's the secret?"

"Attitude, man. Attitude." That, he explained, was how he survived his assignment to clean the filth in the bilge during his Coast Guard duty.

Late one night, a hyper-conscientious new employee on the graveyard shift found an intoxicated fellow stumbling through the halls and threw him out the back door, figuring the drunk had wandered in from Harry's. The next day, his supervisor called him at home on his day off.

"Did you throw someone out of the station last night?"

Yes, sir, the employee said, explaining the course of events.

"Well. That was the owner."

Figuring he was sunk, the employee told his boss to just send his final paycheck in the mail.

"No, no, in fact, Ted wants you to come in and meet him."

And he did.

"So, you're the one," Ted said with admiration. "I wish more people were like you. All I've got is these hippies around here."

Though he had no compunction spending tens of thousands of dollars each year on sailing, he quibbled with a manager for deigning to ask for $212.50 to buy videotape, insisting he forage for used tape in the basement. (The same frugality ruled the Turner home. Janie opined to writer Christian Williams about Ted's prohibition of air-conditioning and heat, and his proclivity for cutting his own hair—and balking when she took the kids for their own seven-dollar haircuts.) Emboldened by his success, Tush—who commanded the princely salary of $200 a week—screwed up the courage to request a clothing allowance. Ted looked at the man he'd started to refer to as his "low-budget Walter Cronkite" and said, "You're about the same size as me. I'll give you my hand-me-downs."

Tush instead ditched the coat and tie, embraced the wide-collared, groovy, casual shirts of the day, and let loose.

From part-time announcer to on-camera
host, new technology (and a sense of humor)
catapulted Bill Tush to become the first
star of cable television. *(Rob Barnes)*

The once-dreaded task of recording the news had become so much
fun, it now served as the repository for the entire crew's outlandish creativity. They all wanted in on the act: Troll, Captain Banana, Mr. Mike
"Dy-nee-mite" Allen, Joe "The Fifty-Year-Old Hippie" Kelter. Tush stuck
a paper bag over the head of one crew member—a guy hired to host a
show Ted had commissioned and then canceled in a matter of days—
and anointed him as his investigative reporter, "The Unknown Newsman." The "news chicken" tackled pressing consumer affairs issues like
traffic flow in the parking lot of a popular bar. Editorial analysis was
provided by "Red Neckerson."

Dressed in black robes, the stout promotions director, Jesse Waller,
delivered impassioned "Reflections from Brother Gold" in a pitch-
perfect impersonation of a preacher—a take-off of the sermonette that
aired on many a station at sign-on or sign-off.

"This morning, the thoughts of Rod Stewart," Waller intoned
at a dramatically lit pulpit, somberly opening his "prayer book" and

launching into a flamboyant recitation of the lyrics to "Da' Ya' Think I'm Sexy?" as if the words were heaven-sent.

When the nation was gripped with fear over the fate of Skylab, America's first manned space station, the crew donned hard hats and frantically ran around the set, as newsman Tush delivered an emergency broadcasting alert that Skylab was falling. (It wasn't, at least not then.)

Breaking news: "The Carter administration has legalized marijuana, and it will be cheaper than cigarettes," Tush read; then, after a beat, "April Fool's!"

Flipping through a book in the graphics department in search of new ideas, Tush spotted a picture of a dog clad in shirt and tie. Next thing you knew, a crew member's German shepherd had arrived in the studio, similarly attired.* Co-anchor Rex the Wonder Dog lumbered all over the anchor desk, helping to deliver the day's headlines.

Even the installation of new linoleum in the studio proved fodder. During construction, Tush and his cardboard desk were relegated to the garage for a week. Each night, he'd cut away to a "live shot" from the scene of a workman in action. He even invited the laborer onto his temporary set for a proper sit-down interview. (The poor guy tripped on his way out.)

As soon as the work was complete, Tush celebrated by enlisting a local marching band, and the camera cut away for a close-up of the gleaming new surface, shot with a star filter like the kind used in Hollywood to imbue movie stars with a radiant glow. Tush exclaimed to viewers, "Look at our beautiful floor." This was big news—at least to the staff. Did news *always* have to be something *tragic?*

Only one staff-person appeared to be displeased by this irreverence. Sid Pike, the station manager, older than the youngest of the employees by twenty years, and one of the few people on staff who'd had experience in "real" television, had reluctantly signed on to work for Ted—and

---

* Tush wasn't alone in co-hosting the news with an animal. The *Today* show famously featured monkey co-host J. Fred Muggs. Even Walter Cronkite appeared with the lion puppet Charlemagne, manipulated by Bill Baird, on CBS's *Morning Show* in the mid-fifties.

now worried that a low-budget UHF station on his résumé would raise a red flag to future employers.* Seated before this rogue employee, Pike scolded Tush, "We can't do the news like that."

"Why not?" Tush countered. "Where's it written *how* you have to do the news?" Who said you needed a serious tone? The Federal Communications Commission hadn't spelled it out. He was simply serving up news, WTCG style.

Pike shrugged. "I guess you're right." He was too busy wading through the ever-expanding film library. They currently owned the rights to enough films, if played back to back, to fill a year and a half of airtime. Ted never met a movie package he didn't buy, said Pike, who was consumed by his boss's erratic schedule and capricious decision-making. After he'd pitched in to help with the beg-a-thon at WRET, Ted had rewarded Pike with a gift of company stock—which he later rescinded, deciding a onetime $300 cash bonus was more fitting compensation. Like everyone else at channel 17, Pike was doing the equivalent of four different jobs, so he didn't have much time to worry about the particulars of the news, anyway.

But he wasn't so busy that he didn't notice Tush's growing popularity. Everyone else in town did, too. Now that he'd infused the news with comedy, people on the streets no longer shouted "Hey, channel 17!" They began to yell, "Hey, Bill!"

And then, something else started to happen—something that didn't make any sense. The fan mail that streamed into the station, along with the orders for merchandise, started to arrive bearing postmarks from far out of the Atlanta viewing area.

* * *

As the crew of Super 17 caroused and laughed and made TV, a quiet revolution was brewing in "television land" that would change the medium

---

* Pike spent the rest of his career working for Ted, ultimately traveling the world to assist in negotiating the carriage of CNN internationally.

forever. A utility known as "Community Antenna Television," increasingly referred to by the shorthand "cable television," found itself at the cusp of explosive growth.

At the dawn of commercial TV, appliance salesmen struggled to sell this pricey magic box in remote areas, "television deserts" where reception was poor or nonexistent.

Three different enterprising men in three different cities—Mahanoy City, Pennsylvania; Tuckerman, Arkansas; and Astoria, Oregon—had independently arrived at the same solution to the problem. Each had erected an antenna at the highest possible point in their communities, allowing them to capture the nearest signal and then, thanks to the magic of coaxial wires, run it into homes. Voilà! Reception! For anyone who couldn't otherwise receive a clear picture, forking over the onetime installation charge of $100 or more, plus a monthly service fee, was a worthy investment in order to participate in this communications revolution.

Dazzled by the larger possibilities beyond the mere utilitarian, these pioneers who believed in the technology's wider promise brazenly imagined the day the entire country would be wired—and entire channels would be created that could be seen only by cable customers.

Traditional broadcasters, meanwhile, fearful of their turf, reactivated their earlier venom against pay television. This time, it was cable in the crosshairs. Viewers didn't want to pay for TV service, they argued. Who would ever want or need more than several television stations? No one wanted to watch *that much TV!*

For its part, the government struggled with how or whether to regulate the burgeoning industry, while the monopoly phone company schemed how to get its mitts on this new, powerful wire that had entered the home and rivaled the one they'd controlled for decades.

For the time being, they'd managed to succeed in blocking cable from entering most of the nation's major cities.

A dizzying matrix of ever-changing rules—or what writer Christian Williams eloquently described as "an opaque cloud of regulatory gobbledegook"—overwhelmed even those whose fortunes were dictated by them.

It was in the muck of the ever-changing gobbledegook that Ted Turner's destiny was to be found.

In 1972, while cable television was still a runt—available in just six million homes—the FCC handed down an industry-altering edict. Cable operators, they decreed, could import the nearest independent station as a bonus offering to their customers.

Here channel 17 possessed a decided geographical advantage. The southeast had few other independent stations. None carried the variety of local sports programming that Ted's station did, much less the vast collection of old movies he offered, and none broadcast all night.

Till now, Ted been hungering and toiling to bring his "underground" station into the light. Now, a way to expand the market itself—to burst beyond the borders of Atlanta—had been handed to him on a silver platter.

While other broadcasters feared the cable incursion, Ted set about wooing and glad-handing cable operators all over the southeast, evangelizing with the fervor of a tent-revival preacher the benefits of adding his station to their systems. From Tuscaloosa to Knoxville to Tallahassee, his frank enthusiasm electrified the industry. Channel 17 was a southern-fried alternative to what those networks in New York had to offer!

In practically no time, seventy-three cable systems across five states were carrying channel 17 into 312,000 cable homes—as many homes as the station reached on its own turf. Within a year, its viewership would triple.

No longer was channel 17 some piddling also-ran on the lunatic fringe. Now it was a full-on powerhouse, a southern *network*.

There was no way to know for sure how many people were tuning in. Ratings didn't measure cable yet. But there was a more powerful indicator, and it arrived in the form of an avalanche of hundreds of pieces of mail a day—fan mail for Tush, fan mail for the wrestlers, orders for products. More than half of that mail arrived from outside the Atlanta metro area, demonstrating channel 17's expanding footprint and the zeal with which the audience consumed it.

There was an added bonus to the excitement. As Ted gleefully sifted through the life-saving bounty delivered each day by the postal service, he'd keep his eyes peeled for stamps the post office had forgotten to cancel and carefully remove them to use again. Every penny helped.

* * *

It was about this time that Reese Schonfeld and Sid Topol had walked in the door to Ted's den-like office, buzzing about commercial satellites and this service called HBO and the transformation of the business of television. Ted was positively giddy about how cable had turned around channel 17, and his growing audience around the region.

While it made sense that people in the southeast were devouring his programming, especially since they loved Atlanta's sports teams, it seemed preposterous, at first blush, to think that anyone outside the area might be interested in what channel 17 had to offer.

Or was it? Why *wouldn't* other viewers in markets around the nation want to see channel 17? Sixty-five percent of the country had never laid eyes on an indie station. And unlike HBO, which cost an additional fee and aired for limited hours each day, his service was free—and on the air day and night.

Airing over cable had stripped away the innate liabilities of the station and had allowed him to compete, side by side, with network affiliates. The potent cocktail of cable and satellite would allow him to compete with the networks themselves.

Yes, it was new and untested and the rules were changing quickly. Yes, some people thought it crazy. But the fact that others saw something as crazy had never stopped Ted before. The riskier the proposition, the more likely he was to take it. As a kid, as he devoured the stories of kings and conquests from the history books, he'd worried that there were no new worlds left to explore. Now it was clear that the unexplored frontier he'd been waiting for was up above, in the heavens. That's when he began to think of himself as a modern Christopher Columbus. Who knew where the skies might take him?

* * *

Ted called his sales staff to order. He'd just reserved his own earth station by writing a check to Scientific Atlanta for $750,000, admonishing Topol not to cash it for a few days while he figured out how to raise that sum. On the conference table, he placed a model of a satellite in the center of the table, a small piece of square-shaped metal that looked as if it had wings. Someone whispered that it looked like the wreck of a car. Ted paced around and around in circles, like a wild tiger, unable, as usual, to sit down. He moved so swiftly that attempting to count his rotations around the room proved futile.

"This is how we're going to become a national network and compete with ABC, NBC, and CBS," he announced confidently, pointing to the sorry hunk of metal. Super 17 was soon to be a *Super Station*.

The staff looked at him blankly, as if he were speaking Greek. Even those who loved him agreed that Ted was nuts, but this cinched it. A satellite? A fourth network? Channel 17, with a bunch of wrestling and reruns and old movies and a goofy middle-of-the-night comedy newscast? Transmitted over a twisted hunk of metal shot up into the sky?

Look at what they'd built by linking up to cable, he told them. That distribution system could take channel 17 only so far. This would allow all of America to tune in, crystal-clear! Here was their chance to become "the superstation that served the nation," to give every television viewer in the nation a choice. When they got up on the satellite, he proclaimed, "ABC will shrink down to a puddle like the witch in *The Wizard of Oz*."

Having said his piece, he looked around the table, in search of a positive reaction that didn't materialize. Relying on cable operators outside of Atlanta to import their signal to other markets had been a strange enough concept for most of his team to grasp. TV wasn't supposed to work this way. The networks were based in New York and provided programs, over AT&T lines, to affiliated stations around the nation. Together, they dominated the television roost. Then, there were the independents, like channel 17, that cobbled together their own programming and hoped for the best. Other attempts at turning a string of indies into a network had failed. Television had been this way for the twenty or so years since it became commercially available. What Ted was proposing made no sense. It had no precedent.

A couple of guys bravely piped up with concern. Colleagues in the business disparaged satellites as bunk, a fad. Many believed HBO was unsustainable—their battle with the movie companies alone, for the rights to air films, would squash the service! HBO, at least, had the backing of a big corporation. How could little channel 17 possibly hope to compete?

Ted, chief inhabitant of Planet Hope, didn't want to hear one negative word.

"You guys take your lunch and get out of this room!" he shouted. "The only people I want in this room are people who are going to help me."

CHAPTER FIVE

Captain Outrageous

It was bad enough that the carpetbaggers who owned the Atlanta Braves had deigned to award the broadcast rights of the beloved team to a crappy, fourth-rate television station. In the sacred year that marked the two hundredth birthday of America, word came that the group of businessmen in Chicago were selling the team to the owner of that very station. So eager were they to dispose of the cellar-dwelling drain on their finances that they allowed the cash-strapped Ted Turner to buy on an installment plan, like a car or a BarcaLounger. Fittingly, when the news first leaked out that an "Atlanta advertising executive and internationally known yachtsman" was about to seal the deal, where was the mysterious newest owner in Major League Baseball to be found? Off sailing.

The Braves' original lineage dated all the way back to Boston and the nation's centenary year, 1876. By the time the team took up residence in Atlanta in 1966, after a dozen years in Milwaukee, the south was in the throes of the civil rights movement, and the city sorely needed a boost. The installation of the first Major League Baseball team south of Washington, D.C., also raised the city's profile. Now, on the sports pages of national newspapers, the word "Atlanta" would appear. Icing on the cake: superstar Hank Aaron, who had debuted with the club at age twenty, broke Babe Ruth's home run record, hammering home his historic 715th home run in April 1974.

As the town buzzed with speculation about this wild-card new owner, observers consoled themselves with the fact that while they didn't know much about this Ted Turner fellow, at least he had local roots. As local sports columnist Wayne Minshew observed, "It is a peculiar trait some Atlantans, southerners, have to 'trust our own,' and Turner is 'one of us,' having grown up in Georgia and lived here since he was nine." He was also a "wild man" with movie-star good looks—the opposite of dull. Plus, the columnist reasoned, anyone who could turn around the left-for-dead channel 17 with wrestling, shlocky commercials and a pratfalling news anchor who lampooned the news—anyone with the temerity to float the station hither and yon, all over the southeast—well, imagine what he could do for the Braves.

In truth, the Braves couldn't sink any lower. In their entire existence, they'd called more cities home (three) than they'd had forays into the World Series (two.) Even their devoted promotions director, Bob Hope—an inventive young fellow saddled with the same name as the famous comedian—didn't mince words: "No other team in American sports history has put together a longer span of ineptitude: 2,137 losses out of 3,975 games over 25 years." Their attendance figures matched their performance record—pathetically low.

So why would a two-time yachtsman of the year who spent at least a quarter of his time away from the city on a boat, a man no one remembered ever seeing at the ballpark, wish to be bothered with this money-losing dud of a team?

At his press conference debut, seated behind outgoing owners Bill Bartholomay and Dan Donahue, he pledged his allegiance to the game by wearing a maroon commemorative Hank Aaron tie as he spun the acquisition as a love letter to his adopted city.

"Atlanta is my home and I love it here," he said. "I've been all over the world racing and stopped in Tahiti on the way back from Australia, which I read a lot about as a little boy, and I decided the closest thing to paradise on this earth is Atlanta, Georgia, and aww . . . It's not an economically wise move to buy the team, but, aww, money itself is not the prime motivation here. I believe I'm doing it primarily for the city and the southern part of the country, believe it or not." He was thirty-seven years old, he told the press corps, and he intended to keep the team for the rest of his life.

And he intended to turn headlines that declared Atlanta "Losersville" into ones that proclaimed the city "Winnersville." If anyone understood hard-fought victories, it was him. It had taken him eight years to win his first sailing race, and look at how he'd beaten the odds in turning around the fortunes of the wretched channel 17. The Braves, he promised, would win the World Series in five years.*

The desire for victory and to bolster civic pride, in fact, had very little to do with why Ted had just signed on to baseball. The truth was, the Braves were a crucial component of his burgeoning media empire, and he dearly needed them to stay put in Atlanta. When the owners had revealed at the end of the previous season that they were through with baseball and planning to sell, he'd flipped. Whoever else might have bought the team could very well have opted to move them away or sever ties with the station. Aside from his growing film library and television reruns, the Braves had become the oxygen of Super 17. Airing their games had imbued WTCG with a veneer of legitimacy, not to mention the airtime it filled and the advertising dollars it generated. As the number of cable systems carrying the station around the region continued to grow, the Braves were becoming "the south's team." And just imagine what would happen when permission was finally granted to shower the signal across the nation. That would catapult them to become "America's Team." That next step in his space-age aspirations was currently held up in a tangle of anxiety-inducing governmental bureaucracy and legal challenges that rattled even the ever-optimistic Ted. His earth station had been installed and was ready to go on a special plot of land he'd found ten miles out of midtown Atlanta, but, much to his dismay, he still hadn't won permission to use it. For now, he could brag about this latest feather tucked onto his railroad cap.

* * *

As the city settled into news of the new owner, a thousand of the team's toniest fans jammed the grand ballroom of the brand-new Peachtree Plaza Hotel in downtown to get a glimpse of him. Patrons donned their

* They didn't win the World Series until 1995.

finest for the annual Braves 400 Eddie Glennon Gameboree, named both for the batting average that eluded most mere mortals who played the game and the long-time sales manager for the team, who had been so dedicated to the sport that he'd managed to die while listening to a game on the radio.

More people showed up for this fancy pep rally than had appeared in recent years on an average night at the stadium. The record crowd was eager to hear from this man who owned the rerun station many wouldn't admit to watching, who'd they'd heard couldn't tell a "ball from a balk."

Glasses clinked as the assembled crowd feasted on salad, London broil, and parfait.

Ted, wearing that commemorative maroon Hank Aaron tie again, wasted no time in revealing himself. In his trademark buzz-saw squawk, he told the crowd he planned to make baseball fun again. "I'm sick of mottos. If we have one at all, it's gonna be 'Victory or Death.'" Then he revealed a bombshell: He was thinking of changing the team's name to the Eagles—the name of one of his yachts, he explained, but mostly because "it's cheaper to feed a bird than an Indian."

Lighting a cigar for dramatic effect, Ted the bombastic raconteur reveled in his place at center stage. While he was certain he was a terrific public speaker, his off-the-cuff meanderings confounded audiences. His inability to stop talking, much less self-censor, would soon yield a nickname he abhorred: "The Mouth of the South."

"We may lose it all on this deal," he told these most ardent cheerleaders of the Braves, "but if everything goes down the commode, they'll have to come get me, and channel 17, too. If things get bad enough, and aww, they may, we'll lock up the stadium, play day games to save electricity, and by God, if anyone asks what the hell we're doin' in there, I'll tell 'em—we're learning how to win! I've got some friends in the Mafioso up north and as much as I'd hate to resort to those tactics, we'll rough up Pete Rose or Dave Concepcion if they start playing too well."

After a half hour of speechifying, rambling Ted admitted he'd been asked to keep his remarks to just five minutes and explained he got "kinda carried away." In the next day's paper, sportswriter Furman Bisher observed that for the bewildered boosters, going from the stoic, starched previous owners to Ted Turner was "like switching from Mozart to Lynyrd Skynyrd."

Ted continued to rock and roll on his get-to-know-you publicity tour. Next stop: the Atlanta Chamber of Commerce breakfast, where he fielded questions that included one about what he intended to do regarding the crime issue in the area surrounding Atlanta–Fulton County Stadium.

His solution? He planned to run buses from the stadium to the north side of town during games, so the thieves could steal from those more affluent neighborhoods, then board buses back home afterward.

In wandering introductory remarks to the curious employees in the Braves front office, he evoked Hitler and Alexander the Great and likened their quests to conquer the world with his own. From now on, he declared, the workday would start at eight thirty, not nine—the early bird/worm theory. Environmentally unfriendly Styrofoam cups would be eliminated from the office. Next, he appealed directly to fans in a newspaper ad, asking them to write in with suggestions but advising, "Please do not be too lengthy in your comments since I will have a lot of reading to do."

Later, Ted summoned team promotions and publicity director Bob Hope to the station, asking him to bring along a Braves cap, bat, and script so he could tape a commercial promoting season tickets. He told the man he had another important goal besides winning: to put the fun back in baseball.

"Hope, I want this team to be like McDonald's," he said enthusiastically. "I want an atmosphere built here that will make kids want to come to the games. Excitement isn't the success of one individual promotion. It's the chemistry of everything combined. We've got to do enough to create the chemistry."

After years of grappling with conservative ownership, this was music to Hope's ears. He proceeded to lay out thirty pages of theatrics designed to pack the stadium and distract fans from the team's lousy ballplaying, including organizing bathtub races, conducting weddings at home plate, and enlisting local ham radio operators to summon a UFO to the field.*

The more outlandish Hope's ideas, the more Ted whooped with approval. "Keep the smoke going after the fire goes out!" he cheered. Then he offered up a few ideas of his own. When the team lost, fans could release their anger with Slug the Players Night. Okay, he admitted, he was only kidding about *that*. But he was dead serious about something else. He didn't just want to publicize the team. He wanted publicity for himself. Hope and the Braves were going to help him become a celebrity—as famous as Muhammad Ali.

He was on his way.

Baseball had never been Ted's sport as a fan or player, but his purchase of the Atlanta Braves placed him side by side with one of baseball's greats, home-run king Hank Aaron. *(Budd Skinner/Atlanta Journal-Constitution via AP)*

* Hundreds of ham operators participated, and fifty thousand people sat hushed in the darkened stadium as a small circle of lights formed a landing pad on the field. The crowd booed.

Proprietors of a local clothing company asked to feature the handsome Ted, nattily dressed, in their ad campaign, sliding into first base. There was particular irony in this, since not only had Ted never played baseball, he also looked, as one player observed, like he got dressed in the closet. (Or in the dark. Once an interviewer noticed he was wearing one black and one brown shoe.) In an effort to jazz up his wardrobe, Janie had bought him Gucci loafers. If he knew they cost $150 a pair, he'd have freaked. He insisted on cutting his own hair to save the seven dollars for a barber.

People magazine called. Ted was to be included in their "most intriguing people" list. A dashing young media mogul who raced yachts, now insinuating himself into America's pastime, was as juicy as headline-grabbing hamburger king Ray Kroc emerging in the eleventh hour as the unlikely savior of the San Diego Padres. The editors proposed a photo shoot that included three pillars of Ted's passion: Ted posing in a rowboat, holding a portable television set, wearing a Braves cap. The only thing missing was a billboard—and blondes. Though the weather was bitter cold, Ted mugged happily for the cameras.

Nowhere did he hunger more for approval than with the players. Back when he was merely airing the Braves games, he'd lamented that the boys of summer were nothing but an anonymous "bunch of stiffs." The fans needed to know these young, uniformed athletes were real people—individuals. Be nice, he advised. Amp up the theatrics. Take bows: "It will mean more money for you and more for me." Together, they appeared in a commercial touting "The Big League Team with the Little League Spirit." Come on out and see the Braves at your "Atlanta Teepee," the proud new owner twanged with P. T. Barnum flair. The players smiled like awkward teenagers next to their outgoing dad.

To illustrate his approachable nature, he admonished them to "Call me Ted. I ain't no Mister." (After he upbraided his secretary for using "sir," she'd taken to calling her boss by the decidedly informal nickname "Teddy Baby.") He invited the incredulous bunch over for dinner at his house, personally greeting them at the door as if they were old friends. The planned entertainment for the evening? A screening of a film of his failed America's Cup bid in 1974—his worst defeat ever, and the one from which he'd learned the most. His plans were dashed when the projector didn't work.

It was if he'd acquired not just a sporting enterprise but a whole team of fellas to pal around with. After all, he was a jock, too, just like them. He didn't care—as other owners did—what they wore off the field, or about the length of their hair, or whether they grew beards and mustaches. ("Just as long as he wears something over his cock," he told a reporter.) This being the cusp of the era of free agency, when the average ballplayer earned less than $50,000 a year, he invited them to come work at the station in the off-season to learn new skills and pick up extra cash.*

Another culture clash: spiriting the boys of summer during an April series with the Mets to the vaunted New York Yacht Club—the same club that had reluctantly admitted Ted after rejecting him twice because of his bombastic personality. Ted himself still couldn't believe he was allowed to enter the storied limestone mansion on West Forty-Fourth Street, much less that he belonged. Just thinking about it made him particularly wistful for his father, who'd regaled him when he was a kid with descriptions of how "swank and ritzy" the place was. Ed Turner would never have imagined his own son might be awarded membership. "Lord, it would blow his mind," Ted said. Now, here he was wrangling a pack of young baseball studs, awkward in their sportscoats, down the streets of midtown Manhattan. He'd arranged for a private bar and a dinner of prime rib with horseradish sauce served by tuxedoed men carrying towels over their arms. The gentility quickly devolved into schoolyard recess when shortstop Darrel Chaney destroyed the decorum by letting loose his handmade fart machine, which he then gleefully passed around to the others.

As a member of a very different exclusive club—owners of Major League Baseball teams—Ted plunged into every facet of the game, the

---

* For a look at average salaries before free agency, please see https://www3.nd.edu/~lawlib/baseball_salary_arbitration/minavgsalaries/Minimum-AverageSalaries.pdf.

kind of total immersion he'd indulged in when he'd first purchased channel 17. By day, he'd deliver speeches to the community on the breakfast and luncheon circuits. Come afternoon, he'd busy himself with personnel issues and plot pregame promotions. In between, he'd help sell television ad time.

At the stadium, he installed Atlanta's first electronic scoreboard, a million-dollar state-of-the-art screen, the ultimate modern billboard, on which he planned to flash instant replays as well as Ted-isms like NOT TOO SHABBY after a good play, or quippy bits like: "The Civil War was a boon to baseball. Union soldiers played the game for recreation. The Confederates learned it from captured Union soldiers."

As general of this joint, he ordered the visiting team's dugout emblazoned with the words THE ENEMIES and the first few rows of the stands moved a bit closer to the field. This would be the perch from which he'd lord over the games—no luxuriating in the air-conditioned isolation of an owner's box for Ted, who fancied himself "Mr. Every-man." After each game, he planned to head to the locker room, where, just like one of the guys, he'd shower with the team.

After the very first game, Ted frolicked on the ball field, running the bases, turning somersaults, and delighting in leading the crowds in a rousing rendition of "Take Me Out to the Ballgame." Something about baseball unleashed his inner good ol' boy. Off came his shirt, away went his pricey Cuban cigars, traded for a bag of Red Man chewing tobacco, which remained perched on the roof of the Braves' dugout for the season. He'd pinch and cram a generous wad of it inside his jaw, hooting and hollering with glee. Fans unabashedly approached him for autographs—women, on occasion, pointing the pen at their bosoms—and he happily signed away. Sitting behind Ted during a game, one visitor observed, was "like sitting behind Caesar at the Colosseum."

Caesar who threw tantrums. Once, after the team lost, he retreated to the locker room, angrily hurled an onion against a wall, and upended a table of sandwiches.

Not everyone was enthralled by the irrepressible volatility nor the wild ideas of "Teddy Baseball," the snickering nickname the team's staff bequeathed on him (behind his back) for his zealous and seemingly sudden conversion to the religion of America's pastime.

The idea of changing the Braves to the Eagles crashed with a resounding thud. Ted shrugged off the deluge of angry mail he received in response, singing to a reporter a few lines of Glen Campbell, that "Like a Rhinestone Cowboy" he was "getting cards and letters from people I don't even know." He got the message and dropped the idea.

After offending the fans, he'd offended the sportswriters by asking them to quit writing negative stories about the team. They explained that it was hard to write positive stories, since the Braves were so bad. *Atlanta Constitution* columnist Ron Hudspeth was appalled when Ted told him that baseball was for "little people" who had nothing else to live for. "Can you imagine your happiness hinging on the Braves winning or losing?" he said of the loyalists whose happiness did.

Ted's decision to start charging members of the press for lunch and booze they were accustomed to receiving free was nothing short of a declaration of war. It was hard for anyone to believe his penny-pinching excuse for scuttling the grub: "My wife and I are unable to have friends over for dinner—and I mean that—and here I am feeding sixty people every day Swiss steak in the press box. I know every other team does it, but I'm gonna be the first to stop it."

The only thing worse than messing with the sportswriters' free food was firing their drinking buddy, a longtime Braves staffer who'd logged thirty-eight years of service with the team—an allegedly profligate man who happened to be a dwarf. ("What does he need a hotel suite for?" Ted demanded to know of the man's penchant for luxury on the road. "All he needs is a closet!") The spurned employee's wife, a practicing witch, retaliated by casting a hex on Ted *and* the team. Voodoo or not, there wasn't much lower the Braves could sink.

Atlanta Journal sportswriter Frank Hyland expressed his disgust not with a spell but with words: "Ted Turner has money. Ted Turner has a lot of money. Ted Turner has enthusiasm. Ted Turner has his own baseball team. Ted belongs to some of the world's most prestigious clubs. But Ted Turner has no class."

Ted's classy response?

"The guy wrote that I have no class. Well, I don't consider myself a classy person. Class is very low on my list of priorities. I'd rather have traits like courage and tenacity. For this particular guy to say I have no class, he's a slovenly character who doesn't even take care of his teeth. His teeth are rotting out of his face. I pay janitors more than he's probably making. I bet ninety-nine point nine percent of the people would say I have more class than that guy."

People in Braves Land were being treated to a crash course in what those in TV Land, Billboard Land, and Yacht Land already knew: Ted Turner was "a package of dynamite in those days with a bit of loose cannon thrown in," observed Roger Vaughan, a Brown classmate who'd sailed with Ted and later wrote two books about him.

"Ted," said front-office veteran Bill Lucas, "would make coffee nervous."

And as Ted's star ascended, Hope observed, what may have been seen before as simply crazy became legitimized as eccentric. That did not excuse, in his estimation, Ted's penchant for telling people (including his own wife) to shut up or chastising them as "stupid" and "numbnuts" and "dummy." When he dared to call his devoted promotions and publicity chief an "idiot," Hope angrily retorted that he must never do that again.

"I call people that all the time," Ted said with a shrug. "It doesn't mean anything. You're one of my best friends. I was nervous. I say all kinds of strange things. I don't even know what I'm saying sometimes."

Was that his explanation for his behavior toward women? Pitcher Dick Ruthven outed Ted for making several passes at his wife. (For his part, Ted said he was a "friend" to the Mrs. and that he liked her husband, even if "he was a little bit of a head case.")

"Nothing stops the guy—even the woman's husband standing twenty feet away," professed one Turner watcher. Or his own spouse. Ted's frequent accomplice, a gorgeous Frenchwoman who liked to lounge naked on the hull of his boat, now enjoyed a new place to sunbathe topless—by the pool during spring training. Never mind if wife

Janie was around. When concerned staffers tried to hush their conversation about the nude nymph as Janie approached, she waved their concern away, dismissing the woman as "Ted's French whore." At a society party, Ted explained as he left the dinner table, "Excuse me, I have to call my mistress," while dumbfounded guests watched his scorned wife storm after him and pound on the phone booth door.

Just five months into his tenure, the National League president, Chub Feeney, hauled Ted in. The conduct unbecoming that broke the camel's back occurred when he shouted out from the stands at pitcher Al Hrabosky that he shouldn't bother signing his contract. Baseball brass also advised him to stop offering cash incentives to players to win, cease playing poker with them, and ditch the use of nicknames instead of surnames on the backs of jerseys.

This practice had begun when he signed pitcher Andy Messersmith for an eye-popping salary of a million dollars—heralding the free-agency era that changed the sport forever. The new addition to the team, who happened to wear number 17, quipped, "Boss, the kinda money you're paying me, my nickname's gonna be 'Channel,' OK?" While Ted loved the idea of his pricey new ballplayer doing double-duty as a human billboard for his beloved television station, Chub Feeney did not. "Channel 17" the ballplayer was exiled to extinction, while channel 17, the formerly downtrodden station on the lunatic fringe, continued to soar.

* * *

The Braves finished the first season of the Turner era with seventy wins and ninety-two losses, cementing their last-place standing. But other vital statistics vastly improved in that summer of 1976. Attendance had almost doubled, in no small part because of the wild entertainment provided to divert from the lousy baseball: wrestling matches, home-plate weddings, postgame fan appreciation spaghetti and pizza served on the field, and, on occasion, Champagne. (A wet T-shirt contest was in the works for next season.) As Hope described it, "Every pig in the southeast was pursued in a greased-pig chase, and every little leaguer appeared in a pre-game show." No matter how inventive the theatrics, the main draw was indubitably Ted. It was worth coming to the park just to see how he would fare *this* time, in competitions for mattress stacking, bathtub racing, and the baseball nose-roll (Ted won that contest, and had the bloodied face from pushing the ball around the diamond with his nose to prove it.) He'd almost backed out of the ostrich race (and lamented that it lasted only one lap) after learning that the plan was to ride not on the back of the bird but rather in a cart. That seemed like cheating. Short of hanging upside down at second base or spitting BBs two hundred yards out of his mouth, Ted said, he was happy to participate, parking himself at home plate to shake the hands of victorious home-run hitters, helping the bat girl sweep the bases, or spontaneously breaking into backflips on the field. (That exhibition of superpower even mystified him—he'd never done one before.)

"I may look like a clown," Ted told an interviewer, "but I'm a very deadly serious person in trying to accomplish things just for the satisfaction of accomplishing them. Struggling hard to achieve something is the most fun I get. All my life is a game. Everything is a game. And the game goes fast, too."

Time wasn't all that was fleeting. So was his sense of satisfaction. All he had ever wanted, he said, was to be rich and famous. "Now everybody knows me, and I have more money than I could possibly ever spend, and I'm still not happy."

His innate restlessness was intensified by his impatience as he continued to wait for the green light to beam his space-age TV station up to the heavens. The earth station was primed and ready in northwest Atlanta. (Bill Tush was pressed into service to host a recorded tour of the highly sequestered high-tech facility that would make the "space-age station" possible.)*

Meanwhile, Ted just couldn't keep from getting into trouble. Blame this next monumental baseball gaffe on the '76 World Series—and six

---

* To take the satellite facility tour yourself, please see https://www.youtube.com/watch?v= RV8YRqBUnMI.

vodkas. After rain postponed game four between the New York Yankees and the Cincinnati Reds, a member of the press had tipped Ted off to an impromptu party where the booze flowed. In a blustering move to show he wasn't a cheapskate, he bragged to the owner of the San Francisco Giants, Bob Lurie, that he'd top whatever offer he made for free-agent outfielder Gary Matthews.

After a sportswriter who'd overheard the exchange wrote about it, and Lurie received a complaint, Ted was slapped with a $10,000 fine for tampering. Sick and tired of the Mouth of the South, Commissioner Bowie Kuhn threatened to suspend him from the sport.

An outraged Ted exclaimed that he hadn't been suspended from anything since college! Even the aggrieved Lurie felt the punishment didn't fit the crime. "If all charges and kidding at cocktail parties were taken this seriously," he said, "there'd be nobody left in the game."

Irate fans spurred to action on behalf of their good ol' boy. Burger King printed protest postcards for customers to send to the commissioner's office. The mayor of Atlanta, Maynard Jackson, delivered a petition filled with forty thousand signatures. A "Ted Turner Task Force" distributed red-and-white bumper stickers, funded by a local tire company, that announced, "WE SUPPORT TED TURNER." At the Atlanta Flames hockey game, a gigantic sign was unfurled: "Who Cares About Ted Turner? ATLANTA DOES!"

In the outpouring of public support, Ted saw an unbeatable PR opportunity. After all, he said, Jesus Christ "never got rolling till they nailed him to that cross." Without crucifixion, he "would have been considered just another longhaired hippie freak." Indeed, a suspension further elevated Ted's status as a hero—and it was perfectly timed, too. He had other plans for next summer that involved the sport he *really* cared about. After his crushing elimination from the 1974 America's Cup, he'd plunked down a quarter of a million dollars to buy that year's winning boat, *Courageous*, on the condition that he would get to skipper it the next time around, and 1977 was to be the year.

The oldest sports prize in the world, the Cup was considered the most prestigious on the racing circuit—the Mount Everest of sailing.

Ted had been dreaming of the chance to participate since his college days, when he'd first laid eyes on the majestic twelve-meter boats in Newport, Rhode Island's Bannister's Wharf. To young aspiring warrior Ted, they looked like Viking ships poised for battle.

The three months of preliminary competition took place right smack in the heart of baseball season. How could Teddy Baseball, Mr. Everyman, explain being away for so long? He'd become an indelible part of the Braves draw. Taking off to sail would flush his good ol' boy persona right down the drain. "People might suddenly realize he was not only rich but also an elitist," observed Bob Hope. "Or even worse, they would realize yachting came first with him since he'd be missing all the baseball games."

But if the commissioner suspended him for an entire season . . . then the stadium would be off-limits, and Ted would have the perfect excuse for not being around all summer.

As the verdict loomed, all involved in the business of the sport gathered in Los Angeles for its annual confab, the Winter Meetings. Ted talked to anyone who would listen about how he was being harassed, castigated, and crucified by commissioner Bowie Kuhn—that he was worried for his life and feared Kuhn was going to kill him. "I double locked my door last night," he told a reporter, and went on to lament that he had "as much chance of winning this case as Czechoslovakia had against Hitler." At the hotel restaurant, he got down on his hands and knees and ranted and raved and barked like a dog, rambling incoherently in the lobby for a while and then, observed an increasingly concerned Hope, disappearing with some woman.

A few days into the meetings, a radio reporter approached Bob Hope with a troubling audio recording. It was unmistakably Ted, saying that he was going to get a gun and kill the commissioner before the commissioner got him first.

Hope and the team's general manager, Bill Lucas, took their boss by either arm to a lobby bar.

"Ted, there's a fine line between being outrageous and being absolutely out of your mind," they told him. "You've gone over the edge."

"Do you think I should get on a plane and fly back to Atlanta?" Ted asked.

"Yes, if you can't get your mind together and act right," Hope responded.

"Do you think I've convinced him I'm crazy?" Ted asked. That would certainly cinch his suspension.

Yes, Hope answered. He was convinced himself.

* * *

Just before Christmas, Ted received the gift he'd long been waiting for. The Federal Communications Commission gave the green light for channel 17 to beam its signal to cable operators via the satellite. The switch was flipped on the fortuitous *seventeenth* day of December. By launching into space, Ted had leapfrogged his once-destined-for-the-graveyard local station into a SuperStation. From the ghetto of the lunatic fringe, all the way up to the stars, and back down to the nation's television sets.

Though not terribly many of them. To start, only four systems were equipped to receive channel 17—in Grand Island, Nebraska; Newport News, Virginia; Troy, Alabama; and Newton, Kansas. Twenty others, from as far away as Canada, Puerto Rico, and Hawaii, had applied for and received FCC permission to come online by January. Satellite dishes and the right to transmit were tightly monitored by the government. Soon, though, regulators began to ease up on the size of and price of receiving dishes, making it cheaper and easier for even the smallest cable companies to afford to link up to the satellite. In an instant, instead of having to fork over a hundred grand for a thirty-foot dish that ate up the parking lot, you could pay ten thousand bucks for a dish small enough to install on the roof of your building. The more cable operators could offer subscribers, the more subscribers they could attract and the more cable would grow.

By April, channel 17 would have a half million viewers outside the Atlanta area; by the fall of 1977, double that.

To help him wade through this new complex terrain, Ted hired one of the few people in the nation who actually understood it. From his perch at a cable trade association, Donald Andersson had intently studied the rules and the maps of the nation's systems and television stations. Now, a soldier in Ted's army, he trundled around the southeast to cable companies large and small, encouraging them to, as the button he took to wearing on his lapel invited, "Steal This Signal." But this was hardly a theft: It was a game-changing rule that was about to catapult Ted to new figurative heights.

From the ladies in the brothels in Nye County, Nevada, to the captive audience at the Granite State Prison in Oklahoma, the potential to reach a national audience was, for Ted, more electrifying than all the fireworks ignited throughout the bicentennial year.

Doubters persisted. A dubious reporter had wondered who would care to watch channel 17 outside Atlanta. To prove how widespread and devoted the fan base was, Braves announcer Skip Caray read the doubting reporter's phone number on the air. The surge of calls overloaded and ultimately blew out the telephone exchange.

Now, with this latest development, another reporter asked, "How many people in Alaska are going to want to watch the Braves?" In short order, another answer arrived. To serve as grand marshal of its annual parade, the city of Valdez, Alaska, invited none other than cable television's very first star, the man who entertained them every night—Bill Tush.

* * *

The verdict on another bit of business that had vexed Ted arrived just after the first of the year. Baseball commissioner Bowie Kuhn handed down his sentence: a $35,000 fine for tampering and a year's suspension for "conduct detrimental to baseball."

This didn't stop Ted from making a major announcement the very next day. He was buying another dog of a team whose games he already aired. Purchasing basketball's Atlanta Hawks might have seemed as pointless as "taking over the Confederate Army on the steps of Appomattox Court House," he said. "Hitler was more likely to get elected President of Israel than the Hawks were to win." But owning the team, no matter how losing a team it was, was a key pillar in his new dream, to build a sports network. He planned to supply up to sixteen pay cable sporting events a month.

But first, it was time to hit the road in the name of preseason baseball and the annual Winter Caravan. Along with the usual stops—Macon, Columbus, Savannah, Augusta, Valdosta, Rome, Gainesville, Albany, and Dalton—this year's goodwill tour to press the flesh and peddle season tickets had expanded to include cities where cable had made the team more beloved, like Chattanooga, Nashville, Knoxville, Montgomery, Anniston, Birmingham, Huntsville, and Dothan.

But the most important stop would be first—Plains, Georgia, hometown of Governor Jimmy Carter, just days away from his inauguration as the thirty-ninth president of the United States. Baseball plus the new president's slice of small-town America equaled the perfect media pit stop.

Everyone, even Ted, angled for a seat on board. The procession grew to include three buses, two station wagons, and an RV—bigger than the caravan had ever been before. Hope worried that his boss would explode with disappointment if the president-elect himself didn't show up—an amusement, since Ted was an avowed Republican who'd supported President Ford in the election. Without making any promises, Jimmy's brother, Billy Carter (sporting a shirt that proclaimed he was a "Redneck Lobbyist"), assured Hope not to worry.

It was warm and sunny, after days of rain and cold, when the caravan pulled into town and paused at the appointed location, the Plains Country Club, which turned out to be little more than a beat-up old shack near an abandoned motel. The players and their entourage waited for an hour before a limousine peeled into the parking lot. Jimmy, Rosalynn, and Amy, enjoying their last weekend before taking up residence in the White House, had arrived.

Ted presented the president-elect with a blue Braves warm-up jacket emblazoned with his name and the number 1, the perfect page-one shot for the next day's news.

"We're trying to get their minds off their troubles," Ted said—meaning their lousy record. "You're doing a good job," the president-elect said to Ted—one Georgia boy to another.

"This is strong," Ted responded. "I was there when you announced you were running and I said, 'He might do it.'"

"You win a World Series," Carter replied, aware of Ted's ambitions for the team, "and we're even."

In truth, Ted had developed even grander ambitions than a championship. He himself was considering a run for the presidency. Perhaps he'd first have to wet his feet by winning a more junior office, but he was certain he could. The outpouring of support he received during his scuffle with the baseball commissioner convinced him of his mass appeal. He was certain he could count on the support of the press, too. Wouldn't the media love to see one of their own run for the highest office in the land?

For now, Plains, Georgia, felt like the center of the universe, as a feast of barbecue chicken was served up on paper plates, accompanied by plenty of beer. Later, what seemed like the entire town (population 653) packed the high school stadium. The soon-to-be First Mother, Miss Lillian, arrived around the second inning and cozied up in a lawn chair. Billy Carter pitched to Hank Aaron, and the Plains All-Stars walloped the pros, seventeen to five.

And on the way back home on the fancy coaches hired for the trip, the boys of summer were treated to a present from Ted: porno films.

* * *

Presidents. Satellites. Suspensions. Basketball teams. As if that wasn't enough drama, late one night, the FBI trailed Ted's French lady-friend, now a suspect in a matter of international espionage, all the way to a

Holiday Inn in St. Petersburg, Florida. Much to their surprise, they discovered Ted in the room she was headed for—waiting in bed with a bottle of Champagne, cheerfully wondering what took her so long. He was there for a yacht race the next day. The alibi she gave the embarrassed agents exonerated her on the spot.

Ted began to wonder if the FBI had tapped his phones or the lines in the commissioner's office. Speaking before the National Sportscasters and Sportswriters Association in Salisbury, North Carolina, he speculated about both in a breakfast speech that was pure Mouth of the South. First, he lamented that no book existed with the title *How to Be an Owner*. Next, he advised never taking more than five drinks at a baseball cocktail party. Then he swore off the parties themselves: "I want to keep a low profile, keep my mouth shut and be a good boy. I'll do whatever the commissioner says. If he says, 'Step 'n fetch it,' I'll step 'n fetch it."

The only person he disliked more than Commissioner Kuhn and Adolf Hitler, he said, was sports agent Jerry Kapstein. He promised to explain why he didn't like the man, for, after all, "You should have some reason to dislike a guy besides the fact that he wears a full-length fur coat and is a Jew." Frustrated by the piles of money he extracted from owners like Ted on behalf of his clients, he'd written Kapstein a letter decrying his tactics and signed it "Yours in Christ."

After his remarks were published, the Anti-Defamation League expressed outrage, and some members of the New York Yacht Club pushed to have him ousted, Ted issued an apology. In a letter to the local Jewish paper, several Jewish employees of channel 17, including Pike, loyally rose to Ted's defense. Really, they explained, Ted was not an anti-Semite. Fallible, but not anti-Semitic. He was, they knew, equal-opportunity offensive.

Keeping his mouth shut—and keeping a low profile—was simply not in Ted's DNA. Frustrated by a sixteen-game losing streak, he thumbed his nose at baseball's establishment yet again by sending his manager, Dave Bristol, off on vacation and announcing that he'd manage the team himself. If he had "enough brains" to buy the club, surely, he believed, he had enough brains to run it. "I could make them winners. Hypnotize them—*you are winners*," he said. Whatever tactics he might deploy to improve the team, his knowledge of the basics was sorely lacking. Observers looked on with amusement as Ted clumsily suited up in his uniform with the stirrups on backward.

His self-appointed managerial role lasted exactly one game—after he added another loss to the Braves' dismal streak, dropping their record to 8–22. Finally, mercifully, his suspension kicked in, and he was free to go sailing.

But he didn't leave baseball behind. Trailing behind him as he pulled into Newport was a "portable" ten-meter satellite dish that got planted behind the twenty-two-room English Tudor lodge he'd inhabit with the crew for the summer. By day, he'd walk the two miles to the docks to sail. By night, after the endless parties that were part and parcel of racing season, the dish would allow him to tune in to the Braves

How hard could it be to manage a baseball team? Harder than it looked, Ted discovered, when he took the helm for one game—and added to the loss column. *(AP Photo/R. C. Greenawalt)*

and channel 17. Onlookers attracted by the space-age curiosity gathered around and wondered in amazement if the dish radiated light. They'd never seen such a thing. The biggest marvel—and the main attraction—was not this hulking piece of newfangled technology but this strange, larger-than-life specimen of a human.

The flap about his suspension had put yachting, and specifically the America's Cup, on the populist map. Most of the nation couldn't tell a luff from a tack, nor did they care to, but that didn't stop the crowds from swarming to the quaint town of Newport in support of Ted. Fans mobbed him, rock-star style, rushing out of restaurants and chasing him down the street to snap a photo or beg an autograph. Street vendors peddled buttons that proclaimed *Ted Turner for President*.

A faction of haters sported competing buttons featuring a cartoon of a mustache and wagging tongue with the caption *Beat the Mouth*, a riff on the nickname he despised. Spotting one on a lapel, Ted grabbed it and threw it on the floor, inviting its owner outside: "If you want to beat the Mouth, I'll give you a chance to do it right now if you want to follow me to the parking lot."

The motto he chose for his crew, "Acta Non Verba," belied his garrulous nature. The theme song of the newly released movie *Rocky* became their anthem. Just the first rousing bars of the tune gave them all goosebumps, they said.

Though Ted told his tactician, Gary Jobson, that he'd never felt as prepared for anything as he was for that year's competition, this now three-time yachtsman of the year was still considered the underdog. No one imagined or expected he could win. And that made his desire to win all the more ferocious.

How do you spell fun? W-I-N, he said, but he and the crew were having plenty of F-U-N, too. Frat boy style, they'd raise their shirts and scream off the side of the boat to pretty passersby, "Show me your titties," and some women, dazzled by the intoxicating allure of dashing seafarers, happily complied. At one of the seemingly endless society dinners, Ted caused a fracas when he asked an attractive young woman if she got enough loving from her companion, who looked to be twice her age. It made no sense to him that a beauty would be wasted on an old guy. When she admitted, "I'm horny as hell," Ted said he thought he could help take care of that—later backpedaling by saying he was offering up his young, single crew members.

"There are times you'd like to bash his head in with a baseball bat," said crew member Dick Sadler. "But there are more times you want to hug him. You know he's conning you, but you can't help but love it."

No matter how crude or bombastic, his performance on the water couldn't be denied. One fateful day in August, the venerable selection committee, the old guard of yachting, arrived on board *Courageous*, neatly attired in their traditional blue blazers and straw hats, to pass along good news.

"Captain Turner, we appreciate your hard work. You've come a long way. We'd like to inform you that you have been selected to defend the America's Cup." Ted's eyes welled up at the news of his victory, and his men erupted in jubilation. Now they needed equal parts luck and skill to win the best-of-seven competition against Australia. At the press conference later, cocky Ted nonchalantly toked on his cigar, blowing smoke rings, declaring that he felt like the luckiest guy in the world.

"This has to be a dream," he said. "I've been dreaming of this so long, I had to figure I was still sleeping when I got the news. Then I heard the guys yelling and celebrating, so I had to think it was real." There would never be a time in life as good as this.

With the *Rocky* theme serenading on an endless loop, and a masterful performance by the entire crew, over the next six days *Courageous* easily took the four victories in a row in a pitch-perfect performance, clinching the Cup. And all of Newport erupted, a "floating Times Square on New Year's Eve," as one observer described it, an explosion of horns and screams.

As was tradition, his men threw Ted into Newport Harbor, and everyone jumped in next—everyone except for Janie, who didn't want to ruin her hairdo. Back on the boat, before he peeled off his wet clothing, the victorious captain posed in front of a mirror and announced, "You are the fucking greatest," flanked by two young groupies who'd appeared from God knew where, as women always seemed to when Ted was around. "Captain Courageous!" the mobs shouted as he staggered past hundreds of spectators over to the victory press conference, fortified by champagne and beer and Aquavit and bottles of rum that had passed his way. He'd had so much, he kept tripping out of his shoes.

The Aussies sang Dixie, and as he entered the room he was greeted with thunderous applause. He and his tactician lit up cigars and belted back more booze. Two more bottles of rum suddenly appeared on the folding table in front of them.

Hovering in wait: Two creatures from his other life in Atlanta, channel 17's Sid Pike and R. T. Williams. Hyperaware of appearances and the fact that the international press was present and cameras rolling, Pike slipped up to grab the booze and hide it under the table—attempting to keep Ted from getting even drunker. Ted, chomping on his cigar, melted down to the floor in search of them, shouting as he slithered, "Pike, give me that, you dumb fuck!" Despite his inebriation, he managed to hoist himself back up, bottles in hand, and burble out words of thanks:

"I'm happy to be alive and be in the US and able and healthy enough to compete with my good friends on the *Australia* and to be in the US and be fortunate enough to be competing in this competition with my good friends and it's bit overwhelming to see all the nice people who've been so kind and everything," he slurred. And his crew spirited him off the stage, back to the lodge, and tossed him into bed. "Captain Courageous" had cinched his place in yachting history.

Later, the earnest Pike wondered out loud to Williams whether he'd done anything wrong by moving the liquor. All he'd been trying to do, he explained, was protect Ted in front.

"Shoot, Pike," Williams said, "you can't protect Turner from himself. Everyone knows that."

CHAPTER SIX

"No News Is Good News"

To enter the majestic art deco building at 220 East Forty-Second Street in New York City was to instantly become imbued with a sense of urgency and importance. There in the center of one of city's finest lobbies spun a gleaming, twelve-foot facsimile of the earth, rotating faster than the actual one, symbolizing the expansive action that transpired thirty-six floors above. Dramatically lit like a Hollywood movie star, the globe was framed overhead by a golden sun. News was collected here and pumped out to the world, in a variety of formats. Here on these premises, the New York *Daily News*, the paper for which the building had been erected in the 1930s, was created and printed each day. Radio and television and wire reporters worked frenetically in their respective media. So dramatic was the structure that Hollywood had chosen it as the backdrop for one of the world's most famous fictional broadsheets, *The Daily Planet*. This dazzling building was worthy of Clark Kent and Superman.

What Reese Schonfeld was himself trying to accomplish in these hallowed halls required a superpower. Each day, he arrived and rode the elevator up to a modest office that housed an organization known only to a few—the Independent Television News Association, his tiny bid to upend the news establishment.

Nine independent television stations around the country had signed on to the service, including WPIX, housed here in this building. Reese had launched it just two days after Coors's TVN had shut its doors in the fall of 1975. His grand plan to pump out news on the satellite had never reached fruition. Stations simply didn't want those massive dishes eating up spots in their parking lots and saw no reason for the nuisance simply to receive a daily news feed. And then Joseph Coors had decided to ditch the news business.

Just as a wire service spat out text and photos to subscribing news entities, this collective Reese had cobbled together would provide filmed stories and footage from around the nation to its member stations. Late each afternoon, the ITNA fed out a half hour's worth of material for subscribers to use in their newscasts as they wished. In those first weeks, KTVU in San Francisco contributed coverage of the latest in the saga of kidnapped heiress Patty Hearst, while KTXL in Sacramento sent updates on the trial of accused presidential assassin Squeaky Fromme.

"The invisible newscast," Reese called this offering—not a show but, rather, elements for producers around the country to use in building their newscasts.

This was his best salvo in combatting what he called "the golden age of network arrogance." In order to bolster their ratings and preserve their domain, networks didn't want to share their abundant footage with their affiliates before they had the chance to air it. What Reese had created might not have been much, but it was a start—and it was a paycheck. For the service to work long-term, he'd need twice as many stations to subscribe.

The holdout independent that drove him craziest continued to be channel 17. At the annual convention of the Association of Independent Television Stations, Reese would grab Ted and state his case about news. Invariably, Ted, flanked by a couple of convention babes, pontificated for the amusement of all who could hear. Ted had not budged on his declaration that "No news is good news." News was depressing, an endless parade of gloom and doom, depicting the worst of humanity, dragging down anyone who tuned in.

"I hate the news," he'd say. "I'll never do news. I don't believe in news. I've got entertainment programs stacked up in my basement that I could run until 2000." Those programs he ran—*I Love Lucy, Georgia Championship Wrestling*, endless hours of old movies—were the ultimate in escapist fun. Benign as a pussycat! Invariably, he'd sum up his rebuff of Reese's advances by railing against the networks and their unfair domination of the American mind.

While they disagreed on news, the two men did agree on *that*.

He longed for the day when news was front and center, when technology allowed it to flow freely around the giant, spinning globe, educating the audience and inspiring change. For now, he toiled away in these hallowed halls of journalism, a pipsqueak among giants, the overlord of a tiny service he'd concocted out of need and despair, dreaming of the news revolution.

Eventually, Reese was able to hire a few young staff people to help him on his mission. During long days, they'd sit with telephone receivers stuck to each ear, brokering and bartering for stories, all in the service of preparing their invisible newscast. He also attracted a small crew of other news veterans, exiles from greener pastures who'd left indelible marks on the industry of broadcast journalism.

One of them was a television producer from the Bronx, a legendary New York newsman named Ted Kavanau. Some believed Kavanau to be a genius, others a madman. Then there were those who thought him a combination of both. "Mad Dog," they called him. He possessed, in the eyes of at least one old boss, the perfect blend of showmanship and journalistic judgment. This approach had shaken up news in his hometown.

With the handsome looks and impeccable attire of a New York City police detective—replete with a pistol strapped to his shin—Kavanau buzzed with the frenetic energy of a bookie. It had taken him a while to find his way to the profession. Though he felt himself to be a poor student at DeWitt Clinton, the prestigious, public all-boys high school he'd attended, he'd managed to pass the challenging entrance exam for City College, a tuition-free oasis of higher learning considered to be New York's "Jewish Harvard." Kavanau's contrarian attitude was already evident. Asked to explain logarithms on a crucial math test, he sketched out a cartoon of a dancing log.

Unsure at graduation what to do with his future, he settled on the practical idea of becoming a teacher in the New York City schools—until he discovered what it would take to obtain the credential. His fates tilted in a completely different direction when he learned about a master's at Syracuse University that seemed a far easier course of study—in the relatively new medium of television. Once he graduated, he became an instructor at Ithaca College, where he produced public service shows for one of the nation's earliest cable television providers. When a local professor named Martin Abend agreed to appear on a panel discussion program there, the two men struck up what would turn out to be a lifelong friendship.

After producing documentaries and public affairs programs in Boston, Kavanau made his way back to the city he loved and where he belonged. As the producer of New York's first ten p.m. newscast—for independent station WNEW Channel 5—he was well aware how challenging it would be to convince viewers to switch over from prime-time network entertainment. And yet, he also believed the degrading spectacle of the New York streets could be as exciting and outlandish as any drama—and certainly more relevant.

Each night, a menacing announcer opened the show in the same foreboding tone—"It's ten o'clock. Do you know where your children are?"—leaving even those who'd just tucked their kids in with a grave sense of unease. In the moments leading up to airtime, Kavanau would announce to his startled staff that he was tossing out the show's rundown. He'd rush into the field with the night crew, scrounging around for the freshest morsel of news. Inevitably, they discovered *something*—a fire likely had just flickered to life or a dead body was sure to be lingering somewhere. After filming the scene, they'd spirit back to the station, rush the footage into the on-site lab for processing, and interrupt the newscast with a this-just-in breaking missive.

While WNEW was financially better off than most independents around the nation, it was still a scrappy operation compared to the local network owned-and-operated stations, propelled by buckets of money and four times the number of crews. Kavanau's intrepid news teams (who proudly described themselves as "The Jew Crew," "The Fascist Crew," "The Hippie Crew") scrambled each day from story to story, with help in the field from a motorcycle courier who'd meet them to replenish their film stock and other supplies, then ferry the film they'd shot back to headquarters. The urgency they felt as they navigated the streets, rancid with decay, was what he wished to convey to the audience at home. He reveled in conveying to New Yorkers images of their beloved city in all its raw ingloriousness, as if it were not just his job but his moral obligation.

"We'd chase people down the street," he said with pride. "We'd do anything to get a story."

As he'd hoped, the viewers lapped it up like a soap opera or a Knicks game. This was no humdrum newscast. The newscast became a nightly *event*, and every second of airtime had to pay off.*

The mob! Methodone! Mayhem! The police blotter, animated by Mad Dog Kavanau. Television news had never moved with such alacrity.

His obsession with the crime rampant in Gotham reflected the harsh reality of the time. The undercurrent of fear that was the hallmark of 1970s New York had compelled Kavanau and several others on his staff to pack heat. You could never be too cautious or too prepared.

"Ted's idea of continuity was to put a rape next to a murder next to a robbery—an entire violence section," observed Bill Jorgensen, the station's star anchor, with whom "Mad Man" Kavanau was forever at odds.

Technological limitations aided and abetted Kavanau's creative flair. Since reporting live from the field was still, without planning and vast resources, but a dream, he resorted to skits filmed on location, "like-live," that illustrated in technicolor what newspapers could only convey in humdrum text and black and white. When ruffians unleashed a spate of robberies of *shtreimel*, large, expensive fur hats worn by Hasidic men, Kavanau rented the garb from Eve's Costumers, suited up reporter Steve Bauman, wired him with a hidden microphone, and sent him into Williamsburg, a neighborhood in Brooklyn populated predominantly by Orthodox Jews. The crew hid nearby in the unmarked news van and

---

* For a glimpse inside the newsroom, see part one of WNYW's "25th Anniversary of the 10 O'Clock News Special," https://www.youtube.com/watch?v=XyNTKg7ZeKY.

filmed Bauman as he glided down the street to the joyful strains of *Fiddler on the Roof*, waiting for a would-be thief to appear.

Suddenly, a young Puerto Rican kid—a would-be *shtreimel-snatcher?*—approached and implored, "Rabbi, Rabbi, I've got to talk with you."

"Yes, my son."

"I fell in love with this Jewish girl, but her parents don't approve."

Relieved not to have been the victim of a mugging for his sacred chapeau, the rabbi shared paternal wisdom.

"You must persist, son. Love will conquer all."

When sightings of the hulking, mythical ape-like creature Bigfoot dominated headlines, Kavanau returned to Eve's, this time renting a gorilla costume and donning it himself. Standing in Central Park, Bauman explained to the camera that the creature had been spotted there. On cue, the camera panned thirty yards in the distance, revealing a large, hairy figure sneaking for cover from tree to tree. The intrepid newsman approached the beast without a shred of fear and, pointing his microphone into his face, posed the question, "Bigfoot, what brings you to New York?"

The faux giant replied sweetly, addressing the believers in the audience, "There's one person in New York who believes in me." This A-number-one menace, as imagined by Ted Kavanau, could speak!

* * *

To the blood, gore, and theatrical, add: Reviews of schlocky restaurants by a "Masked Gourmet," clad in top hat and tails. Juicy bits by a young gossip columnist named Rona Barrett. A consumer reporter who crusaded against fraud and abuse—all under the rubric "Action News." A righteous undercurrent swept through many a Kavanau opus. During a sweltering summer heat, Kavanau dispatched an older staffer out onto the streets with a hidden camera crew as he searched for a Good Samaritan who might offer a drop of water.

Thus he endeared his station to the audience, which included the likes of Mafia boss Joe Colombo, who was grateful to Kavanau for not propagating what he saw as anti-Italian bias by the media. "If you ever need help with anything, give me a call," he'd said.

The effete, urbane intellectual was not his intended audience; the working-class New Yorker was, and he attracted them readily, rendering WNEW the number one local station in Gotham. So devoted was he to his craft, Kavanau never took a vacation, much less a day off. Indeed, he wished to live in the newsroom. And since that wasn't allowed, he'd tried to enlist his colleagues to chip in for a crash pad near work—the next best thing in his Ben Hecht *Front Page* fantasy of nonstop, in-your-face, madcap news.

For his thousand percent devotion, the staff loved Mad Dog, and they simultaneously hated him, too. He meanwhile confessed a love/hate relationship with the medium in which he dwelled and all who worked in it. Broadcast news did not equal print journalism. Newspaper reporters, he knew, were expected to dig, to deeply understand the beats they covered. A television newsman, on the other hand, dwelled in shorthand and vagary. He might be gifted socially and verbally, but when you got down to it, most of his stories were cribbed from print and brought to life with pictures and sound. Television reporters, he believed, "don't know anything. If you sat them down and tested them, you'd find a massive amount of ignorance." Success in television required tenacity and performance, not necessarily intellect. The footage that wound up on the cutting-room floor to protect a reporter from "looking imbecilic" on the air showed the true nature of the person—and of the medium.

"Never a friendly question" was one of his mantras. So was "There are two sides to every story. How many did you get?" Though he was staunchly conservative politically, he'd crusade on behalf of the almighty First Amendment—for all. Once, he got into a brawl defending Vietnam War protestors' right to speak out against the conflict, though he didn't agree with their position. The creeping liberal bias apparent in network newscasts distressed him not because he disagreed, but because it meant the omission of other points of view.

To offer a sense of balance, he brought in his friend the professor, Martin Abend, as a commentator. Abend was rabidly pro-gun, pro-war, pro–death penalty; he'd recently sparked an uproar when he'd said the United States had always been a white country and that it would be dangerous to allow in more blacks.

The mere suggestion that this radical conservative would share the station's airtime lit the newsroom on fire. Enlisting a liberal commentator for balance didn't appease the staff. All but one employee signed a petition. Star anchor Jorgensen threatened to quit.

Still, Kavanau claimed an important ally. Gabe Pressman, the most revered television newsman in the city—an ace reporter who'd jumped over from a network affiliate for the chance to work in Mad Dog's shop—confessed that while he found Abend's ideas repugnant, he had to admit that Kavanau was right. There *was* a liberal bias in television.

Ultimately, Kavanau's righteousness did him in. Rather than agree to upper management's insistence that he read, approve, and tape Abend's commentaries, Kavanau quit. The day he did, the latest ratings book hit. His newscast had achieved its highest numbers ever.

For a while, Kavanau bounced around other newsrooms, including a brief stint as a news consultant. He was less inclined toward theoretical meetings and more toward practice. In Minneapolis, he asked the news director to anoint him reporter for a day. From the local paper, he ripped an ad for a porno theater and went in search of the manager to ask how much business it generated. Next, he stopped off at a shelter for abused women and interviewed a resident about how smut had ruined her life. Finally, he visited the paper's publisher and asked, as the cameras rolled, "How do you feel about pornography?" After his predictable response that it was a terrible scourge, Kavanau held up a copy of the newspaper ad. The man steamed in the face of his outed hypocrisy. The television staff could see how to take a thread of an idea and inventively string together a compelling story.

Despite other gigs and opportunities, this once–star newsman now found himself out of work. He took up residence in the dusty basement of his friend Abend's home in Brooklyn, walking over the Williamsburg

Bridge to midtown Manhattan in order to save subway fare, hanging around the ITNA offices in the hopes that Reese might send him out on a story, when the budget allowed such a luxury. A fierce warrior of a newsman with no platform—the worst sort of clipped wings for a man who'd lived to have a voice.

* * *

Another of Reese's ITNA cohort was also an industry veteran experiencing a juncture in his own long, storied broadcasting career—although that career had taken a decidedly different turn out of the Bronx. Nearly twenty years before, Kavanau had attended DeWitt Clinton High School and City College, Daniel Schorr had attended those schools, too. He'd always known he wished to be a newsman.

Like any serious journalist, he set his sights on working for the *New York Times*, and in the most rarefied of jobs, as a foreign correspondent. Editors at the paper advised the ambitious young man to send himself overseas and file freelance reports for whatever news outlets he could. Off he went to Holland, where he contributed stories to whoever would take them, from the *Christian Science Monitor* to the English-language service of Dutch radio. Emboldened by his experience, he returned to the *Times* a few years later, hat in hand, seeking a staff job. This time the response was: maybe.

On February 1, 1953, devastating storms swept the North Sea. In the Netherlands alone, several thousand people drowned—leaving a third of the country underwater. Schorr flew on rescue missions with army helicopters as they plucked survivors from trees and filed dramatic reports for CBS radio. In the aftermath, he received a telegram from the venerable broadcaster Edward R. Murrow that would have sent any young journalist over the moon:

WOULD YOU AT ALL CONSIDER JOINING THE STAFF OF CBS NEWS WITH AN INITIAL ASSIGNMENT IN WASHINGTON. STOP.

While it was immensely flattering to receive this invitation, for Schorr, it was the equivalent of catching the attention of the second-prettiest girl in the class. He sent a telegram to his *Times* contact, explaining the Murrow overture, and quickly got a reply:

SUGGEST YOU TAKE THE OTHER OFFER. STOP.

Rebuffed by one of the most prestigious news organizations in the world, wooed by another, Schorr accepted the consolation prize and headed to the nation's capital as a diplomatic correspondent.*

Becoming one of the vaunted second-generation of "Murrow's boys" and studying at the feet of the man considered the master of broadcast news was a fine second-best for this "immigrant from the world of words." The voice and presence of Murrow, his integrity, his reverence for news, propelled him.

In time, he was sent to the Soviet Union, where he was given a camera and a clunky recording deck, allowing him to file reports for the emerging division of CBS television—the medium, Schorr began to observe, whether he liked it or not, was becoming America's "giant classroom." Ejected from the country for refusing to kowtow to censors, the newsman next found himself stationed in Berlin. Tipped off in the middle of the night that a wall was to be erected around the eastern part of the city, he and his producer, Av Westin, corralled a news crew to film the giant barbed wire coils being dropped around the city. Armored cars and tanks from the east rumbled at intersections where barricades had yet to rise. It wasn't until days later that his colleagues received the pictures, which had been shipped via plane for the long ride to New York, then ferried by motorcycle courier from the airport to CBS headquarters in midtown. Even the mighty CBS then was constricted by the limits of intercontinental communications.

Though he still considered himself a journalist "*in* television" rather than one "*of* television," he confessed to enjoying the "ego reward" that came when strangers recognized him. Like other serious reporters, he had been loath to embrace TV. The glamour of traveling first-class and

---

* A few years later, he was told in confidence why he hadn't landed his dream job. Tensions were rising then in the Middle East, and having more Jewish staffers would make the staff inflexible. The irony was not lost on Schorr that this discrimination had come down from a Jewish-owned newspaper.

unquestioned expense accounts helped to offset the frustrations and limitations of the medium that had now become his bread and butter.

"I chafed at the straightjacket of the conventional TV news story—a brief introduction, voice-over silent film, a snippet of somebody speaking a brief conclusion," he said. "Any story on a controversial subject that is packed into so small a container tends to burst on an interested party like a hand grenade."

Television, in his estimation, was a "lumbering King Kong that altered the landscape by weight and force, brushing aside complexities and seizing upon a few concrete images"—which made covering a story as important and complex as Watergate a particular challenge.

"What's the visual?" his producers would counter when he enthusiastically revealed the latest twist and turn of the unfolding scandal. Without pictures, it was tough to justify much airtime.

Far worse than the limitations of the medium in which he dwelled was his discovery that the great democracy into which he'd been born, and the vaunted network that employed him, were rife with imperfection. When his superiors complied with a White House demand not to provide critical "instant analysis" after a presidential speech, Schorr balked, as he did when told to read the names of commercial sponsors, a task he believed impugned his journalistic integrity. Ordered by network brass not to speak in public after criticizing them for what he felt was a soft stance on President Nixon, he felt as if he were back in Russia. Fissures emerged in the house of Murrow when CBS buckled to public demand and aired a rerun of *I Love Lucy* instead of an important hearing regarding Vietnam. News president Fred Friendly angrily resigned. A scathing report Schorr delivered on pollution in the fishing industry led to an internal inquiry—after Bumble Bee Seafoods pulled their ads—and schooled him in the power of the sponsor.

"TV exists on ratings," he observed. "The only real standards on TV is in what sells and what doesn't sell."

The worst was yet to come. After refusing to reveal who'd leaked an explosive congressional report on illegal CIA and FBI activities, he'd graduated from newsman to news maker, a true cause célèbre. Reporters leapt to defend his right to protect his sources. TV comics and political cartoonists riffed on the situation. Hollywood came calling, offering him a variety of roles as a newsman. He even ranked a crossword-puzzle clue in the *New York Times*—the vaunted institution that had unwittingly launched him into fame. He marveled that the brouhaha obscured the contents of the report. All the while, ratings soared.

Unsure now whether he was a "refugee or exile" from TV, he set about investigating what he saw as the decline of CBS—of broadcast journalism, of civilization—in a book he titled *Clearing the Air*. Freed from daily deadlines, he wished to understand more about the relationship between the $2-billion-a-year world of prime-time television and its "brash little appendage of news." "The reality that television presents, however imperfect, has become, for all practical purposes, the only important reality," he wrote. Television, he concluded, "was a magic electronic circle, a séance. A force like nuclear energy, its effects could be beneficent, destructive and incalculable."

Reduced to a mere mortal in the "humdrum real world," now he labored, like Kavanau, as a newsman without an affiliation. A syndicated column he'd been hired to write was failing. A stranger's greeting—"Hey, didn't you used to be Daniel Schorr?"—stung. Occasionally, he'd pick up work as a moderator or narrator, file a freelance report for $75 for National Public Radio, or do a turn on the speaking circuit, where he found being "journalist Daniel Schorr" didn't have nearly as much heft as "Daniel Schorr of CBS." Despite his misgivings about Reese and his past connections to that rogue Coors-owned news service, Schorr agreed to contribute commentaries to the ITNA. Having four letters after his name offered some validation, even if it was with an "invisible" outfit whose initials spelled little in the way of prestige.

* * *

If the growing cluster of pins on the map in Donald Andersson's office wasn't enough—signifying 465 cable systems now carrying channel 17 to twenty-seven states—the mail continued to cinch it. When it was dumped out each day on the conference room table, stacks were made, one for everything postmarked Atlanta, another, from everywhere else. Fan mail for Bill Tush and the wrestlers, and orders for merchandise—now comprising a quarter of the station's revenue—streamed in from Juneau to Honolulu, from Bangor to the Virgin Islands' St. Croix. Ted would rush to the mail room, straight out of a scene from *Miracle on 34th Street*. "The postmarks tell the tale," he'd exclaim, as he rooted through the pile for more uncanceled stamps.

So did the growing coverage. A story in *TV Guide* posed the question those who already had cable didn't need to ask: "Why are they watching a Georgia station in Nebraska?" The answer was simple: because they could. Most people didn't understand how it worked, nor did they need to, really. All they knew was what came out of their televisions—and that now there was more to see. The ad guys commissioned the art department to work up a cartoon illustration of lightning bolts radiating upward from a receiving station on the ground to an orb in the sky, which then showered bolts back down, like rain. It wasn't quite *so* simple, of course, but, then again, it was. It was a miracle—TV from Atlanta without being there.

As the seventies marched on, the networks anxiously monitored the public acceptance of HBO and the "Super Station that Serves the Nation" with mounting terror. The government, in whose hands their fortunes rested, kept relaxing the rules that allowed this parallel medium of cable to continue its expansion—these rogue newcomers swashbuckling away decades of an entrenched system and eating into the traditional television audience. Hollywood was keenly tuned in, too, as were the sports leagues and the phone company. Advertisers were also flummoxed. It had never occurred to any of them that one day a brash man in the southeast would wish to air games, and movies, and television reruns, beyond his appointed region—nor that technology would enable him to.

As the old guard argued that the new guard did a disservice to the industry, the new guard argued that the old guard did a disservice to the audience. The arguments all traced back to money and power and fear as technology accelerated and collapsed time and space, destroying television's status quo.

Maverick Ted delighted in charges he was a rogue and a thief and a pirate for wishing to air the programs he'd been buying to the widest possible audience: "Who had the devious and cunning mind who figured out how to disrupt the world?* *Me me me me me me.*" It wasn't his fault that his great idea was crushing the establishment.

While he gloated, though, he was deathly afraid. If the winds blew in a different direction and the mighty lobbyists working on behalf of establishment television and Hollywood prevailed on the FCC, in an instant, rules might be rewritten, and the right to transmit channel 17 around the nation might disappear.

This harsh reality necessitated a brainstorm. Where should he set his sights next? What kind of channel could he create that was immune to the whims of regulation, one that would be wholly his own?

He called to order a meeting of his top men. Gathered around the conference room table, they braced themselves for whatever he would hurl their way. Perhaps this was to be another dramatic reading of another story about Ted the Great. Since he'd won the America's Cup, his already outsize ego had puffed to the size of Antarctica. Recently, he'd subjected the men to a word-for-word reading by regional sales manager John Withers of his thirteen-page *Playboy* interview. The journalist Peter Ross Range had spent months following Ted from his home to office to stadium, talking with him on boats and planes and in cars, yielding a wide-ranging interview that touched on love, sex, sports, competition, Russia, and Ted's hobby of photographing nude women. Transcribed, the conversation totaled eight hundred pages. Range pointed out to readers what his sales team and anyone close to him already knew: Ted "the radio" never stopped talking, even while he was in the john.

---

* Another force upending media consumption at about the same time was the new technology, the home videotape recorder. See https://reelrundown.com/film-industry/The-History-Of-Home-Movie-Entertainment for more information if you didn't live through this period.

Range concluded that the mogul was a "blithe spirit," a fanatically positive thinker who advocated "lots of sex" as a solution to the world's problems—because, after all, "only horny people shoot people. I mean, you never feel aggressive just after you've gotten laid, right?"

On this day, though, Ted was not engaging in self-congratulatory behavior, for once. He wished to discuss new channels they might create.

HBO had staked its claim on a channel dedicated to newer films and entertainment.

What about all-sports? Ted had hoped to parlay his ownership of teams into a regional cable sports network. But that would mean losing sports on channel 17, decimating their core business. Besides, rights issues for sports were a different sort of complicated and thorny than rights issues for entertainment.

What about all-music TV? said one man, riffing on the success of the all-music weekend show, *The Now Explosion*. Boring, someone said. Who would watch music on television?

After entertainment and sports, what else was left?

Someone chimed in: All-news radio was the fastest-growing commercial radio format in the nation. Why not all-news TV?

But, the men wondered, wasn't that like the six-o'clock news over and over again? That would be *really* boring! Who would ever possibly watch *three hours* of news a night? Was there even enough news to fill twenty-four hours every day? Might they have to blow up old motels or something on slow news days?

The all-news format did offer an advantage, though. There would be no copyright issues, no complex negotiations with the entrenched Hollywood establishment that had been trying to block channel 17 every step of the way. As difficult a proposition as it seemed, producing news suddenly sounded grand and important.

Other rationales clicked into place: Half of the nation didn't bother to read a newspaper anymore, opting to get whatever news they did from television. Network television news, by Ted's estimation, had destroyed the faith of the citizenry. Part of the reason America had so many problems, he believed, was because his fellow Americans were so ill-informed. There was no better place to promote a variety of opinions than on almighty television. With a news channel, he could quite possibly help save the world.

Running for president still seemed a bit far-fetched—and expensive. But this idea felt right. Suddenly, the man who for years had decreed news evil and boring and depressing had seen the news light—a "born-again journalist," a friend described him. Wherever he went, whoever he spoke to, he glowed about what he planned to do next. The next great cable service, he had convinced himself, was news.

* * *

The call Reese had been hoping for his entire life came without warning in September 1978, and it was initiated by the last person he'd ever imagined. Over the past year, it seemed everyone in broadcasting had been flirting with an exploration of the new wild west, cable-satellite, hoping for a slice of the success HBO and channel 17 had discovered.

As the only provider of news to independents, Reese himself had fielded inquiries from a variety of organizations attracted to the possibilities of an all-news format. Stations owned by the Post-Newsweek group had studied and tabled the idea as too risky. Tantalized by the unfurling ticker tape of news on the wire machine in his office, Jerry Levin over at HBO had commissioned Reese to produce a pilot for an all-news channel. To Levin's lament, even after the pilot was completed, an executive at his parent company, *Time*, ultimately nixed the project.

When the phone rang, Reese took the call out in the open space of the ITNA newsroom and then rushed to his office for privacy after he realized who was on the line. Ted Turner.

Ted explained that he'd been asking around for the name of the best "guerilla fighter" out there, a man who understood how to work with a scrappy budget and help him launch his new idea. There were plenty of news executives from the networks, accustomed to fat budgets and generous expense accounts, guys who sent reporters out into the field on chartered Learjets with suitcases of cash, while filling only a half hour of airtime a day. Those guys wouldn't cut it.

That had led him to Reese.

Could an all-news network be done? he asked the newsman.

Yes, Reese responded.

Would Reese be interested in doing it?

"Of course," he answered without hesitation. "I've been waiting for this for twenty years." Later, he wondered if he should have played harder to get.

Ted confessed that he knew "diddley-squat" about the news business. That didn't bother Reese. *He* did. He had lived and breathed it for two decades now.

A flash of concern tempered his excitement. Did this Ted Turner have a political agenda, like Joseph Coors? For years, he'd heard Ted's homilies against the news. He was accustomed to dealing with unortho-dox station owners through the ITNA—one, a former used car dealer, another whose family had been in the produce business, a third with ties to a gambling concern in Vegas. That Ted himself wasn't a starched-collar traditional broadcaster wasn't the problem. But he had met his second wife at a Republican party function and was an avowed patriot, nation-alist, and conservative, railing against the networks for their family-unfriendly programs that he believed promoted violence and debauch-ery. Then, there were the remarks Ted had made about the agent Jerry Kapstein—as a Jew himself, Reese wondered if he should be concerned.

Ted promised that promoting a political point of view was absolutely not a motivating factor. All those times he'd said, "No news is good news"? His aversion to news all these years, he claimed now, had really been about cost. Though Reese didn't quite buy the back-pedaling, like any starry-eyed person in love with an idea, he was so tantalized by the possibilities that he focused only on the fact that his dream job had just arrived, tied up in a neat little bow. Other people may have been talking about all-news, but here was Ted Turner declaring his intent to invest in it—and he had the power, and the gumption, and, presumably, the money to make it happen.

Look at how wrong he'd been a few years earlier, Reese told himself, when he'd dismissed Ted as an idiot for thinking anyone outside Atlanta would watch his dinky UHF rerun station. Ted was imbued with something most media executives in New York did not have: a sense of the world outside the island of Manhattan.

Reese flew to Atlanta to continue the conversation. Ted picked him up at the airport in his beat-up Toyota. They headed back to midtown, to the same ramshackle building where they'd met four years earlier. Though the station's fortunes had continued to rise, the office seemed worse for the wear.

Ted explained that this creation would be the first business he started that did not bear his name. He planned to call it the Cable News Network. How could the nation's cable systems refuse to carry a channel with the word "cable" in the title? He'd been working hard these past years to make friends in the industry and wanted to make sure they all identified with the idea, to feel as if it belonged to them. He'd rise or fall on their decision to carry it.

What was the minimum budget? Twenty million, said Reese, to get up and running, and $2 million a month after that. A bargain, considering that each network spent $100 million a year to provide a fraction of the coverage, a ridiculous sum given that their flagship newscasts were just a half hour.

Reese was certain staffing would be no problem. Plenty of people who toiled in local television news would work cheap for the chance to do national news. Jobs at the networks were hard to come by.

Which star, Ted wondered to his newly enlisted partner in crime, would they sign to make a splash?

"Dan Rather," Reese said cockily—optimistically. He was playing in the big time, now.

"Who's Dan Rather?" Ted responded. He knew Walter Cronkite largely as a hobbyist sailor and because Cronkite had profiled him on *60 Minutes* after the America's Cup win—but not because he watched him on television.

"The CBS anchorman-in-waiting," Reese explained, surprised that

Ted honestly didn't seem to know Rather's name. He was one of the top stars in the business, and Reese hoped he just might be up for grabs. Recently, Rather's income had plummeted after the cancellation of the gossipy interview show he helmed, *Who's Who*.

"How much would he cost?" Ted asked.

"A million dollars a year," Reese answered.

"A million dollars a year just to have a guy read the news?" Ted asked.

"A million dollars a year to get a guy away from CBS network," Reese said.

"Well"—Ted shrugged—"I just offered Pete Rose a million dollars to play baseball and he only works half a year."

No matter who they hired, Ted was firm that this Cable News Network had to be headquartered in Atlanta. Why did media people think New York City was the center of the universe? News happened all over! And great companies were headquartered all over, too, like Procter & Gamble in Cincinnati, for instance, Coca-Cola in Atlanta, and General Motors in Detroit.

There were upsides and downsides to building a home base outside the northeast, said Reese, who had proposed Arlington, Virginia, as a more palatable alternative to Atlanta. In both places, it would not be necessary to hire union labor—the unions being a costly element of television production. On the other hand, convincing the best talent in the business to live down south was not going to be easy. But with the budgetary concerns a factor, Atlanta it would have to be.

Reese was firm with his own nonnegotiables: There could be no cumbersome film in his newsroom. State-of-the-art gear that recorded pictures and sound on videotape had begun to transform newsgathering, allowing stories to move more quickly to edit and air.

"With film you needed a cameraman, a sound man, and a lighting man," Reese explained. "With tape, all you needed was a cameraman and a tech who did the lighting. And you didn't need the same skill level to operate a tape camera, so you could hire people at much lower pay. You saved more [in salaries] in one year than you spent on the camera."

He'd also need something that was only in the process of being invented: a computerized newsroom. At a trade show, he'd seen a demo of a system in development that promised to allow the wires to tick in silently—as opposed to the belching teletype machines that chomped through reams of paper. These terminals would also allow writers and producers to craft rundowns and scripts on one machine. Finally, to send and receive news feeds, seven satellite dishes would be necessary. Ted swiftly green-lit it all.

With those loose plans, Ted made his way in December 1978 to the Western Cable Show in Anaheim, where he intended to drum up support among the nation's five thousand cable operators. As prices and size continued to fall, more and more of them had begun buying and installing the satellite dishes necessary to pull down feeds.

Standing before the power elite of the industry, Ted felt invincible as he described his idea for a new, revolutionary, twenty-four-hour news channel. Channel 17, along with HBO, were each now available in two million homes. They'd unleashed a frenzied rush of programmers eager to seize their momentum. In this industry, Ted was a hero.

To get this Cable News Network off the ground, he now told them, he would need their buy-in, as he'd supported them these last years. If he could line up only half the nation's fourteen million cable customers, CNN would be golden. A representative of Turner Broadcasting worked the room, handing out contracts, asking operators who were present to sign up on the spot. They hesitated. They refused.

It wasn't just that they didn't believe in this far-fetched notion. It was difficult to imagine an audience for round-the-clock news—since news frequently ranked among viewers' least favorite programming. Of equal concern was the purveyor of the idea. The only news Captain Outrageous had produced was, literally, a joke. How could anyone be sure that the man who collapsed drunk after winning a major sporting event, who had the temerity to believe he could, without a shred of baseball experience, manage his own baseball team, who made rude and crude remarks and deigned to talk about running for president, how could *he* launch a news network?

The vice president of planning for the *Washington Post*, which had been nosing around the idea of an all-news service itself, summed up the skepticism: "The cable industry doubts that Ted Turner knows his ass from a hole in the ground about news." The TV critic for the *Charlotte Observer* had long been appalled by Ted's wanton disregard for public service, especially after he busted WRET for running news headlines recycled from Atlanta's channel 17. He considered Ted's foray into broadcast journalism like "Attila the Hun deciding he's going to do a summer camp for the elderly."

Back at the *Daily News* building in New York, Reese learned the bad news. The plan had thudded. Under pressure to sign a contract with ITNA, he finally relented. He needed the medical insurance the company was offering. So much for his dream.

* * *

In the spring of 1979, Ted had been fighting with his Braves general manager, Bill Lucas, about what to do about third baseman Bob Horner, whose agent, Bucky Woy, drove Ted nuts. Free agency had made baseball a bear.

Lucas was settling into his third season since Ted had elevated him as the first black man in the sport to serve in this prominent position. An easygoing former player who'd worked his way up in the front office, Lucas saw his success in the Turner empire helped by being unafraid to stand up to Ted.

One day at home, Lucas suddenly grabbed his head and fell over. His wife had him rushed to the hospital. Days later, he was pronounced dead. He was just forty-three.

The news of this untimely death of a beloved figure shocked and shattered the entire city, including and especially Ted. Lucas was only a few years older than him. "Seeing such a young, vibrant guy taken away," he said, "made me stop and think about what a short time we all have on this planet." This bolstered his already fierce determination to achieve something grand.

Overcome with grief, Ted did what he did so well. First, he ranted and raved to reporters, blaming the sports agent Woy for killing his friend with stress, as if he'd pulled a trigger on a gun.*

Then, he picked up the phone and called Reese in New York.

"None of us are going to live forever," he told him. "Let's do this fucking thing."

Reese arrived in Atlanta hours after the funeral, at which Ted had eulogized Lucas as having been called back by God to the "big baseball league in the sky."

On that bittersweet day, the madman and the newsman convened at the ballpark.

Reese asked who was going to run this Cable News Network.

"You," Ted told him. "It'll be all yours."

That, Reese explained, meant he must have total control over format and the hiring of personnel. He also, he added, had to make enough money "so that when you fire me, I'll never have to work again. Because we're not going to get along."

"What's your astrological sign?" Ted asked.

"Scorpio," Reese responded.

"We're not gonna have any trouble," Ted, a Scorpio himself, said.

CNN, they decided, would start in a year. Wait any longer, and someone else might beat them to it. They signed a letter of agreement.

"This is gonna make me the most powerful man—" Ted said, before stopping himself. "This is going to make *us* the two most powerful men in the world."

The time was right for Reese to confess a possible wrinkle. That contract he'd signed meant he was obligated to his current job until November. Ted absolutely did not care or understand.

"You're gonna let those ITNA guys run your life? You're afraid . . ."

Reese's board was firm: He couldn't leave until he found a successor. The obvious choice was hanging out in plain sight in the ITNA

---

* Woy later sued him for $17 million in damages for defamation. After an eight-day trial in 1983, a jury deliberated for an hour and cleared Ted.

newsroom: Ted Kavanau. But his reputation preceded him. The board nixed the idea. For the moment, Reese remained locked into his job.

Ted didn't give a damn. He expected Reese by his side at the upcoming cable convention in Las Vegas in a few weeks, where he intended to hold a news conference announcing to the industry, for a second time, the launch of the Cable News Network. This time around, he did not plan on *asking* the industry for their blessings. He would *tell* them his plans. It was, he felt, a worthy gamble. If he could just get CNN on the air, the concept would sell itself and the money would begin to flow.

With the help of a talent scout, Reese had begun to enlist time-filling "columnists" against the possibility (probability?) that there wouldn't always be enough news. Having taped essays on the shelf would be a balm for anxious producers. Among those hired were political commentators Rowland Evans and Robert Novak, psychologist Dr. Joyce Brothers, and astrologer Jeane Dixon, who'd predicted great success for CNN.* Then came other specialty beats—the pet reporter, veterinarian Steve Kritsick; style reporter Elsa Klensch; and chief of the financial desk, veteran business reporter Myron Kandel. Reese intended to build out economic news in a way television had never covered it before. But CNN still needed to announce a full-time marquee staffer with serious journalistic chops.

Conjuring up Dan Rather proved folly. Ted dropped a note to Walter Cronkite, who politely rebuffed the overture with an invitation to sail. Former ABC correspondent Howard K. Smith didn't return calls. Most other A-list anchors were locked into contracts or disinterested in window-dressing at a crazy start-up on what they perceived to be more lunatic than the lunatic fringe: cable.

The biggest star Reese had at his command was fallen CBS newsman Daniel Schorr, a "Big J" journalist who had three Emmys on his

---

* Whether it occurred to Ted or Reese that employing an astrologer as a television commentator echoed the fears proposed by Paddy Chayefsky in his acclaimed film *Network* (where "Sybil the Soothsayer" is hired to boost the news ratings) isn't clear.

shelf and was as serious about news as Ted was about sailing. His credentials were impeccable. He balanced Ted in another important way—he was a liberal.

The speeches and moderating and $100-a-shot commentaries Schorr had been filing for ITNA did not add up to the steady salary he needed to support his young family. Since his departure from the grand network, Schorr had experienced an identity crisis. Did he miss working on television, or did he just miss the thrill of being recognized? Was he now, without this mighty platform, in danger of vanishing altogether? How intensely had he derived his identity from being on the air? He'd relished the notoriety that led him to once rankle President Nixon so intensely that he'd been included on his famous enemies list. Dan Schorr from the Bronx, despised by the president! He was no faceless newspaper reporter. At the same time, he decried the base commercialism of television, what he called "that make-believe world." Of course, he acknowledged, it was far more comfortable to poke holes in the medium when he was a star.

But did he wish to be back on TV badly enough to work for Ted—a "drunk" who "sailed ships," who mocked the news with pratfalls and German shepherds—that was a whole other matter. As dubious as he was about Reese, he was even more worried about Ted.

Lending his name and his reputation to a new venture in an untried medium about which he confessed he knew very little seemed a revolting twist to his vaunted career. What *was* a cable news network, anyway? Who would want to watch twenty-four hours of news a day, and how did Ted know he could make it work? Then, he remembered his initial reaction to television, how dismissive he'd been of the newer medium.

The carrot of a six-figure salary allowed Schorr to rationalize that this Ted Turner must truly be committed to something important and serious. Why, otherwise, would he pursue a craggy, sixtysomething-year-old journalist such as himself? It certainly wasn't his looks Ted was after. Still, it wasn't clear to Schorr that Ted even knew who he was exactly, or his reputation, other than the fact that Reese had told him he was important.

The prospective boss persuaded the dubious journalist to meet him in Vegas at the cable convention to talk things through. When he arrived at nine a.m. sharp at Ted's penthouse suite in Las Vegas, a beautiful blonde with a big personality named Liz Wickersham was present. She was so dazzling that judges had overlooked the fact that she was wearing a cast on her ankle during the 1976 Miss Georgia competition and crowned her the winner anyway. She'd made it to the semifinals in Miss USA. Ted explained that she was his secretary.

At dinner the night before, she'd impressed Reese when she refereed an awful row between him and Ted, who'd fallen in love with the idea of a wheel format for CNN: a half hour of news, then of sports, then of business, and then of features. He was also pushing Reese to commit to an afternoon children's news show.

No way to both, Reese protested, flexing his muscles as president. If Ted didn't want to honor his promise that *he* would control format, content, and personnel, then he shouldn't have hired him.

In reality, Reese had more of a vision than a plan for CNN. That vision involved news floating into headquarters from all over the world, producers building their newscasts on the fly, keeping viewers guessing what was coming next, in a sort of fluid, random fashion. "Live, live, live" would be their métier, he told Ted. This was how CNN could set the news agenda for the world.

"What makes you so fucking smart?" Ted countered, angling for a fight, as the plucky Wickersham attempted to soothe the dueling stubborn egos. Reese retorted, "You picked me." The two men laughed.

Now, as Ted entertained Schorr over breakfast in his suite, it was his turn to offer up his own theory of news. As he paced in his customary circles, he explained to the man who had spent thirty years at CBS that the networks were dinosaurs. The future was in delivering what was happening now, instantly, to the audience. Newspapers were not sustainable, environmentally, and they weren't fast enough. They would not and could not last, he explained.

That was all very interesting, Schorr said, but what about that German shepherd co-hosting the news on his station—the mockery you've made of journalism in the past? Ted admitted that, no, he hadn't taken news seriously. But everything was different now. Schorr could be the very first employee—since Reese had not officially signed on. He'd earn stock options and could make up whatever title he wanted. He could be a vice president! But he needed to say yes, now, because later in the day, he planned to make a formal announcement about Cable News Network, and he needed Schorr right next to him.

The news veteran explained that he had no interest in serving in any managerial role. That had never been his ambition. He was a journalist, a news analyst—not a suit. As such, he could not be expected to read ads, or to do anything that would violate his journalistic standards. After all, with what had happened to him at CBS, imagine what could happen in the hands of Captain Outrageous?

Schorr permitted himself to see some upside to this twenty-four-hour news idea—and to his embarking on this marriage of convenience. For years at the network, he'd had to condense his reports to fit an abbreviated format. News always ranked second to the entertainment programs that were the network mainstay—and cash cow. He recalled the struggles at CBS to deliver breaking news after the nightly newscast had aired. A channel independent of the mighty networks might also be less likely to collapse to government pressures. Yes, Ted had come from a different planet than him, and he certainly sounded different. But it seemed a worthy gamble for the possibility of reviving his career.

Ted was eager to lock Schorr in.

"You write an agreement that says you won't have to do anything you don't want to, and I'll sign it," he said.

Schorr rode the elevator down to the lobby, conferred on the phone with his agent, and, then, on Las Vegas Hilton stationery, scratched out a page-long summary that read, "No demand will be made upon him that would compromise his professional ethics or responsibility." Reese was impressed. He'd never seen such a contract provision before. If Ted was willing to promise that in order to get Schorr, he was serious indeed.

* * *

The energy in the small hotel conference room was intense as the three men filed in at four-thirty p.m. on May 21, 1979, to announce their plan to conquer the world. In the six months since Ted had last made this pitch, the exuberance over the union of cable and satellite had continued to sweep the industry. Another wave of new cable services had been announced, from a kid's channel called Nickelodeon, an entertainment service called Showtime, and a variety of religious channels. Fifteen hundred earth stations had been installed at cable systems coast to coast, ready to receive and transmit new signals.

Standing in front of the trade press, Ted introduced his confederates: Reese Schonfeld as president, a veteran broadcaster who'd been longing for this day forever, and former CBS correspondent Daniel Schorr, who said since Ted was willing to stake his entire fortune on CNN, he was willing to stake his reputation.

The seed funding for CNN, Ted told the group, would come from the sale of WRET in Charlotte, which he'd just put on the market. In a year, he declared, they would launch Cable News Network, the very first all-news network. Ever the salesman, Ted promised it would be nothing less than "the greatest achievement in the history of journalism." He preened triumphantly, a man who'd watched hardly a frame of what either of the two men beside him had created—a man who hardly ever watched the news.

CHAPTER SEVEN
Every Drop of Blood

Ted paced his office, brandishing his sword, slicing the air as if destroying the evil television networks with the blade, as he announced his intentions to annihilate time and space by making news available twenty-four hours a day. Histrionics from his swashbuckling boss didn't faze Bill Tush, but this day's diatribe felt more ominous.

By providing better access to information, Ted blustered, he'd be creating a better world. And because of this, he told his "low-budget Walter Cronkite," a change in the programming was going to be necessary—effective immediately.

This did not mean the end for his star announcer. Back when Tush amazingly, unwittingly, was emerging as the first star of cable television, Ted had promised that as long as he himself had a job, so would Tush.

But now, the unorthodox news shenanigans simply had to stop. No more reading the headlines in a bunny suit. No more sermons from Brother Gold; goodbye, special reports from the News Chicken. From that day forward, Bill Tush would have to play it straight.

In a flash, like that, goodbye to all the fun, and hello, self-serious journalism. Tush felt crushed by defeat—as well as ridiculous. Who was going to take *him* seriously? He had never wanted to be, was never going to be, a bona fide journalist. Making him act like a real reporter, he said, was like asking kid's comedian Soupy Sales to change his outfit and put the pies away.

Ted made it perfectly clear that it wasn't *he* who had a problem with his approach. Too many others had pointed to it as the chief reason why they couldn't take his Cable News Network seriously. (And they hadn't, as Tush had, witnessed Ted roaming the halls of the station donning a purple wizard's hat topped with a satellite dish that someone had sent him.) And right now, getting this project off the ground was his number one priority.

Chief among the detractors was Reese. Even with Schorr on board, he'd been encountering skepticism from many a potential recruit. There was something suspicious about a non-journalist committing his fortune to something as risky as an all-news channel. Was CNN Ted's master plan to control the news? Did he harbor ambitions as an anchorman? When he said CNN was a "crusade," that he was starting it to "straighten this country out," what exactly did he mean? What, asked a reporter, was to keep him from inserting himself into editorial operations at a news channel of his own creation?

"Nothing, dummy," Ted responded. "Of course I'm going to manage the news. Sure, if I want to. I'm paying for it, why shouldn't I?"

Reese scrambled to do damage control, explaining that Ted simply didn't understand the language of journalism. He didn't mean control or manage as in inserting himself *editorially*. (At least, Reese was pretty sure he didn't.) What he meant was that unlike the networks, CNN would not be beholden to the whims of advertisers. The all-news channel, under his control, would be a citadel against manipulation. The networks, he continued, lived by the clock, which by itself altered how and what got covered. "Somebody forced to make a public statement can wait until the deadline is at hand, speak his piece, and flee," he said. "He knows it will be reported on the evening news more or less as he said it because there was no time to check it out. But we're not just on for a half hour. Our reporters can come right back on the air forty-five minutes later, correcting and amplifying. On CNN, the news will keep on unfolding all night, and you'll be watching our reporters at work." Despite that ample airtime, he intended for it to be dedicated to real stories, important stories, not just tales of rapes, murders, plane crashes, and fires in abandoned buildings.

The ultimate public skepticism had arrived in the form of an article in *Newsweek*. The magazine ran pictures side by side—one of Tush, seated behind his ticky-tacky anchor desk with his paper-bag-clad special correspondent, the Unknown Newsman. The other of Daniel

Schorr, principled and Emmy-winning steward of the Fourth Estate. The caption asked what everyone in the media world was wondering: "Can Ted Turner go from *this* to *this?*"

Ted needed all the help he could get turning the doubters of his unprecedented idea into believers—and, more important, into subscribers. Only when there were enough eyeballs would CNN pay for itself and become sustainable. Like it or not, he told Tush, playing it straight was how it had to be. And so, the "fancy news set" sign came down, and the cardboard news desk got turned over and recast. Introducing Bill Tush, anchorman.

Panic and confusion began to spread around the dumpy halls of channel 17. Even Ted's devoted employees were doubtful this could work. Earlier chatter about an all-sports cable network evaporated. Suddenly, the engineers were ordering up two dozen three-quarter-inch videotape machines on which to play back news stories? The idea that a purveyor of wrestling, old movies, and *I Love Lucy* reruns suddenly wished to stake a claim in the news business, said his ad salesman, Gerry Hogan, was as preposterous as if "some little company making seat belts suddenly decided to build a revolutionary new automobile that would change the face of transportation." The precariousness and the struggle of the earlier WTCG years were still visible in the rearview mirror, even now that millions of viewers across forty-six states could tune in. This new, crazy idea could very well kill Ted's finances—destroy their beautiful little television cocoon and free-form fun. They'd all be out on the street.

To reinforce the fear that gripped the staff, Hogan fashioned a two-foot-high cardboard sign, in heavy type, and perched it on Ted's desk—almost like a ransom note:

Turner Be Sure
That The News
Operation
Doesn't Bury Us
Don't Get
Carried Away

Be Absolutely
Positive
It Will Work
At Least Don't
Put Us Against
The Wall

Before he could stash this entreaty away behind his bookcase, a reporter for the Atlanta paper who'd come to interview Ted got a gander at it. Ted waved away the negativity and insisted to the curious journalist that he had no intention of jeopardizing his cash cow. In fact, he was about to spruce it up even more, starting with its name. Finally, he was in a position to chase the call letters he'd long desired: WTBS. Turner Broadcasting System.

His query to the original WTBS—the college radio station, Technology Broadcasting System, at the Massachusetts Institute of Technology in Cambridge, Massachusetts—turned out to be perfectly timed. Student management had been struggling with how to raise the money to pay for a new transmitter when a man claiming to be Ted Turner rang up. The timing was so uncanny that, if it wasn't a prank, it seemed a sign from the heavens. Ted offered $25,000, they countered with a request for the $50,000 they needed, and, after he readily agreed, they wished they'd asked for twice as much. The MIT station was rechristened WMBR (Walker Memorial Basement Radio, after the building where they dwelled).

In short order, Ted's promotions people were readying revamped logos and station IDs to promote their new identity. WTBS, the Super-Station, was born. Inside, doubters remained pessimistic. They were sure these new call letters stood not for "Turner Broadcasting System" but Watch Ted's Boat Sink.

Channel 17 had grown out of more than its name and approach to news. As a dribble of staff arrived to plan the news channel, the run-down building appeared ready to burst at its decrepit seams. As a short-term fix, space was taken in an even more ramshackle structure, a decaying white building up the block on the other side of a cluster of old oak trees, a place its new inhabitants imagined, because of the rusty towel bars attached to the backs of the doors, had once served as a rehab center or house of ill-repute. (It actually had done turns as local headquarters for both the Girl Scouts and the Georgia branch of the American Automobile Association.) The mere rumbling of a passing bus down West Peachtree Street set coffee cups perched on desks to quake-like chattering. Here, the employees soon to come would plot out the "greatest achievement in the history of journalism" while awaiting more permanent quarters.

With just eleven months before launch, building a studio from scratch that could accommodate both channel 17 and CNN was out of the question. One of the few ready possibilities was the dilapidated Brookwood Hotel, an old colonial masterpiece, situated on five acres a few miles north of midtown. It could be had for a million dollars. Over its various incarnations, the hotel had served as a swingers' club, a spot for gay and lesbian cruisers, and a home for elderly ladies. Some believed the structure was inhabited by ghosts from Civil War battles fought adjacent to the property. An earlier potential buyer, who'd eyed it for a recording studio, felt the structure so psychically polluted that he considered bringing in an exorcist.

There was symmetry in this possible locale. The old hotel had once been owned by none other than Jack Rice, the man who'd started channel 17 and thus provided Ted's entry into television. Another plus: The old hotel happened to be a stone's throw from Harrison's, the bar where media types in the city loved to gather.

The Brookwood, it turned out, was simply not big enough to accommodate Ted's growing television army and the Jetsonian satellite farm that would be necessary to allow CNN to bring in news from everywhere.

Another fallow building, just a few blocks from existing headquarters, offered far more promise. The old Progressive Club, once a social and recreational haven for Russian Jews, featured a ninety-two-thousand-square-foot white-columned mansion with three swimming pools and tennis and handball courts on twenty-one acres of

The former Progressive Club sat empty for years, just blocks away from WTCG, before Ted Turner purchased it for $4.2 million in 1979. Some early employees recall attending social functions there back when it was still a country club. *(Jeff Jeffares)*

land. The faded beauty was surrounded by a tangle of highways, the campus of Georgia Tech, and Techwood Homes, the nation's first public housing project. On the day in August 1940 that the stately, columned brick structure at Tenth Street and Techwood Drive had been dedicated, prayers had been led by Rabbi Harry Epstein and a time capsule tucked away in the cornerstone for the distant future when the club might outgrow this grand new facility. From that moment on, the Progressive Club thrummed with life, its cavernous halls filled with the sounds of dances, card games, slot machines, Hadassah Club meetings, and a winning basketball team.

By the mid-1970s, club leaders followed a dwindling membership north from midtown to a new, smaller facility at 1160 Moores Mill Road.* Twice since, developers had announced intentions to transform that sprawling enclave into towers of condominiums, office space, and a thousand-room hotel. But those plans had fallen through, and now, this once vibrant, majestic property sat empty, a gem forgotten by all

* As for the new Progressive Club, it was ultimately dissolved, and the new facility converted into a branch of the Young Men's Christian Association.

141

except vagrants who took shelter there, frat boys from Georgia Tech who snuck in to party, and rats.

Reincarnating this parcel as the home for a growing, futuristic television empire seemed preordained. These twenty-one acres were capacious enough to accommodate the necessary "dish farm," especially once the swimming pools were filled in. The listing price was $5 million, but Ted picked it up for $4.2 million. It would take an equal sum for the renovations.

Instead of turning to architects in New York or Los Angeles experienced in building television studios, Ted enlisted his childhood friend Bunky Helfrich. A sailor himself, Helfrich had served as a sail trimmer on Ted's victorious America's Cup crew. Most of his professional work involved the restoration of private homes in Savannah and the verdant Low Country. He didn't have an office in Atlanta, nor had he ever created a television studio. Then again, no one had ever before dared to launch a round-the-clock newsroom, much less one that had to coexist with a so-called SuperStation that hosted weekly wrestling matches and did a brisk business peddling vinyl repair kits and Super-Bad Party Rings. A crew would need to work mighty fast to transform "Tara on Techwood" into a state-of-the-art broadcasting palace. (New hires cheekily referred to this building as the "news kibbutz" and "Kosher Kolumns"—and were quickly admonished by Ted's assistant to stop.)

Along with choosing the architect, Ted made another crucial decision about the newly acquired building that chafed Reese. The plum first-floor space was to be reserved for cash-cow channel 17. The 80-by-140-square-foot ballroom, once resonant with the big-band sounds of Tommy Dorsey and Xavier Cugat, seemed a natural location for the likes of Dusty Rhodes, the Masked Superstar, and Nature Boy Ric Flair to toss one another around in front of a live studio audience. Cable News Network, as the newbie gamble, would be carved out of the locker rooms in the basement.

Reese worried what else Captain Outrageous might do without his approval while he was riding out his ITNA contract in New York. Would he try to hire his girlfriends? Ted had hastily gone and commissioned a logo for the channel, balking at the $5,000 fee he was charged and, ultimately, forking over only $2,800 for the simple design he chose—which featured the letters C-N-N bold, in red, bisected by a white line, presumably signifying a cable. To Reese, the logo looked, depending on your point of view, like either the Canadian railroad logo or "snakes fucking."

Wishing to employ a set of eyes and ears on the ground since it would be months before he himself could arrive in Atlanta full-time, Reese offered Mad Dog Kavanau a job. Sure, he was tabloid, and yes, he carried that pistol, but his news instincts, drive, and energy were unmatched. Kavanau refused. The newsman couldn't fathom leaving his beloved New York again—much less for rinky-dink Atlanta and a speculative operation run by some misfit sailor.

"I think I'd rather be broke and miserable up here," he said, "than employed and miserable down there." As much as he loved news, Kavanau included himself in the camp of doubters who could not possibly imagine how an all-news television operation could work. To agree to be part of CNN, he said, "I'd have to be even crazier than I already am."

Fortunately for Reese, his old boss, Burt Reinhardt, now an executive at Paramount in Los Angeles, had no such hesitations. He eagerly agreed to step into the role as his former employee's factotum— especially after Sid Pike assured him that Atlanta was a "safe and welcoming place" for Jewish people.

Reese finally convinced Ted and channel 17 to join the ITNA, which achieved two goals: a guaranteed, steady flow of legitimate news for Bill Tush to run on his grown-up newscast and, equally important, the right for Reese and Ted to be in touch every day before Reese could migrate south for good. He counted the minutes.

Of crucial concern to CNN's founding president was the design of the newsroom. This would set the tone for the entire channel. The space, as he imagined it, should be the opposite of polished and perfect. It had to look giant, buzzing, *important*—a nonstop hive of activity. The gathering of news and the people collecting it would be as much a part of the story as the news itself. "The idea was to demystify news," he explained. The set had to allow viewers to peer behind the curtain the networks

The basement locker rooms were cleared out and
prepared for conversion into . . . *(Jeff Jeffares)*

held up to shield the newsgathering process. They only took to the air
with their ties perfectly knotted, presenting fully formed, slick stories,
polished to a sheen. Reese's roughhewn approach, he believed, would
allow his audience to create a personal relationship with the network.

Behold: The director in the control room, "the pit," situated in the
center of the action. The technical director calling up shots on the Grass
Valley 1600 switcher, breezing from one story to another. The crew on
the studio floor, stage directing and operating the cameras. A never-
ending stream of video feeding in on the monitors.

The doors on the edit bays must be glass so the cameras, and thus,
the viewers, could peer in at stories as they were formed. This, Reese
believed, would create a sensation of excitement, especially on days
when there wasn't much of consequence to report.

At the same time, what CNN absolutely could in no way afford to
resemble was some homespun, third-rate public-access cable facility.

Channel 17's engineers argued that Reese's open-newsroom plan
was too much of a technological challenge—particularly because of the
sound issues posed by such an active space. To them, this demanding

man from New York personified the division between the old WTCG guard and the new, and why some felt this ridiculous CNN idea was going to destroy the company. Dozens of people bustling around a newsroom would surely drown out the most important voices: those of the anchors.

... a state-of-the-art television facility, which included a Grass Valley 1600 switcher (top; such an impressive bit of technology it made an appearance in the first *Star Wars*) and a mechanized turntable set that never quite worked (bottom). *(Jeff Jeffares)*

To convince Helfrich his idea could work, Reese—paranoid that his ITNA brethren would take umbrage—would sneak into Atlanta for clandestine meetings conducted in the men's room at the airport. Meanwhile, from a tiny desk in the station's temporary work quarters— a seventy-year-old white house that another new hire described as "a place Sherman forgot to burn"—Helfrich worked from copies of the blueprints given him by the original architect, scrambling to draw up sketches for one part of the building while workers brought them to life blocks away.

Even before a strike of sheet-metal workers slowed progress on the studio transformation, building and wiring a newsroom proved to be the least of CNN's problems—which now piled up each day into an overwhelming heap.

Ted had run off to sail again, this time to England, for one of the most challenging races in all of yachting: Fastnet, named for the lonely rock at the southern tip of Ireland that served as the midpoint of the competition. Back in 1971, on his boat *American Eagle*, Ted had performed respectably well, earning a fourth-place finish. Now, with his sixty-one-foot *Tenacious*, he was resolved to add that victory to his list of triumphs. It would not be easy: the 605-mile course ran through the English Channel from the seaport town of Cowes on the Isle of Wight to the rock and back down to Plymouth. The trip got off to an inauspicious start when Ted forgot his briefcase in a taxi en route to the airport and then wrangled his entire posse into the VIP lounge for cocktails, much to the consternation of the beleaguered flight attendant, who threatened to call airport police.

Once overseas, as they embarked on several shorter races, he subjected the crew, which included his namesake eldest son, now sixteen years old, to a week of shouting and berating.

As the day dawned on the main event, an ominous weather forecast loomed. Hurricane-force winds were predicted in the Irish Sea. When the storm blew in on their third day out on the water, the angry gales proved worse than anticipated—howling, as one crew member described it, with the force of a bomber.

Among the 303 yachts from around the world that had entered Fastnet, some were half the size of Ted's. Many were far smaller, and ill-equipped. Having whipped his men into shape, Ted was by then confident in their ability and certain that his boat was prepared. He'd learned that he needed to be ready for anything. The first time he'd raced to Europe, in 1966, proved to be a sleepless twenty-day journey where he'd run out of drinking water and other supplies while dodging whales, icebergs, and waves. The unpredictability of the ocean and Mother Nature was exactly why he loved the sport.

The winds howled from the west, and the churning waters pierced like a sniper assault. Fighting against these winds, the state-of-the-art *Tenacious* suddenly became a surfboard, riding thirty-foot waves and narrowly escaping ones twice that size. The worst of the storm hit during the black of night, and Ted's crew steered in the dark, entirely by feel. Night—when others dared to sleep—was typically prime time to master this kind of race. But this was no ordinary competition. The seasickness among the men was so fierce that even the well-stocked porno locker went untouched.

Frantic, crackling radio calls of "Mayday! Mayday!" painted an ominous picture on the seas. Rescue operations had begun, and many boats were missing. Ted knew the situation for his fellow sailors was dire, but he'd been so far out in front that his crew hadn't themselves witnessed the carnage. The reality was far worse than the reports he heard. Later, he would say that what got him through was his fear of losing. It was more intense than his fear of dying.

News of the worst disaster in the history of yachting reached the studios of independent station CHAN-TV in Vancouver just before Reese arrived with Bunky Helfrich to survey the station's news facilities. Reese had overcome his resistance to this friend of Ted's and had actually grown to like him. The two men had traveled to Canada to scope out a newsroom they'd found that seemed to riff on Reese's open-concept dream, featuring the studio control in the center of the newsroom and the action unfolding around it. Perhaps they could learn something to convince the engineers in Atlanta that the idea actually was technologically viable.

Rescuers in helicopters had not been able to find Ted or his boat. Other sailors had been plucked dead from the waters. The *Tenacious* crew was assumed to be among the fatalities.

An anxious station employee greeted his visitors with the terrible news. "Go home," he said. "Your boss is dead."

Having crewed with Ted in stormy waters, Helfrich didn't believe it. Ted was no doubt screaming at his men, slapping them, riding them like mules, as he always did, yammering nonstop. His nervous fidgetiness escalated to new heights when he was racing. Once during a competition as he worked to "hike" the boat upwind, his foot began shaking so uncontrollably he fell out of the straps and nearly lost his footing. Most likely, Helfrich reasoned, the weather had knocked Ted out of radio contact, or, perhaps, he'd sequestered himself safely in the cabin below. Landlubber Reese could not be so sure. He was swept by panic. If Ted was gone, since it was on Ted's name and personal fortune that CNN was being built, the news channel would evaporate without a trace before pumping out one frame of news. In an instant, his opportunity to change the news business would go up in smoke.

Since they'd bothered making the trip, they figured they might as well take a look around CHAN-TV's facilities. And as they did, there on a studio monitor, as if a mirage, appeared Ted, drawling to a reporter in England about how much he liked rough weather. *Tenacious* had crossed the finish line, seventy-nine hours, fifty-two minutes, and twenty-two seconds after launch, and Ted was very much alive.

"That ain't the ultimate storm," Captain Ted said dismissively of the devastating force that had demolished nearly two-thirds of the competition. Human fatalities were still being tallied. Eventually the death toll would reach nineteen. Sniffed Ted, his trademark arrogance proof that he was very much alive: "It's no use crying over the dead."

In Colorado, Daniel Schorr was moments away from delivering a speech at a cable convention when he learned on the evening news that Ted was missing. Since he had signed on to the network in May, there hadn't been much else to do but trundle from one speaking engagement to the next, opining about freedom of the press and, thus, the need for CNN. His initial dubiousness about Ted and his "frivolous" new venture had morphed into admiration for what he'd come to consider the man's "enormously adventurous vision." In his new boss, he'd begun to see shades of the legendary, dashing broadcasting pioneer William Paley, who'd parlayed his family's cigar fortune and a handful of radio stations into a powerful idea: the CBS network. On several occasions now, Schorr had obsequiously compared the two men. Seated beside him on the late-night talk show *Tomorrow* with Tom Snyder on NBC, he even went so far as to praise Ted as a "cultured gentleman."

But most of all he'd begun to believe in the mission: "The public is manipulated in a savage fight for ratings," he'd say. "People feel control of their lives and their institutions slipping away under the impact of the media giant. Twenty-four-hour news will allow people to regain control of their lives."

Stunned by the possibility that Ted was gone and the implications for his future, Schorr made his way to the hotel lobby, where he was greeted by young Turner executive Terry McGuirk, who shared the important update: Ted was, indeed, okay. This fact became a blinding glimpse of the abject unreliability of the networks for conveying the most up-to-the-minute information. Denver was two time zones behind New York. Of course! The newscast Schorr had watched had been taped hours earlier. By the time the show aired in Mountain Time, network news staffs in New York were busy ordering their second post-show cocktails. For the veteran newsman, this realization reinforced the need for an all-news station, as well as his enthusiasm for this new direction in his career.

To the audience he'd been invited to address, the situation offered the perfect proof of concept.

"If you've been watching TV and if you heard that Ted Turner is missing, let me tell you that he's not missing," he told them. "The reason you might have thought he was still missing is because you were looking at old-fashioned television, which is delayed across the country. And that's one thing CNN won't do. Because it'll be carried live everywhere."

Because of a complex handicapping system, it hadn't been immediately clear if *Tenacious* had indeed won. Surviving Fastnet should have been triumph enough. For a moment, a declaration of victory in Ted's favor was rescinded. Then came the official, bittersweet, final award of first place. Despite the fact that lives had been lost, Ted complimented himself for his triumph. "We won because we had a good crew and a strong boat and a lot of experience, and the people who didn't have those went to the big regatta in the sky. I'm not going to say I'm sorry I won. I'm not going to say it."

"This," he preened, "was the greatest sailing accomplishment in a long time."

* * *

The next disaster to befall the nascent news channel involved not a missing boat but a wayward hunk of crucial technology.

It was sheer coincidence that the launch of RCA's Satcom 3, the satellite that would soon carry CNN's signal up to the heavens and down to the nation, had been set for early December, just as everyone who was anyone in the cable industry was gathering in Anaheim, California. It had been exactly one year since Ted had first floated the idea for the all-news channel at the Western Cable Show—a year since the industry had spurned him. Now, here he was returning triumphantly, with just five months till launch.

Nearly four thousand conventioneers jammed the Disneyland Hotel for the largest of these gatherings to date—half attendees and half exhibitors, all eager to seize a piece of what an ad in a trade magazine declared were "the three biggest words in television: Cable, cable, cable." The cautious interest had roared into a gold-rush stampede. Programmers hawked their services, all evidence of the focused narrowcasting cable could allow—an all-sports channel called ESPN, a public service channel called C-SPAN, forays into highfalutin arts programming from broadcasters CBS and ABC, which promised theatrical programming that would never fly on mainstream TV.

Also on display: a revolutionary new technology that would allow cable operators to provide customers an unheard-of fifty-two channels! Satellite dishes kept shrinking in size and price, making it possible for still more cable operators to join the revolution. One day in the not-too-distant future, the cord would be fully cut, with the arrival of personal dishes installed in one's home.

As the regulatory "gobbledegook" continued to tilt in cable's favor, cities and suburbs around the nation frantically sought bids from companies that wished to wire their municipalities for service. Other topics on the wide-ranging agenda included the continuing drama over complex, thorny issues like copyright and advertiser skepticism of this emerging medium.

All of the chatter quickly subsided as news of a mysterious and devastating development swept the convention floor. RCA's Satcom 3 had gone missing. The bird should have been safely in place by the time the trade show doors opened. But as it was about to ascend to its permanent orbit, it had simply vanished. The apogee kick motor that would push it into its final orbit had failed.

Missing? Ted asked, incredulous. Well, that's RCA's problem. As a charter customer, surely he'd be fine. There had to be a backup bird or someone who could do *something*, he observed, like when your car didn't start.

The trouble was that the "someone"—in this case, skilled engineers overwhelmed by a "deep sense of doom"—didn't know what to do; nor could they explain what had become of their $50 million satellite, much less what happened next. RCA's next Satcom wasn't set to launch for eighteen months, and already that one was fully reserved. Even powerful radar that could detect basketballs from twenty thousand miles away couldn't locate this box-shaped ton of technology.

"We are searching the heavens," RCA vice president Robert Shortal said. "Other companies with satellites are searching the heavens. The

United States Air Force is searching the heavens. We honestly don't know what happened. For all we know, it's on its way to Mars." Had space aliens captured Satcom? Did this mean Jupiter was receiving *I Love Lucy* reruns? "Cable TV's Bye-Bye Birdie," joked the *Washington Post*'s Tom Shales. "Keep watching the skies!"

As the harsh reality of the loss and its implications became clear, Ted quipped to an audience at the show that he must have lived through the Fastnet disaster so he could witness this new one—though this new disaster might very well prove his demise. The networks must have shot down Satcom, he postulated, just to undo him.

The gallows humor masked his terror. Everything he had was riding on the news channel. If he couldn't launch on time, his entire business would collapse. Still, Ted went ahead with a planned major announcement. The network had managed to land its first advertiser, Bristol-Myers, based on CNN's dazzling promise to deliver half of all cable subscribers as their prospective audience. The pharmaceutical giant had pledged $25 million over ten years to sponsor consumer medical segments. Considering that commercials on the nightly network newscasts commanded $50,000 each, what amounted to sixty bucks a spot for CNN was hardly a coup. The investment was a crucial show of faith that signaled that someone other than Ted believed in CNN. Even the guys behind the Ginsu Knife, who'd made a fortune advertising that and other direct-mail products on channel 17, had refused to invest in Ted's crazy idea: "Who the heck will watch news twenty-four hours a day?"

The Bristol deal had almost skidded when executives demanded editorial control over the segments, which Reese refused to give. Then, the would-be advertiser insisted on approving the on-air talent who'd deliver the medical segments. "I can't do that," the newsman explained. "You'll have to trust me—you'll never, never have to be concerned about the credibility of a newscaster." They relented.

No amount of advertising would matter if Satcom couldn't be found. Media swarmed to the parking lot of RCA Americom in Vernon Valley, New York, eager for the latest word.

Back in Atlanta, the skeletal staff couldn't mask their distress. You didn't have to know a thing about cruciform and spin precession maneuvers to understand this was trouble. Reese had an impossible time spinning the silver lining of this obstacle. He was sure they were a goner. Why would anyone upend their lives now to join CNN when it was in such limbo? Cable operators who already thought Ted was "looney tunes" would never waste their limited channel space on CNN now. Who would ever lend Ted the money he needed to keep up operations until there was enough revenue coming in? The precariousness of the Turnerverse now became clear to Reese. He'd been sure Ted's financials wouldn't possibly be an issue. He'd been wrong.

Ted set about calming the troops, ordering them to continue hiring, full steam ahead. "We will not be stopped! No matter what it costs, we're gonna go on!" he said, brandishing his sword before a roomful of worried broadcasters before heading off to another yacht race in the Bahamas.

On his boat in the gleaming waters around Nassau, Ted soon received even worse news. RCA had revealed a solution to the missing satellite—and the solution was a disaster. The company planned to rent time for its aggrieved Satcom 3 customers on a competing bird. Yes, there were two empty channels on the existing Satcom 1, but that wasn't enough to accommodate all the stranded customers—including the new National Christian Network; a new Time-Life service featuring BBC programming; an entertainment service called Showtime; a superstation out of New York, WOR; and a network for people over the age of fifty called Prime Time. So instead, in the interest of being equitable, all would be rented space on another company's bird.

This wasn't like an airline booking you on a rival carrier when your flight got canceled. What RCA proposed was like offering up an eight-track tape machine on which to play an LP when your turntable died. Having to debut on another satellite meant CNN would launch, out of the gate, into instant obscurity. The earth receiving stations were not interchangeable. Most of the dishes cable companies had bought could only pull down signals from RCA's birds because that's where HBO and channel 17 were. It was highly unlikely they'd invest in an entirely new receiving station. Ted hastily departed from Nassau, collected his team in Atlanta, and headed to New York, loaded for bear.

At RCA's headquarters high above in 30 Rockefeller Plaza, an executive explained that Ted would just have to live with the decision—the space on the existing satellites was off-limits.

With that casual dismissal of his dire conundrum, Ted flew into an uncontrollable rage. He pulled the man by his shirt collar and erupted into a tirade for twenty minutes straight—the "Rasputin Mad Monk" routine, as his young executive, Terry McGuirk, described it. He had staked his own personal fortune on CNN. He was a charter customer! He had helped put them on the map! What about the people he'd hired away from other networks, who'd left secure jobs, who he'd now have to fire? Was RCA, parent of NBC, intentionally screwing him? His mother was so distressed about this, she'd had to have a hysterectomy! There were just ninety days to go till CNN's planned debut, and if he couldn't launch on schedule, it would be a disaster. A catastrophe! His ruin!

"I'm a small company, and you guys may put me out of business. This is my death if you do this to me. This is my blood you're getting. For every drop of blood I shed," he roared, "you will shed a barrel."

If he was going down, RCA was going down with him. He intended to sue them and blast them to smithereens.

Go ahead, they said, calmly and clearly. "We can't give you a transponder if we're denying one to everyone else, but if you sue us and win, we'll be forced to give it to you."

So, on February 28, 1980, Turner Broadcasting filed suit against RCA for $35 million, asking for an immediate injunction that would guarantee CNN a spot on Satcom 1. And while they waited for a verdict, a new heart-stopper of a problem emerged.

The tens of millions of dollars he was counting on from the sale of his station in Charlotte was now in jeopardy.

As soon as Ted had announced plans to sell WRET in order to finance CNN, several eager prospective buyers emerged. Ted's finance officer, Will Sanders, coaxed up broadcaster Westinghouse's offer to an eye-popping $20 million—the largest sum ever commanded by a UHF station. The lunatic fringe didn't seem so crazy anymore.

As the station's fortunes had soared over the decade, Ted, as promised, had dutifully paid back the donations viewers had doled out in response to the televised beg-a-thon—with interest. (The most devoted viewers refused to accept the money, happy to have invested in a winner.)

But a lingering scar marred WRET's standing with the FCC. A group called the Charlotte Coalition had called out station management for "insensitivity in programming and discrimination in hiring and promotion." Coalition activists had requested that the station's license to operate be revoked. Though it hadn't been, the government had renewed it only on a limited basis.

When WRET had added a newscast to its programming, another incident had lengthened the station's bad report card.* A job offer made to a black woman hired for an on-air slot as a weathercaster had been rescinded because someone in management worried Charlotte wasn't ready for a newscaster of color. Naturally, she'd filed a complaint.

Because of sanctions imposed on the station, Ted couldn't sell until its record was clean and he was deemed a fit broadcaster. Given this complication and delay, Westinghouse threatened to scrub the sale.

And that had a cascading effect. Anticipating the cash infusion to come once the sale was complete, Ted had secured a $20 million line of credit against which he'd already borrowed $12 million. Now that the transaction was in limbo, the loan had been called, at an interest rate of 25 percent—$400,000 a month.

Now, he lamented, he found himself just about flat broke. Reese felt as if he'd been conned. He had no idea how precarious Ted's finances were.

---

* The newscast at WRET launched on September 1, 1978, after the station had been awarded the NBC affiliation earlier in the year. In his bid, Ted had to promise to spend a million dollars to begin a local newscast. It's not entirely clear why he wished to affiliate the station with a network, given his misgivings about the television establishment, except perhaps to bolster the value of the station in order, ultimately, to sell it.

Desperate, he arranged a meeting in Charlotte with the local activist group. He brought along with him a baseball superstar, the home run king, Hank Aaron, currently serving as vice president in charge of the Braves' farm teams.

Ted began by apologizing for the past bad behavior of WRET's management. He took full responsibility for their actions.

"You know, I don't blame you guys for being mad at me. I'd be mad at me, too," he told them, gesturing toward the legal team. "It looks like you got the same problem I've got in my company. You don't have any blacks in high places either. You got three guys here who are doin' all the talking—and they're all white."

With that, Ted fell to his hands and knees to underscore his contrition and begged.

"You gotta let me sell this station, or I'm a goner."

The soft-spoken Aaron backed him up, pointing out that Ted had pioneered the promotion of blacks in baseball, like him and the late Bill Lucas, to managerial roles. Ted talked frequently of his brotherly love for Jimmy Brown, a black man hired by his father decades before who'd continued to work for the family.* "This guy isn't prejudiced," Aaron assured them.

A deal was brokered: Ted agreed to fund $400,000 worth of grants to minority groups, internships, and scholarships at several historically black institutions of higher learning. It was a worthy chunk of cash to allow the sale to proceed.

* * *

To be invited to speak before the top editors of the august *New York Times* was a sign of acceptance by the vaunted media establishment Ted reviled. The walls of the paper's boardroom were lined with pictures of esteemed visitors who'd graced the room for the weekly publisher's lunch. Nineteen presidents had spoken before this group, along with

---

* Ted had said of Brown, "I guess you could say it's an Uncle Remus–type relationship."

luminaries like Thomas Edison, Andrew Carnegie, Mary Pickford, and Douglas Fairbanks.

Now, Ted was to join these illustrious ranks.

To help bolster Ted's image among the New York media elite, Reese had hired a former CBS public relations man named Ben Kubasik. So far, it hadn't helped. Ted had managed to offend just about everyone in the audience when he'd appeared recently at the New York Academy of Television Arts and Sciences. Before a roomful of broadcasters, in a speech Reese described as Ted's "brilliant best and off-the-wall worst," he lamented the bygone days of more genteel programming and explained that the reason he'd gone into TV was because *they* were doing such a lousy job.

"Unless television changes a lot in the eighties, this nation isn't going to be around the way it is today," he told them. "No one industry or one group of individuals is as guilty for the demise of this country as the television networks and over-the-air broadcast stations—the cartel that has been feeding us so much garbage for such a long period of time."

When star reporter Gabe Pressman raised his hand to ask Ted's definition of good local news, Ted asked where he worked.

"WNEW," came the reply. Mad Dog Kavanau's old station!

"That's a tabloid station, and you're a yellow journalist," Ted countered.

The event devolved into a bit of a brawl as WNEW's current news director leapt to Pressman's defense.

"You're talking about the most respected reporter in New York!" shouted Mark Monsky, a former colleague of both Reese and Kavanau. Monsky and the ITNA were preparing their own salvo in the news wars, a half-hour nightly newscast that would appear on half the nation's television sets—a potential forty million viewers on thirty stations. The *Independent Network News* would begin airing the week after CNN debuted.

Yet another colleague rose and began attacking Ted's lampoon of the news on channel 17.

Riling up a bunch of local television brethren in New York was one sort of poor showing. But screwing up an audience with the newspaper of record could have disastrous consequences. If the paper wrote a scathing take on Ted, his bad behavior, and CNN before it even launched, they'd be toast.

That day at the *Times*, Ted's handlers advised him to table the attitude and stick to the notes.

As they walked into the beige marble lobby of the Grey Lady, as the respected, starched paragon of journalistic integrity was called, Ted demanded of Kubasik, "What the hell am I doing here?" Emblazoned in bronze letters on the wall was the newspaper's slogan: TO GIVE THE NEWS IMPARTIALLY, WITHOUT FEAR OR FAVOR, REGARDLESS OF ANY PARTY, SECT OR INTEREST INVOLVED. Ted and company made their way up to the private dining room high up in the building. The Mouth of the South kicked into drawling overdrive.

"Don't you know we are going to bury you?" Ted asked the men who ran the world's most influential newspaper. It was no secret that newspapers were in a state of flux in the face of the expanding television universe and widening expectations for faster news delivery. Rising costs of labor and newsprint were hammering the industry. Circulation at the *Times* had been declining, as it had at other papers. To bolster relevancy and readership, editors had been adding new lifestyle-oriented sections like "Living" and "Weekend," though it had recently tabled a planned national edition.

"You are putting out a paper tomorrow," Ted taunted, "and we're putting our news out for today." Newspapers were simply out-of-date—unsustainable!

First, he pontificated, you've got to buy a whole lot of land in Canada and plant tree seeds on it. Then you wait around for ten or twelve years to let those trees grow. Then you cut them down and truck the logs to a sawmill, then turn them into pulp and newsprint. Then you load those giant rolls onto a truck, carry them to New York City, and unload them into the heart of Times Square. Then gangs of union workers load them onto the printing presses, while the printers bang out type on linotype machines to make plates for the presses. They crank up the press runs, then load stacks of newspaper bundles on dozens of trucks and fight traffic to distribute them to tens of thousands of individual apartments, houses, vendors, and airports over hundreds of square miles and across the country.

"We," he concluded, flashing his broad, winning grin, "do that whole process of getting news to our viewers by pressing a single button!"

But, an editor asked, what was this Cable News Network going to do that the networks hadn't done?

"We're going to do live news and more live news like it has never been done before," said Ted, parroting Reese's vision.

"But in reality, aren't you going to wind up covering a lot of little, two-alarm fires that don't amount to anything?" another editor asked.

Reese fielded that one. "Until the fire is over, no one knows whether it's a one-alarm fire or the one that burned down Chicago," he answered confidently. "What we want to sell in terms of live coverage is a role in the process for our viewers."

"Awwwright!" Ted cheered. "Strong!"

No advance story on the new network made it into the paper. Perhaps it was because the *Times* didn't wish to hasten a discussion of the demise of print, or perhaps the editors simply found themselves perplexed, as so many did, by Ted Turner.

* * *

It was in March, ninety days before launch, when CNN won a merciful reprieve. A federal court ruled that Ted did have the right to one of those empty transponders on Satcom 1—but only for six months. To boast about the victory, Ted called a press conference at the budding Tara on Techwood—conveniently omitting the six-months part. Visiting journalists wore hard hats adorned with the CNN logo as they toured the facilities and heard Ted preen about his emerging facilities. It was hard to imagine this place would be ready for showtime by June.

But this was all about bolstering PR. The court ruling would allow CNN to launch on time and, he added, "Barring satellite problems, we won't be signing off until the world ends. We'll be on, and we will cover the end of the world, live, and that will be our last event. We'll play the national anthem only one time, on the first of June, and when the end of the world comes, we'll play 'Nearer My God to Thee' before we sign off."

If planning to stay on through the apocalypse didn't show he was serious about news, what possibly could?

A schedule was distributed to the curious pack of reporters. The programming day would feature a farm report at six a.m., a two-hour news and features show at noon, a two-hour nightly newscast at eight, a national call-in talk show at ten, and sports highlights at eleven p.m. Next, a slick promotional film was screened. It promised "news when it's news, not history" and "the kind of news the world's been waiting for." The world had been changing, but television news hadn't kept up. It continued:

Recent national surveys show that 36% of all TV viewers want more TV news. They want better reporting, better coverage, more follow-up. National newsmen may tell you that's the way it is. At the Cable News Network, we believe that's the way it was, and that's why you'll be looking to CNN.

That is, if you could find it. For it turned out that the seven and a half million homes Ted had been promising prospective advertisers would carry CNN at launch—half the available cable audience—hadn't materialized. Though salesmen scrambled to sell the service, the projections kept being sliced in half.

Now, after having survived seemingly insurmountable obstacles, it seemed only 1.7 million subscribers would be wired for this revolutionary new service at its debut—a tiny sliver of the network audience of seventy-six million people. Channel 17 had a wider audience.

This was also a fraction of what Reese's old pals at the ITNA would soon reach with the new nightly half-hour show, *Independent Network*

News, about to debut on thirty indie stations around the country. This offering was a natural outgrowth of the ITNA news service Reese had launched years earlier, and another testament to the growing zest on the part of stations, and viewers, for news. If Reese had stayed put, he could have had his own show without leaving New York.

Instead, he'd traded the city in order to build a network for Ted, and now, yet again, the network was on shaky ground.

The paltry audience CNN would reach was not just a matter of vanity and relevance. It was practicality. Without eyeballs, the all-news network couldn't sell ads, and without ads, CNN—already a loss leader before creating one frame of programming, and with no fat-cat parent corporation to support it—couldn't possibly last a year.

CHAPTER EIGHT

Reese's Pieces

In the winter of 1979, Jane Maxwell's life was, by most people's measures, moving along at a perfect clip. She'd just married her longtime beau, Rick Brown, whom she'd met at her first job out of college—at TVN, the news service backed by Coors. There, she'd worked her way up from secretary to news assistant at a time when women were finally making inroads in the business. Reese thought highly enough of the couple that he'd hired them at his next venture, ITNA.

Being Reese's number two meant that Jane's job was to wrangle the day's news she'd gathered from member stations into a package of stories that got sent out late each afternoon, just in time for their evening newscasts. She was famous for sweet-talking non-members into selling her video when the news warranted. Everyone said she gave "good phone."

She and Rick had decorated their apartment on West Seventy-Fifth Street to their liking, installing the perfect curtains and parquet floors. A private garden out back served as their own personal oasis, complete with a hibachi and an umbrella to shield against the sun. It was perfect for the days they didn't wish to venture to nearby Central Park, which they typically walked through on their way to work at the *Daily News* building.

When Reese called before Christmas to invite them to join him at CNN in Atlanta, they found themselves at an impasse. Jane dismissed the offer right away. Rick, however, was intrigued. Since childhood, he'd been fascinated by the power of information and how new technologies could propel communications. At age twelve, he'd sleuthed out the names and addresses of all the kids in his neighborhood, then printed a directory using rubber type. Later, at the Associated Press, he found himself intrigued by a service called LaserPhoto, which could dispatch a picture at high-resolution in just seconds. Transmitting news in various forms, as far as he was concerned, was the highest calling.

Just as Ted needed Reese, Reese needed Rick and Jane, not just because they were longtime allies he knew he could trust but also because, like him, they were guerilla fighters—comfortable with the "Bangladesh bazaar" style of news and not the spendy, Saks Fifth Avenue variety to which network veterans were accustomed. Though his would be the most modern, up-to-date newsroom on the planet—the first computerized, satellite-propelled newsroom on earth!—CNN would have to adhere to a slim budget, a quarter of what the networks had to spend to fill a fraction of the time. Reese needed someone who understood the ins and outs of buying satellite feed time, the politics and pricing of the phone company's "long lines," and negotiating the alphabet soup of call letters, network affiliations, and desk chiefs at the nation's television stations. Jane would diligently scribble updates in her copy of the *Television Factbook*, the industry bible published annually that listed addresses, phone numbers, and market rankings. An explosion in Omaha? A bridge collapse in Dubuque? Jane, ever-composed and perpetually enveloped in a halo of cigarette smoke, knew exactly who to call, anywhere, for film from the scene of catastrophes, natural disasters, and crimes. Rick, for his part, understood how to get that material where it needed to be—like a cabdriver who instinctively knew which streets to cut through on the back roads to the airport. This adrenaline-fueled, air-traffic-control part of the business was hardly glamorous, but it would serve as the crucial backbone of the world's first all-news channel.

Anyone who'd worked in broadcast journalism had, at some point, wondered about whether or how news might one day flow continuously. But nobody was clear, exactly, on the mechanics of such a beast, nor what an all-news channel would or should look like. The very prospect of an endless stream of information was heady stuff, challenging the essence of what "news" was or could be. No longer would it be limited to what three networks could wedge into a half hour. Except in limited instances, a television newscast had never before lasted longer than that. The possibilities presented by a never-ending stream of news were mind-boggling—not to mention the implications. Mind-boggling, too, was the possibility that there might not always be something to report. Then what?

Rick, a pensive fellow who liked to work through problems as puzzles, tried to imagine it.

"You're talking about this as if we're going to accept the job," Jane said.

"Why *wouldn't* we accept the job?" Rick said.

"Look, I don't want to do another ITNA or TVN," she said. Those second-tier news services were synonymous with frustration. The budgetary limitations were just part of it. The deflating and constant reminder that they were David battling Goliath was wearying—the tedium of explaining to friends and family who could not see the product she was helping to create. Yes, she worked in television, but it wasn't a show on television anyone could actually *see*. It was, indeed, as Reese had described it, an "invisible newscast."

Jane's resistance to joining Cable News Network was, lastly, geographically propelled. "I don't want to leave New York," she told her husband. "I don't want to live down south, where Jews are not welcome."

And yet, Rick also knew that the man who'd replaced Reese at the ITNA unnerved his wife and had made life at the office more of a trial.

"Essentially," he asked her, "what are you going to do?"

"I don't know," she said. "I can just tell you what I *don't* want to do."

"You want ABC or CBS to give you a call and make you an offer? You have more power doing what you do at ITNA. I think we should do it."

"Well, we'll have to think about it."

In the spirit of compromise and adventure, the couple accepted Reese's invitation to visit Atlanta, to talk with him and his wife, Pat, a skilled film editor who'd left CBS, where she'd worked for years, to join her husband in the film-free newsroom he was building at CNN. A fact-finding trip down south, to the land of Ted Turner, might help

Jane and Rick make a more informed decision. Maybe, too, they'd get to meet this mythic man.

Since he'd arrived in Atlanta full-time that August, Reese had been going out of his way to ensure that recruits who paid a visit did *not* intersect with Captain Outrageous. An encounter with Ted would inevitably lead to an inappropriate remark or action, causing the prospective employee to flee. He was quite sure that Rick and Jane, in particular, would not find CNN's drawling, hyperactive, motor-mouthed patron to be their kind of guy.

While Ted Turner was nowhere in sight during the couple's brief foray south, they did encounter another Ted on the scene—Ted Kavanau. Unable to get a TV pilot off the ground, he had asked if Reese's previous offer stood. Figuring he could use all the street fighters he could get, Reese made room for him as a senior producer. To Jane and Rick, there was something comforting about having another dyed-in-the-wool New Yorker, and one they knew, in their midst.

The tour of the musty old Progressive Club Reese conducted hardly persuaded Jane to switch her answer to yes. Maybe the place would look fabulous, some day, when it was done—but from the looks of it, a miracle would be necessary for that to occur by June 1. The pungent aroma of vagrancy perfumed every corner of Reese's palace of news-to-be. In the run-down locker rooms that would one day serve as CNN's studios, the proud papa could only see a thing of beauty. His guests, on the other hand, kept alert for scurrying rats.

The condition of the surrounding neighborhood was no more convincing. What redeeming features there might be in metro Atlanta were hardly evident in midtown. A pall seemed cast over this vacant, sad, desolate area. A once-vibrant hot spot of nightclubs called Underground Atlanta had been torn apart by the construction of a new subway system. Where were the pedestrians? There appeared to be no authentic deli, not to mention decent bagels or pizza, to be had here. No newsstands from which to fetch the Sunday *New York Times* on Saturday night. Hailing a cab? Forget about it.

Right before Rick and Jane were to head home, almost as an after-thought, Reese brought up the elephant in the room: jobs. He offered them each an annual salary of $22,500, a tiny increase over what they were currently earning. Jane fumed to herself. What an insult! Reese expected her to leave her family and home and the place she loved to parachute into the unknown in a half-baked city where they were sure to be working round-the-clock? For pennies more than she was cur-rently earning?

But, Reese said, the salary was the same one most behind-the-scenes recruits arriving with television experience would command.

"The other thing is," he added—Big Mo, with the hard-sell—"we have to have a yes or no when you leave today."

"Reese, can I talk to you in the hall?" Rick asked, confiding man to man rather than prospective employee to future boss. "She doesn't want to come to Atlanta. If she's going to come to Atlanta, she's not going to come for that. If we get home and I can talk to her about it for a day or so, maybe, but I can tell you right now she's not going to take it."

"We're not doing that with anybody," Reese said. "We're not giving anyone a chance to think about it." Reese had been waiting practically every minute of his forty-seven years on earth for this chance to have at the networks. He was living his dream! That *everyone* didn't see it as theirs, and wouldn't drop everything to be a part of it, didn't compute.

But Reese was well aware that he needed Rick and Jane among his troops, so he relented and extended his deadline to the next day at five o'clock. Burt Reinhardt ferried the couple to the airport in his boat of a car.

"I don't even know what you guys do, but Reese speaks very highly of you, and I guess I have to go along with it," he said. "This is the place to be. This is the thing people will be talking about everywhere. It's the new thing in news. If you're at all thinking of not coming here, you really ought to."

"Wasn't that our exit?" Rick said, as they sped past the air-port turnoff.

"Yes, yes," Reinhardt said absentmindedly. "I always miss that exit."

Marooned in an antiseptic bar in Atlanta's dumpy, under-construction airport after missing their flight because of the bad driving, Rick thoughtfully considered the pros and cons. Jane was speechless, glum. The distance between them was magnified by the seating arrangement on the plane: Jane assigned to the back, Rick up front. The silence in the taxi on the way home roared.

Almost the minute they got into their apartment and switched on the lights, as Rick was thinking, "I have until tomorrow," the phone rang.

It was Reese—manic and insistent.

"I was giving you time, but if I can't get an answer right now . . ."

"Give me an hour," Rick said.

"Tell Jane if she doesn't want to work here, that's okay. We can get her a job at one of the stations here," Reese said. "But we want you."

Rick steeled himself for a firm round of husbandly persuasion. The curtains she loved laid on the windows just so. He knew from experience as a younger man, when he'd briefly served as a page on NBC's *Today*, that the networks were hulking beasts—vaunted, self-serious institutions that demanded reverence and gave little love in return. Sure, it made for impressive cocktail-party chatter. ("You work *there?*") Rising up the ranks, even for the most talented person, required a combination of timing, luck, and magnificent political maneuvering. Anyone who hadn't themselves worked at the "nets" romanticized them, and just one foot in the door would cure you of that. Even Reese's wife, Pat, had concurred.

"The networks aren't going to knock on the door," Rick told his beloved bride. "You and I have something in common when it comes to this sort of thing. We don't have a lot of energy to go do this. We're not going to go looking for another job." Here, jobs—good jobs, jobs on the ground floor of something new and potentially revolutionary—were being handed to them on a silver platter by a man they knew, who respected what they had to offer. Yes, it was a risky venture. Yes, it required uprooting their lives. But New York wasn't going anywhere. They could always go back.

Jane sighed a long sigh of deep resolve. She knew this was a great opportunity. Interesting, even. Maybe, possibly, exciting. It was the logistics that were awful.

"You want to do it, I'll go along. If you insist we go down there, then I'll go along."

She held up one finger. "One year," she said. "We will work there for one year." They'd need to find someone to sublease their beloved apartment, so it would be waiting for them when they came back. "If they're going to screw up my life like this, then give them a month notice," she said.

Besides, they'd forked over $150 for a pair of pricey tickets to *Evita*, the hottest show on Broadway—a delayed wedding gift to themselves. No reason to ditch that pleasure.

On Sunday, February 10, the couple arrived in Atlanta and headed straight to their temporary home, a motel nicknamed Sleazy Jim's, just blocks from the station, the same place Kavanau had landed. It wasn't the proprietor, Jim, who was sleazy, but the establishment. The kitchenettes were tired, and a perpetual hairball drifted across the floor that no amount of sweeping could make disappear. With any luck, the two tissue-paper-thin blankets assigned to their room had been sanitized. Ladies of the evening milled around the block, hoping for customers. It was impossible to imagine a bright future emerging from this bleakness.

Off they went to grab dinner at Mellow Mushroom, a pizza and sub and beer joint that catered to the nearby Georgia Tech crowd. Even before they took a bite, the couple knew that it could not possibly be a fraction as good as pizza back in New York. So repelled were they by this new city, they decided even the *graffiti* was subpar when they spotted some neatly written on the back of the stall in the restroom ("The Ayatolla is an Assaholla!"). Clearly the work of some lowlife ignoramus who'd never make it defacing the walls back on the Upper West Side. Their exile to a foreign land had begun. New York City was 863 miles away—so close, and so very far. In just 364 days, they could go home.

The next day, the couple trudged out on foot—New Yorkers that they were, they had no car and would need to buy one—to their temporary work quarters at the white house. The run-down channel 17 headquarters at the end of the block seemed palatial by comparison, though that building's inhabitants were more worried than ever that CNN was going to drag down Ted's empire and jeopardize their jobs. A bus rumbled outside, shaking the tiny desks jammed side by side in the warren of rooms. Rick and Jane had been so distracted by the wretched condition of the country club that the state of this place hadn't quite registered. Now, with launch day under four months away, it was beginning to fill up.

It was of some comfort to learn they were in the company of network television news veterans, like executive producer Sam Zelman, perhaps most famous for defying critics in 1961 who said no one would watch more than fifteen minutes of news on television. After creating the first-ever hour-long daily local newscast in Los Angeles, mimicked by news executives in other markets, the networks had been inspired to expand their own newscasts from fifteen minutes to a half hour. By then, Zelman was working at CBS in New York. He recalled the "pandemonium" that resulted. That, of course, would pale in comparison to the "zero to twenty-four hours" ramp-up of CNN.

The affable producer was also legendary for discovering on-air talent, like Jerry Dunphy, who famously began his newscasts with the trademark introduction, "From the desert to the sea, to all of Southern California, a good evening." Zelman knew that to cut it at CNN's seat-of-the-pants environment, good looks and mellifluous pipes wouldn't be enough.

He passionately believed news was "the lifeblood of citizenship" and that the more of it there was, the better. Now sixty-five, he'd traded retirement—mandatory at the network at his age—for this impossible-to-miss opportunity. Goodbye, Learjets and the extravagant silver tea service available at CBS. Hello, Winn-Dixie gift certificates and fruitcakes provided at down-market Turner Broadcasting.

The résumé of another network refugee, Jim Kitchell, read like a timeline of the mid-twentieth century. He'd directed NBC's nightly newscast, *The Huntley-Brinkley Report*, including coverage of the Kennedy assassination, the Cuban Missile Crisis, and Nixon's historic visit to China. He'd won an Emmy for his coverage of the Apollo space missions. At CNN, he'd arrived as vice president of operations at a start-up that was ordering used furniture and old videotape from the network he'd left behind. (NBC, flush with cash, recorded on tape only twice before chucking it.)

Both Zelman and Kitchell didn't mind that they were window-dressing for Ted as he trundled around to potential investors, advertisers, and cable companies, hoping for their buy-in. Their A-list bona fides were prominently featured in a glossy promotional video to add legitimacy in the hopes of offsetting Ted's questionable behavior. An unrelenting critic of their former employers Ted might be, but he wasn't beyond using their clout when it served him.

Among the other hires were, as Reese uncharitably called them, the "rehab projects." He lumped Kavanau and Schorr into that category. Another producer he'd hired despite his history of harassment issues at another broadcasting company. Then there was Ed Turner, an experienced news director who'd lost his television job in Washington, D.C., because of a drinking problem. Kavanau convinced Reese it would be a mitzvah to give the man a chance to get back on his feet. Turner learned quickly to point out he was "no relation" to Ted.

While Ted Turner was thrilled that someone who shared his father's name was on the payroll, Jane was distressed to learn that this Ed fellow had been promised the same title offered to her: managing editor. It fell to Ed to explain that, in fact, she'd have to settle for deputy managing editor. Then, he deigned to ask the young woman to fetch his dry cleaning and make restaurant reservations. No, Reese's assistant made clear: Deputy did not equal secretary.

Adding to the sting, "No Relation" explained that there would be no budget for acquiring news stories. Everything had to be pure trade. Even her finesse and her Rolodex didn't offset the sheer lunacy of asking stations around the country to *give* their material to an untested news network.

"You're being ridiculous," they'd say when they heard her proposal. "Ted Turner can go to hell." It was hard for most people, particularly those in smaller markets, to grok this newfangled system—and how it would be advantageous to be a part of it. Jane knew from her last two jobs how starved local stations were for video, the pressure they were under, and with limited budgets, too. The industry of television news had gone berserk, as local newscasts were continuing to expand and a wave of new technology like minicams and videotape and microwave trucks and news choppers were making it possible to transmit more often from farther away, and more quickly.

On Kavanau's recommendation, Reese had also hired a well-regarded senior producer who'd worked in local news, most recently in the San Francisco television market. His name was Alexander Cooper Nagle III, a prep school graduate who'd attended Dartmouth (like Reese) and Syracuse University (like Kavanau, he'd earned his master's there). "Any similarity between Alec and characters in movies depicting the fraternity life of the sixties is not coincidental," his college alumni magazine said when describing this convivial spirit. At age thirty-five, Alec, as he was called, had already suffered a heart attack. The stress at an always-on news network would naturally be even more intense than in local television, but he couldn't turn down the challenge to invent something new, nor the opportunity to work alongside the legendary Kavanau.

They made for an odd couple. Together, they became the heart and soul and conscience of CNN—Nagle, a blue-blazer, khaki-clad, Ivy League WASP of a gentleman who, a colleague described, "joyously lived in the news," and, as Reese explained, "coddled people into shape," alongside Kavanau, the intensely serious, pistol-wearing "Mad Dog" from the Bronx, who believed the best way to create a great newscast was to keep the staff tense and on edge.

"Kavanau would say tear down the wall with your fingernails," Reese observed. "Alec would say, 'No, let's do it with our teeth, and smile,' and then go knock it down himself and shrug as he was doing it."

Each man possessed an obsessive, tireless commitment to his work that made him perfect for an all-news channel. Nagle followed his wife's orders to keep to a rigid schedule, due to his precarious health. But when he was present at work, he was all in. Kavanau never wanted to step out of the frenzied haze of the news cycle. He asked if he could live at the new studio, as he had wished to in New York—and was told by Ted Turner himself that he couldn't. CNN was no sweatshop! (Though once they went on the air, it wasn't uncommon for a young employee to sleep off the fun of the hours before his or her shift by catching a snooze behind one of the hulking one-inch tape machines.)

Whatever their fundamental differences, Nagle and Kavanau united in plotting out their raison d'être of news, the philosophy of CNN. They fervently believed in populist appeal, creating newscasts that cabbies would talk about with their fares. Zelman concurred. Reese, on the other hand, aimed to be more high-minded. The miner approach, as he thought of it: "Go around with your Geiger counter or whatever and look for the radiation, and if you find it, ah, there's the ore, there's the ore."

In his dreams, he imagined a free flow of news, endlessly unfolding from story to story. No rundown, no format, just anchors responding to news as it was punched up from the satellite feeds. The audience should hang on to their seats, afraid to change the channel, for fear of missing a frame of the action—like a football game. Like the crew of a sporting event, the CNN crew would have to pivot on a dime. A television audience was captive, and therefore restless, and this quick pace was essential to keep them from changing the channel. A newspaper reader might skip around from page to page, but a TV viewer unhappy with what they were watching would suddenly ditch you and hop to another station.

Though he'd been in the business for more than twenty years, Reese hadn't produced one single hour of live television. Nagle and Kavanau knew from producing hundreds of hours of it that some sort of road map to the troops was necessary, even if, along the way, that road map got blown up. The veteran producers knew that Reese's vision of digging for stories required far more people and time than there was, especially given the beast of a "news hole" they needed to fill. Besides, broadcast journalism was built not on what you said but on what you *showed*—not on stories themselves but on the *people* affected by the stories. People power, Nagle called it.

"A bank interest rate increase can be pretty dull stuff unless we show the audience people who can no longer afford something because the price of money just went up," they explained in a manual that laid out their philosophy. "Show them the people. We all must resist the temptation to take the easy route and merely interview the company presidents, who seem to have all the answers. Actually, most stories are far removed from the corporate world, down there where the folks are living."

Their wisdom extended to personal habits.

"The energy that goes into the program comes out the other side of the screen," Kavanau advised in a note to the staff. "If you are a laid-back producer . . . the show you produce will lay back—the talent will lay back . . . the staff will lay back. Personal advice. If you are a low-energy person, that will be reflected into your work . . . lift weights . . . run . . . do pushups. Do what it takes to bring up your life energy so you can pump it into the program."

Finding guerilla warriors propelled by the right "life energy" was the goal. Absent that, they'd settle, simply, for eager.

"It soon became clear that I possessed most of the qualifications for a young producer that they were looking for," said John Hillis, who worked at an ABC affiliate in North Carolina, "namely that I had two arms and two legs and was breathing." Some recruits had been plucked from among the thousands of résumés that arrived at the white house. Others knew someone, or knew someone who knew someone. Still others just finagled their way in the door. There was no rhyme or reason. Kavanau administered writing tests to prospects, aware that he'd need an endless flow of copy to keep the shows going. If a person could rewrite ten copy stories in an hour from wires and newspaper articles, the job was theirs.

To eager would-be producers, Nagle would pose a theoretical news situation.

"Let's say a plane goes down off Tenerife . . ."

"I'd call the network," a confident would-be employee answered.

"But you *are* the network," Nagle explained.

Everyone was making it all up as they went along. The woman hired to start the foreign desk wondered, "How do you start a Foreign Desk?" With personnel elbow to elbow at the white house, she retreated to her car with a bunch of file folders and converted her back seat into her office.

* * *

Finding on-air talent was another matter. In a tiny room upstairs, Nagle, Kavanau, and Zelman inserted demo tape after demo tape into a three-quarter-inch video machine, in search of the perfect faces to deliver news round-the-clock to the nation's living rooms. Reese had budgeted for one anchor per hour, with a decided preference for hiring male on-air talent. Zelman convinced him women newscasters deserved to be equal parts of the equation and that two-person teams were necessary to keep up the pace. The budget for on-air talent immediately doubled.

The résumé tapes, stacked six feet tall and covering every wall, served as a visual reminder they were the epicenter of something hot. How many of the candidates were any good was another matter. Too many in the avalanche of potential newsreaders appeared stricken by what the trio of producers deemed "prompter look," meaning it was obvious that they were reading, or in possession of "helmet hair," that shellacked-in-place coiffure that made them look "stamped out of an anchor production line." If it wasn't their voice or their hair, it might be their clothing that presented gaudy "fashion risks."

Determining a thumbs-up or -down on a candidate took thirty seconds. Prospects were ranked on a scale from one to ten—anyone over a seven got sent to Reese for further consideration.

Zelman's lament? "The good ones are under contract, and those who aren't are reluctant to join in Ted's crazy scheme."

Sniffed Kavanau: "An anchor is an anchor is an anchor."

Burt Reinhardt seconded that: "The news is what people watch. The *news* is the star!"

Few of the candidates wowed all of the men, but for one. Her name was Kathleen Sullivan, and she worked in Salt Lake City—where she was beloved by the Mormons.

With her "wonderful violet eyes," Reese felt Sullivan looked like "pure sex," as if she'd just climbed out of bed with someone, that she was "astoundingly beautiful in a non-conventionally beautiful way."* Exclaimed Nagle, "She's magic. She makes love to the camera!" Hired! To establish her as a hard-nosed reporter, they sent her off with a crew to Nicaragua to stockpile reports for June.

The steely blue eyes of Mary Alice Williams didn't hit the same home run. Zelman found them cold, Reese said, but he himself was impressed by the reporter's journalistic chops. So he hired her for a plum assignment, as anchor and chief of the New York City bureau. She had dreamed in college that there might someday be an all-news channel. The newsroom she'd lead would be situated in an unusual spot, behind a forty-foot pane of glass in the lobby across from the elevators at One World Trade Center. A fishbowl newsroom, on display for thousands of passersby each day.

Installing miles of cable to the top of the towering building proved a particular challenge, given the unions Williams had to wrangle to get the work done.

A woman placed into such a prominent managerial position was a rarity, made possible by this fringy, emerging part of television. "Women are attracted to cable," Williams explained, "because it's new and risky. We weren't raised to think we would have to support a family, so we don't carry that burden."

In Atlanta, Ted was told one day between sailing competitions that the New York bureau chief had arrived to meet him. When the statuesque blonde Williams entered his office, he leapt up from his desk, she observed, as "if red fire ants had bit him."

---

* Once they got on the air, Reese said, "The letters I got could best be described as mash notes; the letters with things men wanted to do with Kathleen were beyond the imagination."

Daniel Schorr on the Cable News Network. Solid Journalism.

When we set out to build television's finest news staff, we decided to settle for nothing less than the best.

That's why we asked Daniel Schorr to join the Cable News Network.

We looked at his record. Ace reporter for the **Christian Science Monitor** and **The New York Times.** A quarter century as one of the key people at CBS News. The first CBS correspondent in Moscow. Other important assignments around the world. Landmark stories on the Soviets in Cuba, the search for Nazi war criminals, Watergate and the CIA Scandals.

We considered the recognition of his peers. Citations from the journalistic community. Praise from citizens' groups. Honorary university degrees. "Emmy" awards.

Most of all, we recognized his excellence as a reporter. This is the man whom the **Washington Post** called "the toughest and best reporter in television news." In **The New York Times,** William Safire said, "He may be the best television newsman in the field today."

And author David Halberstam believes he is "an old-fashioned print journalist—too serious, too talented, and too aggressive for television."

But at The Cable News Network, we think Daniel Schorr is just what contemporary television needs. So, when we begin 24-hour programming on June 1, 1980, he will anchor our Washington desk. Schorr will join a distinguished group of journalists, analysts, and feature talent.

People such as political columnists Roland Evans and Robert Novak, former Treasury Secretary William Simon and psychologist Dr. Joyce Brothers.

Schorr will cover Washington for CNN's two-hour prime-time world and national newscast, a daily report with the kind of depth only print reporting could offer up to now. And the full story continues around the clock, with financial reports directly from Wall Street, exclusive items for women and other groups, national and regional weather, plus continuing updates of the stories behind the stories.

That's solid journalism. That's the kind of solid foundation we're building for television's most innovative news story ever.

Cable News Network

CNN

1018 West Peachtree Street, Atlanta, Georgia 30309
For more information, call (404) 898-8500.

Promotional materials for the first all-news channel included this piece touting the first official hire, veteran broadcaster Daniel Schorr, whose journalistic pedigree offset Ted Turner's reputation as a rogue. It wasn't clear to Schorr that Ted even knew who he was.

"A woman! A woman?" he screeched.

Williams planted herself in the doorjamb, the place she'd been taught you're supposed to stand in an earthquake.

"Do you want to work with me?" she asked, almost as a dare, and then explained that they'd do best if Ted stayed out of her way.

As difficult as it was for a woman to make her way in broadcast journalism, it was doubly hard for people of color, especially on-air talent. Aware that he could hire excellent anchors at a good price, Reese snapped up three African American women: Reynelda Muse, Roz Abrams, and Beverly Williams. Luring Bernie Shaw away from his job as ABC's Capitol Hill reporter to anchor CNN's eight-to-ten prime-time newscast was a coup. It would elevate Shaw to a position as one of the most prominent black on-air anchors in television news. His wife convinced him to take the job; she said he'd be impossible to live with if this grand, oddball journalistic experiment took off and he hadn't.

Trading the prestige of the network he'd worked so hard to reach for the low-rent CNN D.C. bureau situated across from a graveyard on Wisconsin Avenue, miles from the center of media activity in the nation's capital, didn't faze him one bit. "I don't view it as a step down," he said. "Someone told me, 'More people will see you on *World News Tonight*,' than anchoring on CNN. That's not the purpose. [CNN] is pure news—not just once or twice a day. The least of my problems is that it has a small audience."

At television stations around the nation, a pink "while you were out" phone message slip bearing a message from "Diane Durham" became code for "CNN calling." Anchorman Dave Walker in Sacramento got one. The rumor of shabby facilities and the rap about Ted Turner and his messianic vision to inspire world peace and brotherly love among all peoples didn't stop the anchorman from responding. In fact, Walker said, the chaos was kind of appealing—as long as he could bring along his wife, Lois Hart, who worked at another station across town.

Reese and Pat and Rick and Jane had already set the stage for the Noah's Ark of television news. Newsrooms typically refused to hire married couples and would force half of couples that formed at work to leave when they got hitched. For CNN, twofer hiring became a mainstay. So many couples and family members were subsequently brought on board that Ted joked CNN actually stood for "Cable Nepotism Network." (One early employee petulantly referred to them as "nepits.")

Some were lucky enough to receive a personal welcome.

"Dee," Ted shouted to his dutiful secretary when two newcomers were ushered down the block to his office, "get me the basketball team on the telephone! I want the basketball team to welcome these guys aboard."

"The whole basketball team, Ted?" It was just after nine in the morning.

"Awww, well, you pick a couple of players and wake up just a couple of them. I want everybody in our organization to know you're here," he explained to the newbies sitting in his office. "I want everybody in the media and everybody at those big, bad network dinosaurs to know you're here. That way, they'll know we're serious! They'll know we're coming after them beginning June first!"

When Dee shouted, "I got a sleepy Hawk on the line," Ted punched up the speakerphone on his desk that his employees called his "squawk box." The device exaggerated his nasal drawl into a sound like, as a reporter described it, "a mynah bird with an adenoid problem."

"Now we have these good people from the Cable News Network in here this morning. Say hello to them."

"Hello, Cable News Network," the sleepy Hawk said unenthusiastically.

"I just wanted you guys to know they're working with us now and we're going ahead full speed with CNN. I want you to pass on the good news. CNN is now in business! I want to do more than get rich. I want to do something for mankind! CNN will shine a light on the world! That's my real motivation! I want to shine a light on the world."

Ted might have thought himself a modern Christopher Columbus, but others saw in him shades of the strange and arrogant industrialist Howard Hughes, who almost succeeded in buying ABC in 1968.

Alec Nagle offered a better comparison: "Do you realize that Ted Turner is the Wizard of Oz, and all of us are marching down the yellow brick road?"

* * *

The road continued to be riddled with potholes. While a core group of inductees laid the groundwork for his baby, Reese dipped in and out of town in service of the Wizard's creation. He was well aware that he could deputize others to perform tasks like finding the real estate to house the six planned CNN bureaus around the country (Chicago, Dallas, Los Angeles, and San Francisco, in addition to New York and D.C.), or negotiating for a first-of-its-kind switch that would connect Atlanta with New York and D.C. to allow a continuous pipeline of news to flow. (It was so revolutionary an idea that when it began working, even cynical TV veterans gasped with wonder.) Reese didn't intend to miss one single moment of what he deemed "the most exciting opportunity in journalism in this quarter of a century." He had one shot to "do news better," and this pressure propelled his already warp-speed personality into overdrive. In the hopes of tamping it down, his assistant slipped his wife, Pat, some Valium to put in his orange juice, but they all decided it didn't work. A painful hernia that Reese was ignoring in the service of making it to launch day amped up his mania.

Describing Ted's investment in the network as both an "act of faith" as well as an "act of genius," Reese sliced and diced his "pie," the hours of the day, inventing shows and hiring more commentators to record those time-filling "columns." For a morning business program, he wanted to negotiate with the New York Stock Exchange so his team of financial reporters could file from the trading floor for the very first time. In the evening, when the networks ran their obligatory newscasts, he imagined a sports round-up that "every bar in the country will have on," which would please the bookies, too. Just like newspapers ran comics to entice readers to other parts of the paper, he planned on hiring music critics for daily reports "to attract the kids."

Top of mind was whom to hire for what he considered the plum assignment, a nightly, issue-oriented call-in talk show that would be CNN's answer to Phil Donahue. On this ten p.m. program he'd tentatively titled *Backtalk*, newsmakers of the day would sit before a live studio audience for an in-depth interview that advanced the news into the next day. So in love was he with his idea that it never occurred to him that it would be next to impossible to corral Atlantans to sketchy midtown at that time of night, much less that he'd have to wrestle with the phone company for a toll-free number, which they refused to give this untested network. He fretted: Would anyone call if they had to pay?

Maybe all the industry buzz would help him lure what he couldn't before: a big flashy "name." A string of well-known and up-and-coming television personalities turned him down. David Frost. Geraldo Rivera. NBC's wry Linda Ellerbee. Maury Povich, then a sportscaster eager to cross over into regular news. Charlie Rose, who'd been making the rounds in local news. (Thumbs down from Sam Zelman, who declared him dull, dull, dull.) Some prospects parlayed CNN's interest into better deals at their existing jobs. Reese dismissed a local Atlanta anchor named Forrest Sawyer for fear that hiring him would seem too homespun. Sam Zelman pushed an undiscovered gem named Oprah Winfrey, a young, rising star on Baltimore television. Reese nixed her without even watching her demo reel, claiming she was too inexperienced. He didn't want critics to harp on the new network for having a rookie in such a prominent role.

Soon, Winfrey would land a job in a major market because of the person Reese did hire.

Sandi Freeman of WLS-TV's *AM Chicago* had sent in a tape accompanied by an impressive endorsement—a column by Jules Witcover in the *Washington Star* that praised her for a recent interview she'd conducted on her morning news show with the presidential candidate Senator Ted Kennedy. After watching her reel, Reese was certain he could turn this woman into a star—the next Barbara Walters.

A midwestern charmer, Freeman was possessed with good people skills, with the looks to match, but a career in journalism hadn't been her goal. Her passion was singing. She'd appeared with the St. Louis Municipal Opera in her hometown and, after graduating from Webster College there in 1964, had set her sights on Broadway. With only $140 in her pocket, she found herself waylaid in Chicago, where she paid her college loans by working as a cocktail waitress at the Gaslight Club. (Unlike Bunnies at the nearby Playboy Club, fishnet-adorned Gaslight Girls were expected to have some sort of vocal talent to go along with their good looks.)

Mostly, she appeared in big-budget theatrical productions the general public could not see. The lucrative "industrial musical" circuit staged trade-show gems like *Whirlpool Is the One* and American Standard's *The Bathtubs Are Coming*. Along the way, she'd met her husband, John Ivicek, when she joined a singing group he ran called the Ivy Five. By day, he was an editor at the television station where Freeman got her big break.

As second banana on the morning show, she'd sat beside a string of male co-hosts, so many that her colleagues joked she'd had more partners than Elizabeth Taylor.

Consultants, a proliferating force in the local news industry, insisted she cover up her long blond hair with a wig that, to her, "looked like a hard hat with curls and felt worse."

"Her job was to look cheerful and pleasant. But not so beautiful as to make the women at home uncomfortable," local TV writer Fred Rothenberg explained.

When co-anchor Charlie Rose left the program, Freeman asked for solo billing. The answer was no. Her boss didn't think she could hack it. A reporter asked why the mother of three just didn't walk out after the snub.

"What was I going to do?" she said. "Say 'Fine, I'm going somewhere else'? Even in this age of supposed liberation, most married women with children don't think the way a man does about this situation. I didn't want to disrupt my husband's career as a tape editor." She dealt with her frustration by redecorating the house.

Freshly reupholstered furniture hardly tamped down her ambition. The same week that Ted announced CNN in May 1979, NBC confirmed that Freeman was in the running to replace Jane Pauley on NBC's *Today*. Passed over for that job, she contented herself with her local celebrity, expanding her role at the station by contributing movie, theater, and restaurant reviews. Occasionally, she'd sing at station-related public service appearances in the Chicago area, and she picked up extra money as spokeswoman for a chain of women's exercise studios.

Though television critics dismissed morning news as "empty-calorie television," her mettle as an interviewer was on full display in March 1980, when Ted Kennedy appeared on *AM Chicago* in advance of the Illinois presidential primary. A poll had shown that the chief reason women wouldn't cast their ballots for him was his treatment of his wife, Joan—he'd legendarily survived an auto accident in which a younger female companion had died.

"What about the 'Joan factor'?" Freeman had asked.

When Kennedy said he didn't understand what she meant by that, Freeman explained she was talking about his wife's alcoholism and how it might have been brought on by "incidents that happened in your marriage." Kennedy acknowledged that Joan was coping with substance abuse. Women were angry, Freeman told the senator, about the "alleged promiscuity that could have led to her drinking."

Columnist Witcover had been wowed by the doggedness of this "pleasant looking blonde woman with one subject on her mind, and the determination to get answers about it."

Reese found himself similarly enchanted. Tapped for this major career move and, at last, a show of her very own, Freeman felt "ecstatic," like a "kid at Christmas," especially after she learned that the program's name had been updated to *The Freeman Report*. A cross between *Newsweek* and *People* magazines, she described it, with a goal to enlighten and inform.

This shot at the big time helped her overcome her fear of disrupting her family. She moved to Atlanta without her husband and three kids.

"It was very difficult to pick up and leave," she told a reporter in Chicago, where her new job was big news, "but I know it was the right thing for me. And for my family. To be here now, doing what I love to do, when this whole thing is so new and so exciting."

* * *

It didn't really matter who was on the air at Cable News Network if there was no crew to run the studio cameras, to spirit the tapes fresh out of edit to air in master control, and to cue the anchors—thankless jobs in the trenches essential to the smooth functioning of a television operation.

Initial projections called for the hiring of eighty-six crew to cover the 168 hours in a given week, for which each employee would be paid $20,000 a year. In a union shop, like at the networks, camera operators, audio technicians, and tape editors were paid handsomely for their focused expertise. Talent or guests couldn't clip on a microphone without the assistance of a trained technician. Georgia, however, was a non-union, right-to-work state, which meant CNN faced no such restrictions.

Which was a good thing for the nascent network, because Reese had made a major miscalculation. Twice as many crew members would be necessary to keep the place operating—and, of course, doubling the budget was out of the question.

The math startled. Who would work overnights for what amounted to $3.10 an hour? Easy. Recent college graduates! A new, entry-level job category was invented that Kavanau anointed with a vague and lofty title: *the video journalist*. Work as a CNN "veejay" would be like getting a master's in television, without the degree, in exchange for a (barely) subsistence-level wage. The "most important journalistic innovation of all time" would, it seemed, be propelled by an army of newbies! The sink-or-swim school of TV news, Reese called it.

Kavanau, along with Jim Kitchell, fanned out to broadcast journalism schools around the nation, in search of idealistic young recruits willing to join the wild, wild west of news.

The very best graduates of the very best schools would undoubtedly get snapped up for the handful of entry-level jobs that existed at the networks, where, in exchange for the prestige, they'd be restricted by union rules from touching equipment and have to stick to rigid job descriptions. Then, there was everyone else—kids with dreams well aware of the catch-22: they couldn't get a job without experience, but without experience, they couldn't get a job. At CNN, there would be no limitations. If you showed up and performed, and you wanted to try your hand at something, you could. That would presumably make up for the lousy pay and crazy hours.

All who enlisted arrived with different stories and aspirations, and yet, all the stories and aspirations were somehow the same. Take Fred

Cowgill. Watching his father and his colleagues punch the clock at IBM as a kid had inspired him to find a profession that was so much fun he didn't notice the time except for where he had to be next. He was about to graduate with his master's in television from Boston University when Kavanau appeared on campus.

Cowgill was sure he was destined to be, as he called it, the "next rock star of Earth." Kavanau sold him on the adventure.

"We're offering an opportunity to take years off the climb you might have to make," he told the young man. "There'll be lots of opportunity. If you're half of what you think you are, you'll make it."

Caught up in the whirl of excitement at the prospect of something new, and wowed by Kavanau's intensity, Cowgill ignored naysayers who said this move was a crazy gamble. What did he, as a newbie, have to lose? So he said yes to six days of work a week for $9,600 a year.

The weather proved an auspicious start to the adventure. When he'd left Boston in early March, it had been snowing, and when he arrived in Atlanta, the trees were in bloom. The variety of states represented by the license plates on the cars in the parking lot made arriving at CNN feel like the first day of college. He didn't know a soul, he didn't know the city, and he had no idea, really, what he was doing. What he didn't see, couldn't see, because of his own insecurity, was that everyone else around him was just as afraid.*

Like John Towriss. He'd been working for his uncle's construction company in his hometown of Muncie, Indiana, and kept encountering closed doors as he attempted to break into television. Like everyone else, every week he scoured the trade magazine *Broadcasting* for opportunities. During his lunch break one day, he dialed Atlanta's directory assistance (404-555-1212), asked the operator for the number of the Cable News Network, and, when he got through, asked to speak with someone whose name he'd read in some article: "John Baker in operations, please."

---

* After some on-air work at CNN, Cowgill moved to WLKY-TV in Louisville, where he has served as sports director since 1987.

Baker himself answered the phone. Towriss launched into his polite, confident spiel, that he was a kid out of college, looking for a job.

"Sure, we're hiring lots of people," was the response. "Send me a résumé, give me a call in a week."

Towriss did as instructed.

"Well," Baker said, a week later, "do you want to come down and talk to us?"

Of course he did. Towriss loaded up his little Honda Civic and arrived after a day-long drive to find Baker's desk piled with papers. When he couldn't locate the young man's résumé in the avalanche, Towriss pulled out another copy.

"John," said Baker, giving it a cursory look, "you have a little more experience than most people we're hiring right now."

"Mr. Baker, I've never done *anything*," the dumbfounded and unerringly polite twenty-one-year-old responded. "What kind of people are you hiring?"

Baker spent the next twenty minutes trying to talk him out of the job.

"If we hire you, you'll be working overnights, six days a week. We're only paying minimum wage," he said. "We're losing $2 million a month, and we're not sure how long we'll be on the air."

Towriss's construction job back in Indiana paid nine bucks an hour and was a sure, steady gig.

"Well, Mr. Baker, I'm just trying to get my foot in the door, I'm pretty footloose and fancy free. I'd accept all that."

"Okay. Go to that guy over there, see him, tell him to put you on the schedule."

"Wait, does that mean I'm hired?"

There was no human relations department, Baker explained. But that guy over there, he would get him into the system. In other words, yes.

"Hi, Mr. Knott, Mr. Baker told me to come over and have you put me on the schedule for next week," said the young man, not quite believing his good fortune or how easy it all seemed.

"What can you do?" the man responded.

"Not really anything," Towriss replied, ashamed, humble, but honest.

"Great," he said. "I can put you anywhere I need you."

Towriss was afraid to ask the next question: Which day did he start? He had to go home, get his stuff, and find a place to live.

His worry that everyone else who'd been hired had rafts more experience was allayed shortly after he arrived when he'd met a guy whose last job had been playing Goofy at Disneyland. He himself felt like he'd landed in his own idea of an amusement park, a utopia of television news.*

Summer camp, with no curfew! *Animal House* meets *Network*! Kavanau had suggested they build a dorm to house the veejays, but they themselves created their own group homes to cut costs, in some cases "hot-bunking," where one person would sleep in a bed while another inhabitant went to work on a different shift. Absent a formal coordinator, Reese's wife, Pat, stepped into the role of den mother, helping young arrivals connect with roommate-seekers and all else a den mother might do, like fielding calls from a bunch of drunken veejays who'd been arrested and then bailing them out of jail. If she detected addictive substance abuse, she'd track down the parents of the afflicted. If a kid had rent problems, she and Reese would advance them money. If a girl got into trouble, Reese said, Pat would help her do what had to be done. They loved and relied on her.

Toga parties. Skinny-dipping. Sizzling love affairs that lasted as long as a commercial for Zamfir and his pan flute. For the ninety days from March up through launch, life was like an endless convention: Intense focus during the day giving way to wild parties at night. Everyone, all together, from the anchors to the veejays, rushed to the local bar for happy-hour appetizers to balance their otherwise liquid meals.

---

* Towriss spent twenty-two years at CNN in a variety of roles and is now a communications consultant based in the D.C. metro area.

On the weekends, the invitation stood to Reese and Pat's back-yard for a pool party. (Kavanau refused rides and trekked miles to the party on foot, but Pat insisted his pistol must not come inside.) Locals arranged trips for newcomers to raft the Chattahoochee River, or take in southern-fried spots like Aunt Fanny's Cabin or Bobby and June's Kountry Kitchen, to remind them, if they forgot, that they were inhabiting the glorious south. But not everyone wished to be so closely allied with "Reese's pieces."

"I just hope we can avoid network politics. We want to keep it like a family," one of the anchors, Lou Waters, told a reporter, hopefully, of these halcyon days.

A happy little work bubble it was—for now.

* * *

Before they could launch the first all-news channel, they needed to get Ted Turner's Graduate School up and running. To the grizzled "yeah, yeah, yeah, seen-it-all" types, the ones who wondered if their careers might be shot for having taken a job at a risky new venture, fell the task of educating the veejays at CNN College, which opened its doors on March 31 for a limited run. Writing, editing, shooting, Vidifont. "WEL-COME TO THE CABLE NEWS NETWORK," read one memo, issued by CNN College "deans" Jim Schoonmaker and Guy Pepper. "If you have questions, please ask. You should understand, however, that as this is a brand new operation, and as this is an undertaking that has never been done before, there will be questions that will not get an immediate answer, or might even get several answers. This is not an indication of confusion, but rather of continuous creativity. We will be making many, many changes right up to, and even after, June 1. So please understand and go with us. We are writing our own futures."

In six weeks, Reese confidently explained to a reporter, they could train an ambitious young college kid to do the same exact work as some-one who'd been in the business for six to ten years.

Since tarps and exposed windows and mud on the floors kept Techwood off-limits, and with the white house brimming to capacity, "class" was set up over in the Dogwood Room at the Admiral Benbow Inn at the corner of Fourteenth and Spring, a place up the street from Sleazy Jim's affectionately known as the "Bimbo," and at a field shop of channel 17 a few miles up the road.

Never mind that the instructors teaching the newbies how to edit videotape hadn't ever edited videotape themselves. The technology was still so new, few people had. Similarly, hardly anyone in the business knew a thing about the new creations of uplinking and flyaways and live shots, but those subjects were covered, too. The eager, attentive pupils together learned the ropes about rundowns and B-roll and dubbing and the difference between master control and B control, and the crucial role of a tape supervisor. Together, the veejays braved the stressful task of tape playback, learning to queue up four three-quarter-inch tape cassettes that teased the first four stories of each newscast—a bit like that episode of *I Love Lucy* at the chocolate factory where the conveyor belt speeds up and she can't keep pace. Even more vexing was commercial playback, which involved unwieldy one-inch open-reel tape machines.

As soon as someone got good enough on a particular piece of equipment, they'd become tribal elders, expected to pass down their wisdom to the latest crop of hires—because every week, even someone who'd been so sure they could hack the chaos and the pressure inevitably fled screaming from the premises, and a steady stream of new recruits would be necessary. Desperate for bodies, John Baker proposed recruiting from the unemployment line. Fortitude could not be taught, but television skills could.

Everyone at any level of experience was handed a binder containing a fifty-one-page manual called *Inside CNN* that explained the ultimate, lofty hope: "Make our newscasts so good that people across the country will think of us when they think of television news."

It seemed an impossible dream.

In addition to detailing human resources nuts and bolts about health insurance and stock options, not that most people would have extra cash for such frivolity, the guide explained the mysterious ins and outs of the technological heart of CNN, the revolutionary Basys Newsfury computer system specially developed for the network. In an age when computers were gigantic, room-sized beasts touched only by skilled experts, this user-friendly innovation was as revolutionary as the satellite and video porta-paks—but designed to be as simple to use as a typewriter. Into a desktop terminal, the wire machines would endlessly flow—no more changing paper or ribbons. Producers would lay out the elements of their show in digital rundowns created on this multifaceted system, which could time out the show factoring in the individual read rates of the anchors, eliminating the need for back-timing. Writers could immediately see their assignments and craft their scripts on a split-screen feature. In turn, the editor would copy edit and, with the press of a button, feed scripts into a digital teleprompter so the anchor could read unfettered by paper. Everyone could "top-line" messages to one another—an incredible innovation in communications, long before text messaging, that eliminated the hassle of calling on the phone or shouting across the newsroom. Hardly anyone of any experience level had ever touched a computer before, but this system, connected to a custom-designed microprocessor propelled by an Onyx C8000 with an incredible ten megabytes of memory, was, while revolutionary, perfectly user-friendly.

There was only one problem: It didn't work.

That the essential information backbone of CNN was stalled when the troops moved into the old Progressive Club on May 1 wasn't the only looming matter. Other key ingredients remained incomplete: Floors were still mud, and porta-potties stood in for the unfinished bathrooms. Nonetheless, rehearsals, inelegantly referred to as the "dry runs," had to commence. As the crew practiced the theoretical they'd been tweaking for months now, jackhammers reverberated and carpet was unfurled. Every so often, everyone fell to the ground to help the workmen lay cable. Just as it had been on *Courageous*, the energizing anthem from *Rocky* was played in an attempt to pump up the crew, electrifying the converted country club.

But that electric current of discovery that had propelled them for weeks was being replaced by pulsing currents of fear.

Out of nowhere, from time to time, the Wizard himself would appear.

"I don't know a thing about journalism," Ted Turner squawked in the face of this action he'd unleashed. "But I'm betting $100 million that you all do."

Some of them had thought they knew what they were doing. But with each passing hour of error-filled practice newscasts, it was hard to remain positive. Alec Nagle did his best to cheerlead a room full of glum personnel.

"Are we gonna do this network or not, yes or no?" he asked them.

"Yes!"

"We've got a twenty-four-hour news network to run. Let's kick ass, and screw everybody that can't take a joke."

A week elapsed, ten hours of rehearsals each day. Not one single, error-free hour had occurred. A gallows joke made the rounds: "What's

After a month of "CNN College," veejays and other staff were finally able to move into the still-incomplete building and begin a grueling rehearsal schedule in the final weeks before launch. *(Jeff Jeffares)*

the difference between CNN and the *Hindenburg*? At least the *Hindenburg* got off the ground." The act of throwing one's hands up in the air in utter frustration became known as the "CNN Salute."

Fraught with exhaustion and fear, some of the troops became physically ill. Others were racked by intense nightmares, like producer Paul Amos, who woke up in a sweat, screaming, seeing the time clock clicking in his head, his show timing out short. In operations executive John Baker's nightmare, an hourlong newscast would run out of news ten minutes in, and the anchor would say, "That's all we have." Alec Nagle's nightmare: The anchor would keep reading the same story over and over again, and he couldn't stop them.

All the dazzled Reese would confess to being worried about was that this network he was creating would be so terrific, he'd be responsible for a new crop of television addicts: "I think many of our viewers will be people who don't watch television now," he said to a reporter. "I don't know if making more people watch television—when they should, say, be reading books—is terribly good."

It was the panic of the most intense of this fiercely intense bunch, Mad Dog Kavanau, that registered code red. The dry runs had led him to a painful conclusion, intensified by the crippling inability of the Newsfury to work consistently: There simply wasn't enough news to fill each hour, nor was there enough *new* news, from one hour to the next, to update. The entire vision for CNN failed for him with this recognition. It had worked in theory, but the reality proved a disaster.

Deflated, Kavanau made his way on foot back to Sleazy Jim's and formulated a plan: When he woke up in the morning, he'd just disappear, run off to Hawaii. He packed his bags so it would be easy to escape and collapsed into the sorry excuse for a bed. That night his sleep was fitful, punctuated by feverish dreams, and when dawn arrived and the morning light streamed into his window, he found himself refreshed by a revelation.

He dressed and rushed back over to Techwood, finding Burt Reinhardt and insisting he order relics of the past most of his team could navigate: good, old reliable typewriters, as well as reams of six-book carbonless script paper. Crew up a pool of typists, he commanded. The next day, a dozen administrative women showed up, out of thin air, ready to go. Producers would now be permitted to reuse copy stories from one hour to the next, despite his previous insistence that there should be no repetition. The retyping pool pecked away, freeing up time for writers to churn out fresh new scripts.

Certain that he'd conquered the system's kinks, Kavanau stood on a crate to address the other CNN originals who'd been toiling away in the service of this television news revolution.

"I've been hearing that some of you have been saying among yourselves that this thing is not gonna work! That we're not gonna get on the air! That we're not gonna be a success!" He paused, himself a convert from doubt. He pointed a finger at the ceiling. "Well that may be true for everybody else, but not for you! I didn't bring you here to fail! You will not fail! You will not fail because I will not permit you to fail! If any of you cannot work under those terms, leave the room! Right now!"

The startled eyes of the exhausted production team locked on his every move. Whether they believed him, or were too scared to get up, or just tired, or, perhaps, wary of his excitable nature and the pistol they knew he kept hidden on his shin, didn't matter. If Kavanau said it would work, by god, then it would. It had to. They had invested everything in CNN. They all wanted nothing more themselves than for the first all-news channel to succeed.

Everyone stayed put.

CHAPTER NINE
Until the End of the World

By late in the day on June 1, a sprinkling of rain had come and gone, and in the hours just before CNN's debut, the thermometer in midtown Atlanta sizzled at ninety-two degrees. The freshly mowed lawn scented the air, soft and sweet, and the fountain in front of the entrance to the former Progressive Club sparkled bright blue in the afternoon sun.

Party tents striped yellow and white had been pitched to shelter a generous spread of beef tenderloin and Italian sausages and shrimp and, befitting any grand party, bars from which flowed beer and bourbon and wine and margaritas.

At Kavanau's suggestion, the old swimming pools on the grounds had been packed with dirt and converted into gardens beside which reporter John Holliman, previously the agricultural editor for the

Few people, even those who worked in television, had seen satellite receive dishes before, much less so many in one place. This shot was taken from the window of Ted's office on the second floor. *(Jeff Jeffares)*

Associated Press, would fly in each week from Washington to deliver the farm report.* Nearby, a more modern farm had sprouted—six massive white satellite dishes, dramatically tilted toward the heavens, the largest non-governmental array of its kind. The backbone of CNN's very own invisible information superhighway would soon buzz with news. Ted and Reese had marked their territory.

The rats were as much a thing of the past as the peeling paint. But a dead squirrel floating in the fountain out front was a talisman of the chaos still inside. The work was still nowhere near complete. The architect Bunky Helfrich was off with Ted in Newport, Rhode Island, for the preliminary trials of the America's Cup. Thank god for the portapotties, and the trees, because there still weren't enough bathrooms. Glass was still missing from the frames in the windows out back. The turntable set rotated only when propelled by humans. The revolutionary computerized news system still had yet to consistently work.

Still, the $10 million worth of switchers and edit bays and computer terminals inside this converted locker room gleamed to rival *Star Trek*'s starship *Enterprise*. The dozens of panicked people scurrying around this hyperspace needed the force of *Star Wars*'s Obi-Wan Kenobi to be with them. As the clock ticked closer to six, Kavanau huddled with the day's crew and told them again not to worry. By now, he was more pragmatic about a possible failure. If it didn't work out, he said, they'd all disperse to local stations around the country and give one another jobs.

Ted had flown in that morning. If he hadn't promised three years ago, after his triumphant, drunken victory, that he'd race again—if he didn't have baked into him the unquenchable need to win—he'd have sat this one out. He simply hadn't been able to devote the necessary time to practice—although his victory that past fall at Fastnet had earned

---

* There's dispute over whether the garden produced much vegetation. Some recall a bounty of radishes, beans, and zucchini, while others swear it was fallow because of chemicals added by the construction crew. Perhaps the truth lies in a bit of both stories: Research chief Bob Sieber says Ted looked out his office window one day, complained about the horticultural vision, and promptly ordered it removed. (In late 1981, the space was built out into the headquarters for CNN2.)

him the title "Yachtsman of the Year" for an unprecedented fourth time. The thrill had quickly waned. A headline in the *Sarasota Herald-Tribune* captured his current obsession: "America, Not America's Cup on Turner's Mind."

Far weightier matters than twelve-meter boats and silver trophies now preoccupied the brain of the best yachtsman in the world. He believed World War III and a nuclear holocaust loomed. Humanity might soon be extinct, for the Russians possessed more tanks and greater strength, now that the United States had weakened immeasurably. Remember those Charles Atlas muscle-building courses in magazines, where the fabled bodybuilder taught the skinny guy to bulk up in the face of bullies? We needed to fortify, Ted believed, so nobody could kick sand on us.

And what, in his estimation, was to blame for the dissolution of our collective well-being, our great nation's standing in the world? The very invention that had empowered him and made him rich: television. Television, he'd decided, packed far more power than politics. That didn't dampen his glee at the sight of acolytes around Newport sporting hopeful "Ted Turner for President" T-shirts. The thought of running still lingered, but at the very least, he wished to be the nation's Jiminy Cricket—its conscience.

Workmen put the finishing touches on the bleachers and a viewing stand. As the armed forces band enlisted for the day arrived to rehearse, Ted made a special request that reflected his angst. Could they play the hymn "Nearer My God to Thee"? This melancholy tune was said to be one of the songs musicians on board the *Titanic* used to calm the passengers as the legendary ship began to sink. That day's band, standing tall and neatly attired in their crisp military best, assembled in front of the grand columns at the entrance of this Tara on Techwood and complied. At the boss's instruction, a camera crew recorded the rendition to be stashed away on the HFR shelf—hold for release.*

---

* A copy of the tape was discovered by an intern in 2015 and lives online in a variety of places, including here: https://jalopnik.com/this-is-the-video-cnn-will-play-when-the-world-ends-1677511538.

Ted relished the moment. Since he planned for CNN to continue broadcasting until the apocalypse, it would be some time before he'd hear this again.

* * *

The guests began to stream onto the front lawn of Tara on Techwood, commanded there by a simple ivory invitation and an intense curiosity. Microphone in hand, camera crew beside him, and a newly minted security badge affixed to his lapel, dutiful newsman Bill Tush ran around interviewing luminaries for a live, prelaunch special on WTBS, *CNN: The Birth of a Network*. As the clock struck six and CNN began, channel 17 would switch over to the all-important moneymaker, wrestling.

The days when the hulking performers would prop cardboard in the windows of the station's lobby to convert it into a dressing room were numbered. When the rest of the new building was finally complete, fans would line up there each weekend for the theatrics. The thuds of Abdul-

lah the Butcher, Killer Khan, and Dusty Rhodes would startle the news crew on the floor below—a perfect reminder that it was channel 17 that had made this grand facility possible.

From the bureaucratic badge to this stately columned building and the parade of newcomers who sniffed at Ted's rerun station, June 1 was the consummate reminder that life would never be the same for anyone on its staff.

In between asking the military bands to play "Nearer My God to Thee" and officially dedicating CNN, Ted basked in the glory as man of the hour at the gala launch party on the lawn. *(Jeff Jeffares)*

The free-wheeling fun was history. As a nose-thumb to this formality, one employee taped a photo of Humphrey Bogart over his own on his company-issued ID.

"It's not every day of the week that a twenty-four-hour network is dedicated," Tush said to the camera as he approached Ted's long-suffering blond belle of a wife, Janie, neatly attired in a black dress and smiling cheerfully. Sensing that she needed something to distract her from her ever-absent husband, who'd recently been named one of the sexiest men of the year by *Playgirl*, Reese had gone so far as to offer her a job as one of the video journalists. (Immediately, he'd thought better of inviting the boss's wife to work for him and was relieved she never responded.)

This was, Janie said in her lilting southern drawl, all very exciting: "All these people working here together. We feel like this is Ted's dream, something he's looked forward to for so long. He says it's one of the biggest things that ever happened to him in his entire life."

Now, roving reporter Tush happened upon another smiling blonde essential to the Turnerverse, introducing her to the camera as "probably the most proud mother in the world." What kind of day was it for her?

Florence Turner smiled broadly. "The most thrilling day of my life." Unsure what to ask next of this vivacious lady, whose contribution to this monumental occasion was having given birth to the mastermind behind it, Tush posed a question he immediately realized was the kind of vapid softball for which he'd mock a local news reporter.

"What is it like being Ted Turner's mom?"

The proud Florence didn't find the query dumb at all. She beamed with pride.

"It's wonderful. I'm really speechless. I'm so thrilled," she said, pausing to add a confidence. "The only thing I worry about is Ted's undertakings are so great and I always worry about him."

"When he took over the billboard business, did you ever think he'd go this far?" Tush asked.

"Never. This is past any dreams I could have had for Ted."

"Well, we wish you continued success being Ted's mom," Tush said, wincing again at his happy talk.

Besides family, present that day, too, were media revolutionaries who shared Ted's and Reese's frustrations with the established order. Onetime trade reporter and D.C. denizen Brian Lamb had himself recognized the immense power of new technology to upend the "hammerlock" of control long wielded over communications by the networks and the phone company. Imagine, he had said, if when the printing press had been invented only three companies could use it. This was the world they had lived in up till cable had arrived.

As a young man breaking into radio in Lafayette, Indiana, he'd convinced the owner of the local UHF station to let him launch a weekly dance show—a simple one-camera program for which he served as host, casting director, producer, set-builder, and ad salesman. Though sometimes he couldn't lure young dancers to the set (high school sports proved a greater allure on a Friday), he was able to attract big-name talent who came through town, like Nat King Cole, Leslie Uggams, Gordon McRae—luminaries he'd never attract if he'd reached them in New York. The show proved the perfect "laboratory" to illustrate the power of a microphone and air time—and local programs.

Later, as a young naval officer working at the Pentagon, he saw firsthand the distortions and limitations of broadcast news—the short clips and sound bites that distilled the day's events so superficially.

Distressed that the average American citizen couldn't easily witness the inner working of government, Lamb had fought for the right for television cameras to broadcast democracy in action on Capitol Hill. Lawmakers had stalled, and then quibbled, about whether to allow this invasion of their hallowed chambers. Many were horrified at the idea that their proceedings would be made visible to the public that had elected them. For a time, it seemed a divided House might award broadcast rights to none other than the networks themselves. Lamb's push for an independent, nonprofit service had mercifully prevailed. Cable-Satellite Public Affairs Network, also known as C-SPAN, had debuted in March 1979 with remarks from a young lawmaker from Tennessee, Albert Gore,* who extolled the possibilities of the medium to revitalize democracy. "Television will change this institution, Mr. Speaker," he said, "but the good will far outweigh the bad . . . The solution for the lack of confidence in government, Mr. Speaker, is more open government at all levels."

To Lamb, the arrival of CNN was another sign that the entrenched system of reporting, and closed-door government, finally was breaking down.

"I'm as big a booster as you can find," Lamb told Tush. "This is a terrific day in the history of news. It's an important day. This country has been deprived of news that it could have gotten many years ago. So, I'm as excited as everyone else is."

A handful of the thirty on-air "columnists" who'd been hired to fill CNN's empty moments circulated by the food. Psychologist Dr. Joyce Brothers marveled over the dazzling array of equipment inside, the likes of which she'd never seen before. Anti-feminist crusader Phyllis Schlafly engaged in a heated conversation with Reese's wife, Pat, about what became of babies born to mothers denied abortion. Conservative columnist Robert Novak admitted that he didn't really understand cable television but acknowledged that multiplying the number of television channels was a "great step forward"—though toward what he didn't explain.

In his neat white suit, the Reverend William Borders of the nearby Wheat Street Baptist Church explained to Tush that the new network was one of the great things happening in Atlanta. Of Ted and his idea, he beamed and said, "He's absolutely the most fantastic, daring, courageous person of spiritual insight I've ever seen. I just wonder what he's going to do next."

---

* You can see the first twenty minutes ever broadcast from the House here: https://www.c-span.org/video/?318387-1/televised-session-house-representatives. On June 2, 1986, Gore, having risen to the Senate, spoke during the first session televised from that chamber: https://www.c-span.org/video/?45919-1/30th-anniversary-tv-cameras-senate.

Before anyone could find out what Ted might do next was the question of what would become of the venture whose imminent launch they were gathered to celebrate.

* * *

It had been one year, twenty-two days, and seven hours since Reese received the call that CNN was a go. The moment he had been waiting for his entire adult life had arrived. He'd been so eager to plunge in that when he'd agreed to a June 1 launch, he hadn't realized it was a Sunday—typically, a dud of a news day. In a panic, he'd managed to push CNN's debut till the dinner hour, which not only meant fewer hours to fill but a better party start time for the guests. Now if only the news gods would smile down.

Reese knew the critics didn't believe viewers would ever choose news over entertainment. The audience might not know yet that they had an appetite for news, but he was going to prove they did. The greatest moment in history might actually be a heartbeat away. Soon they'd learn that if you dialed away from CNN, you'd risk missing it. What better drama could there be than that?

He had heard the sneering tone in the voices of reporters sent to quiz him these past few weeks, but it wasn't just the journalists who were doubters. One banker, Robert Howitt of First Manhattan, declared it unlikely that CNN would have "any impact on either cable or broadcasting industries or their revenues." Media buyer William Donnelly of Young & Rubicam confessed that in New York media circles, "an awful lot of people" were predicting—and almost *hoping*—that CNN would fail, for its success would upend not just news, but the entire advertising industry. New choices confused the established order. "Any establishment doesn't like an entrepreneur," he had said. "You know, 'It'll never fly, Orville.' A lot of people don't want to face the changes that would be caused."

Bill Leonard, president of CBS News, wondered, "Why would anybody choose to watch a patched-together news operation that's just starting against an organization like ours that's been going for fifty years and spends $100 to $150 million a year?" That top network brass seemed poised for schadenfreude didn't surprise Reese.

To hell with all the doubters, and with this frivolous party. Inside this old country club, converted to his specifications, history was about to be made, and he wanted off the dais so he could get inside. From this day forward, he believed, "presidents and kings, prime ministers and foreign ministers, the Pentagon, Congress, the media, and the public would have to adjust to CNN."

Of the big picture, he was certain. Whether his troops could pull off the next three hours was the immediate concern.

* * *

Twenty minutes before six p.m., Ted ascended the stage and greeted the crowd, gesturing toward the three flags that were flying on the other side of the fountain.

One, he said, represented the state of Georgia, headquarters of the company. The second, of course, was the United States flag, which "represents our country and the way we intend to serve it with the Cable News Network." And, lastly, he'd installed the United Nations flag because, he explained:

> We hope that the Cable News Network, with its international coverage and greater-depth coverage, will bring both, in the country and in the world, a better understanding of how people from different nations live and work together, and within the nation work together, so that we can perhaps, hopefully, bring together in brotherhood and friendship, in kindness and peace the people of this nation and this world.

Now, it was time for the benediction.

"Let us pray," said Reverend Borders, who proceeded to compare his host to Jesus Christ. "We thank thee this day—this day—for Ted

Turner and all those who have worked with him. Continue, our father, in our behalf, in thy name, in thy name, in thy name we pray. Amen."

With just minutes to go before six, Ted amended a piece by the poet Edward Kessler, which served as a mission statement.

> *To act upon one's convictions while others wait*
> *To create a positive force in a world where cynics abound,*
> *To provide information to people when it wasn't available before,*
> *To offer those who want it a choice*
> *For the American people, whose thirst for understanding and a*
> *   better life has made this venture possible*
> *For the cable industry, whose pioneering spirit caused this great*
> *   step forward in communications*
> *And for those employees of Turner Broadcasting, whose total*
> *   commitment to their company has brought us together today*
> *I dedicate the news channel for America—the Cable*
> *   News Network.*

The crowd dutifully rose for the pomp of the color guard, and the band began to play the national anthem. At the final note, Ted shouted his trademark, "Awwright!" as if he was in the front row at a Braves game.

In the mad dash up to this moment, it hadn't occurred to anyone to install monitors for the guests outside to see what they'd come to celebrate. As a drum rolled, a television camera, directed by channel 17 staff, slowly, almost with hesitation, zoomed in on the space-age dish farm. Was anyone out there in TV Land watching? Anyone who was now heard an off-camera announcer's voice speeding through a globeful of cities, a teaser of where those dishes might soon transport you:

Saginaw Washington Birmingham New York US Naples Rome Los Angeles Niagara Falls Paris Tulsa Denver London Canton Newark Peking New Orleans San Diego Reno Nicaragua San Francisco Seoul Perth the Marianas the United Nations Vienna Buffalo Lima Kirabiti Islamabad

"The pit" control room at the moment CNN went live for the very first time on June 1, 1980, just after Ted's dedication (which ran long). *(Jeff Jeffares)*

Decatur Nashville Jamaica Jonestown Chicago Weatherford Topeka Tokyo Madison Fort Worth Fort Wayne . . . *

Inside, the director Guy Pepper, seated in the "pit," the heart of the operation that until recently had been infested with rats, advised his crew, "Don't forget, in television, shit flows downhill." Then, the audience heard him speak the language of television, as CNN launched for business: "Ready camera three. One center up."

The husband-and-wife anchor team from Sacramento had been personally selected by Ted for the honor of hosting the very first hour. For all the deliberations and rehearsals and angst, no one had scripted opening remarks. Moments before the debut, Kavanau, the brawn, and Zelman, the conscience, and Nagle, the heart of the operation, screamed at one another, five feet from the anchor desk. What should the first words uttered on Cable News Network be? Time had run out before a consensus was reached, so the smooth, California-chill anchors stopped wondering what the hell those shouting producers were going to tell

---

* The entire first hour of CNN is available online at https://www.youtube.com /watch?v=rWhgKuKvvPE.

Reese beams with pride on the set beside one of his hires, anchorwoman Reynelda Muse. *(AP Photo/Joe Holloway)*

them and simply dove in, as if they'd been sitting at the anchor desk for time eternal, waiting for their cue.

"Good evening, I'm David Walker . . ."

"And I'm Lois Hart. Now here's the news . . ."

And for anyone in the 1.7 million potential homes who actually tuned in, the Cable News Network began, for the very first time, to hopscotch around the world for headlines.

* * *

"I'm so happy I could die," said Ted, who'd snuck out of the party to go inside and gaze at the wonder of his $20 million investment. "Nobody believed we could do it. But there it is. I got to find a crow. Where can I get a crow? It should be a nice long large dead crow." He planned to send it to that clown in the newspaper business who'd said he didn't know his ass from a hole in the ground.

Reese stuck it to the critics in his own way. Twenty minutes into their maiden voyage, after a commercial for Maalox Plus antacid, the crew broke away from a spot advertising Nestea to a pooled live shot from Fort Wayne, Indiana.* The news gods had answered his prayers by delivering a tiny morsel. President Carter had traveled to the Midwest to visit the civil rights leader Vernon Jordan in the hospital. Jordan had been the victim of a racist gunman several days earlier while in the company of a white woman. Jane Maxwell had spent the better part of the past twenty-four hours talking her way onto this live shot, reminding the local NBC affiliate what Reese had drummed into her: a "pool for one is a pool for all." Now, in living glory, the president appeared live. The networks might include a soundbite of his remarks in their newscasts, but here CNN was beaming the briefing out live, unedited, as it happened—a curiosity rarely seen on television.

"How do you like the way we cut away from our first commercial to go to Carter?" Reese gloated to Ted. "It couldn't have been better if God had written it."

"That'll show them," said Ted, distracted. "That'll show 'em we'll never bow down to the advertisers. You can always run ads later. Who cares about ads anyhow? It's a news operation."

With that, he went in search of a television on which he could watch the end of the Braves against the Dodgers. (They were winning.)

In master control, Alec picked up tiny Jane and twirled her around with delight.

"You realize," he declared, "we've just pulled the blocks out from under the runaway train of news."

* * *

There was absolutely nothing monumental about what unfolded over the next sixty minutes. It looked like news, albeit much of it covering a subject that Ted had so frequently said he despised: violence. Rounding out the hour: live shots from Israel and Miami. Video from New York

---

* The White House Press Pool had been developed as a space saver and a convenience so that each network could rotate coverage of the president's daily movements, freeing up crew time and space and minimizing disruption. The pool is different from the White House Correspondents Association.

of the Israel Day parade. A long report on air safety. A preview of the upcoming Super Tuesday. An interview with the family of a convicted murderer about to die on death row. A teaser of an upcoming "exclusive" pretaped interview with President Carter that would run at eight p.m.*

What mattered was that the first hour was now history, and CNN was now real. Lois Hart signed off for the nightly sports wrap-up, with a neat little bow:

"Stay with us. We're going to have all kinds of news, sports, weather, and special features, coming from now on and forever."

Waves of relief swept over the CNN originals, those lucky enough to have been assigned to work this day. As they finished their shifts, they made their way to a party in the back room, singing and laughing and congratulating one another, relieved to have the laundry list of bewitching obstacles and worry of the past months behind them. Now they just had to do what they'd just done, over and over again.

Against all odds and obstacles, their ship had sailed, and initial reviews were favorable.

"Goodbye, Walter Cronkite," Jonathan Miller of the *Washington Post* wrote. "Hello, Ted."

Since D.C. wasn't wired for cable, his colleague Tom Shales had to trek over the river to Arlington, Virginia, to view the maiden voyage. It was "obvious from the premiere," he wrote, "that CNN means business and that it is anything but the plaything of a playboy. A new day dawned at dusk."

Variety's notice glowed. "Here is news, alive with all its wonderful technical warts and missed cues, and it all worked."

But Dick Williams of the *Atlanta Constitution* posed the most pragmatic observation. "The question 'Will Turner pull it off?' has been replaced by 'How long do you think it will last?'"

---

* Presidents make for splashy network beginnings. When CBS News launched its half-hour news format in September 1963, an interview with President Kennedy was featured.

CHAPTER TEN

Duck Hunting with Fidel

March 30, 1981, started out as one kind of rotten and, by mid-afternoon, had U-turned into rotten of a far more serious type. As the assignment editor of the Washington, D.C., bureau of the first all-news network, Cissy Baker, age twenty-two, faced a dismally boring slate of stories this dreary Monday.

An internship at a local television station during college had indoctrinated Baker in the macabre philosophy of a wizened broadcast journalist. She found herself daydreaming about what might spice up the day—a fire, possibly, or a shooting.

Turning her prematurely jaded ear toward the police scanner, Baker listened intently, hoping a morsel of news might reveal itself.

Desperately attempting to increase its subscriber base, CNN provided ads like these to cable operators around the nation to place in local papers. Other ads proclaimed CNN as purveyor of "the news of your life when you need it most," and described the service as "Television You Can Take Seriously"—a nod to counter Ted's earlier cable offering.

Producers at headquarters in Atlanta had learned, in the short ten months since the Cable News Network's debut, to lean on the bureau to fill the never-ending news cycle. Sometimes, forty minutes into the hour, it would become clear there was simply nothing new to report. A desperate rush to cue up some taped piece that had aired earlier in the day would ensue.

The staff also knew, by then, the ironclad tyranny of Reese, who some called "the dictator." He hawked every moment that went out on what he considered to be his airwaves, sometimes even calling the control room in the middle of the night to back-seat drive the coverage or simply scream about a decision he deemed stupid.

One original described the cascading shouts as the "blame game drill-down." Reese would yell at Kavanau, who would yell at the producers, who would yell at the editors, who'd blame the writers, who lived in fear of the "green book," where poorly written scripts were enshrined each day. "If they were, you were toast," Joan Greig told Atlanta magazine. Gems included a story on an obscure holiday that began: "Yesterday went unnoticed by many people."

The nation's capital city offered a reliable, never-ending source of speechifying filler. The mere presence of CNN's live cameras at press conferences and other events had started to kill the long-standing practice of revealing news under an embargo. No way to "hold for release" what had just been announced when CNN had broadcast out the news live.*

Who was watching, anyway, especially during the daytime? A television positioned anywhere other than a living room, bar, or appliance store was as uncommon a vision as a two-dollar bill. A television hooked up to cable, even rarer. Less than a year after CNN had gone on the air, eighteen million homes—still not 40 percent of the country—were

---

* Still acclimating to the power of live broadcasts across time zones, CNN aired a story about the massive frenzy around "Who shot J.R.?" in the blockbuster CBS series *Dallas*—spoiling the surprise for the West Coast audience. CNN original Tom Gaut says the newsroom was deluged with angry calls.

wired. A little over six million of those sets were able to receive CNN. Cable service had yet to arrive in the nation's capital city.

To overcome that gap, Ted had been gifting satellites around the capital city like hard candies, so that the influencers at the White House, Congress, and the National Press Club could tune in. He'd even installed one on Dan Schorr's lawn. (Dish size and price continued to plunge, and the person who had everything could order one up, fully installed, from the Neiman-Marcus catalog for a mere $36,500.)

The lavish gift to Schorr almost compensated for the time that a studio light exploded while he was on the air, igniting his pants. The endless parade of gaffes continued—revving chainsaws and cleaning crews emptying trash bins as the anchors read the news, to a switching error that transmitted a porn channel on CNN's airwaves for a painfully long few seconds. The bush-league errors, technological or human or both, never ended. Such was the nature of live television.

Shit, apparently, did flow downhill. During the inauguration of President Reagan, Reese—not realizing his staff was about to dump out of a commercial break to a live feed of the release of the long-held American hostages in Iran—threw up his arms in a full-bore CNN salute and shouted, audible to all, "You prime assholes get that off the air." That was one for the blooper reel—and a reminder to everyone to modulate their sound.

Perhaps the grandest mistake to date had involved a brilliant idea Reese had cooked up involving the final presidential debate in October 1980. While President Carter and Governor Ronald Reagan prepared for their face-off in Cleveland, the independent candidate, John Anderson, ascended the stage at Constitution Hall in Washington, thousands of miles from the main event, to participate in Reese's alternative, made possible by a suite of new technology.

The congressman from Illinois had roiled the political applecart with his wildly popular candidacy. He'd polled so well that he'd been invited to appear in the first presidential debate a month earlier. Dismissing Anderson as "primarily a creation of the press," President

Carter refused to participate. Governor Reagan fared so well one-on-one against Representative Anderson that the independent's standing plunged. As a result, he'd not received an invitation to the second match.

In this new era of videotape and satellite trucks, Reese decided, why not give the maverick a platform? Daniel Schorr played the role of moderator—with the help of a stenographer, who transcribed the questions posed in Cleveland and passed them along.

It sounded like a grand idea—until it went awry. In a hulking satellite truck stationed behind the hall, four producers recorded Carter's and Reagan's answers on tape and cut them as quickly as possible so they could play inside the hall and prompt Anderson's retort.* But when a tape operator paused to flirt with one of the producers, the system fell apart. Questions were replayed out of order, and the answers didn't match.

Schorr punted, apologizing, and was grateful that CNN was so invisible many of his friends thought he'd retired. But Anderson's enterprising campaign manager blew his cover. For maximum exposure, he'd made a deal to rebroadcast the experimental debate on PBS, where a far larger audience could witness his candidate's performance. The potential audience for the botched production CNN wished to forget numbered in the millions.

* * *

While Ted Turner basked in his belief that CNN was a "smash success," the network continued to teeter on shaky financial ground, bleeding $2 million a month and often struggling to make payroll.

Employees whispered that revenue from the Braves concession stand was helping to bolster the never-ending budget shortfall. Borrowing a page from his Charlotte days, Ted even took to WTBS to hawk five-for-a-dollar bumper stickers that declared, "I SUPPORT CNN."

* The entire debate is online at https://www.youtube.com/watch?v=dEHGr4VuBYI.

It was time to dig into the piggy bank. A few years earlier, when gold cost $275 an ounce, Ted had invested $2 million in Krugerrands, gold coins from South Africa. He'd taken to carrying one of the glinting coins in his pocket, showing it off by flipping it casually, as if it were a quarter. Now, gold's value had soared to $800 an ounce, and Ted was desperate for a cash infusion; the precious metal might help him get by—for a moment or two. The only trouble was remembering the combination to the safe where he'd stashed the loot. It had to be drilled open.

Los Angeles Times critic Howard Rosenberg didn't realize how correctly he'd assessed it in when he described CNN as a flimsy, carefully wrapped sham: "Several $100 bills are on the outside, but the rest of the roll is wadded paper."

So dire was the financial picture that Ted even entertained the previously unimaginable: an alliance with one of the big three broadcasters he reviled. Lately, he'd revived his crusade against them, aligning with the Moral Majority to rail against the network "oligarchy" as a threat to the United States for propagating sleazy sex and violence. Television executives were, in his estimation, a "greedy bunch of jerks" worse than the Nazis and should be tried for treason!

Nonetheless, he agreed to take a meeting with enemy number one: that "cheap whorehouse," CBS. The disrespect was mutual. CBS President Bill Leonard seemed to have forgotten that he'd dismissed CNN before it launched. Now, as he examined the cost of starting his own round-the-clock news service, Leonard had concluded it would simply be cheaper to just buy it.

For this top secret meeting, the executive flew to Atlanta on the CBS jet and, for maximum privacy, met Ted in a nearby motel. Captain Outrageous sauntered in, chewing his trademark tobacco, casually clad in jeans and Topsiders, sans socks. He cut to the chase.

"I'll sell you CNN. How much of it do you want to buy?"

The answer: 51 percent or more.

"You want control?" Ted responded, aghast. "You don't buy control of Ted Turner's companies. Forty-nine percent or less."

Leonard told him that simply wasn't possible. Ted taunted, "Someday, I'm going to own you, you bet I am. Remember I told you so." Ever the closer, he pushed to make *some* sort of deal. "I can't come away from here without selling you *some*thing. How about my wife? Lovely lady."

Just as acute as the financial pinch was the toll on human resources. Staff revolved in and out of CNN and its bureaus as quickly as the front doors spun at Macy's. Younger employees discovered that with just six months under their belts, they could land better-paying jobs with more humane hours at television stations closer to their hometowns. Veterans like Washington bureau chief George Watson—a big get when he was hired from ABC—couldn't hack the Chicken Noodle News approach. He'd practically sprinted out of the bureau only months after CNN debuted, driven away by the used furniture ordered for the office and the hasty coverage of the political conventions, duct-taped together at the last minute up in the bleachers and micromanaged from a distance (as most things were) by Reese.*

Inevitably, turf wars emerged, especially among a menacing pro-union faction that appeared to be gaining traction. Jim Kitchell, at odds with Reese from nearly the beginning, moved over to work at WTBS.

Elder statesman Sam Zelman didn't try to mask his dismay over the quality of the product. He described it in one word: skimpy. More time to deliver the news hadn't, in his estimation, translated into more thoughtful, substantive coverage.

"I'm concerned about the journalism we practice," he told a reporter. "It's not how long you make it, as the cigarette people say. It's how you make it long."

Others inside CNN put it more succinctly. They dismissed what they were producing as "junk-food news."

---

* There'd been but one triumph at the Republican convention in Detroit, when Bernie Shaw alerted producers in Atlanta to take a live shot from their distant perch in the rafters of Cobo Hall. As a result, viewers got a glimpse of Governor Reagan rehearsing that night's acceptance speech. It hadn't dawned on political operatives that the newbie network might go live in the afternoon.

* * *

On that rainy spring Monday in March, Cissy Baker wound up sending her White House crew to a snoozer of a time-filler: the ballroom of the sprawling Washington Hilton on Connecticut Avenue, where President Reagan was about to address the national Conference of the Building and Construction Trades of the mighty trade labor union, AFL-CIO.

As was the custom in the carefully orchestrated universe of Washington politics, the text of the speech had been released to the press corps in advance. Most television viewers were unaccustomed to seeing routine events of the day in their entirety, but this was the kind of typical governmental affair that helped CNN burn through many an hour. There was always the chance that at some point the affable president might "commit news," as the broadcasters cheekily referred to any unexpected development. Maybe there'd be boos from the audience; a bit of mileage could be had from *that*. As far as Atlanta was concerned, a speech by the president was far preferable to a five-minute, thumb-sucking analysis from Daniel Schorr. No wonder his nickname at CBS had been "Jukebox."

The camera lingered on the president as he shook hands and beamed his movie-star grin. Anchor Bernie Shaw smoothly deployed his inside-the-beltway knowledge in summarizing the remarks. Being able to offer this sort of live, post-game analysis was precisely what had lured him to this job. Who cared if there was no audience?

"President Reagan, in a speech that lasted about nineteen minutes, drew applause four times from this group," Shaw observed, with such authority that a viewer might actually believe there was a significance to the number of rounds of applause.

His midday assignment complete, he tossed the baton back to Atlanta. And during the next commercial break, Cissy Baker's wish for a more interesting day suddenly materialized.

The words rang out from the police scanner at 2:27 p.m.

"Shots fired" followed by "Hilton Hotel."

In that instant, Baker frantically connected the dots: The Hilton? That's where the president was, with one of her crews wrapping up inside. Her mind raced strategically over the map of the city. The chess game of routing personnel, particularly at a time of crisis, was a crucial part of running an assignment desk. Her back-of-the-hand knowledge of the nation's capital was precisely the reason she'd been offered this job. It didn't hurt that she ranked as a Washington insider. Her father happened to be the Senate Majority Leader, Howard Baker.

The next words that bleated out of the scanner offered a disturbing new clue: "Rainbow to GW." Baker knew the code. "GW" meant the George Washington Hospital, and "Rainbow," the First Lady. If Nancy Reagan was heading for the hospital, that must be because the president was headed there, too. But why?

Hearing the fracas among his anxious colleagues, Shaw demanded to know what was going on.

A desk assistant said sarcastically, "I think they're shooting at your president."

"Don't joke," Shaw scolded. For a veteran newsman, he was curiously unjaded—patriotic, and respectful of authority, even. (That didn't equal passive. As a young member of the Marine Corps in Hawaii, he'd tracked down Walter Cronkite when he'd learned the anchorman was coming to town, urgently hoping for guidance on how to get into the business.)

The assistant responded to Shaw: "I'm not joking."

A split second later, Atlanta dumped out of a taped report on education in China to anchor Bob Cain on the set.

"We interrupt . . . there's been a late development," he said urgently. "Shots reported fired outside the hotel where President Reagan spoke a short while ago. Here's Bernard Shaw in our Washington bureau."*

Shaw knew little more than what Cain had just said, but he began to speak, masking the shivers and chills he felt. The mere suggestion of

---

* CNN's coverage of the shooting of the president can be viewed online at https://www .youtube.com/watch?v=9JVKgoQEemM.

an assassination attempt could plunge the world's security and economy into a tailspin. His job—his responsibility—was to inform the public in a measured, sober, deliberate tone. It was crucial not to fuel hysteria.

"Bob, as you can understand, details are very sketchy. We don't know precisely what happened, nor . . . Pardon me."

His voice was hollow. In his rush to get into position behind the anchor desk, Shaw forgot to clip on his microphone. He calmly reached over to grab it and fastened it in place.

"Okay, my apology," he said, looking down to consult the fragments of information being rushed before him by Sandy Kenyon, his producer. The young man had been so eager to work at the network that he'd bought a one-way ticket to D.C. from New York and talked his way into a job. At this grave moment, he sat at Shaw's feet, out of the camera's view, pecking away on a state-of-the-art IBM Selectric typewriter and synthesizing details as his colleagues collected them.

"Details are very sketchy at this moment," Shaw repeated. "We don't know precisely what happened. We don't know the sequence . . . First of all, the president is safe. We are told that shots were fired at his party as he left the hotel . . . We can report that shots were fired as President Reagan left the Washington Hilton hotel following that address we carried live here on CNN. The president did not appear to be hurt, according to United Press International." He continued to read the wire copy Kenyon had handed him.

For this vague report, the upstart CNN could now claim a triumph: It had beaten the other networks in announcing the shooting by four whole minutes. To its tiny audience, this didn't matter. To their broadcast competitors, it was proof CNN meant business.

The only pandemonium greater than the scene of a shooting is the unfolding madness of a newsroom trying to sort out the aftermath. Before now, the mechanics of both were, except for Hollywood depictions and the assassination of President Kennedy, shrouded from public view.

A few minutes later, over on ABC, Shaw's former colleague, newsman Frank Reynolds, took a deep breath as he summarized the same bits of information Shaw had just delivered. He, however, had a visual aid: videotape shot by the White House press pool.

CNN had been angling to join the pool but had been denied admission for several reasons—because it employed non-union labor; because how could anyone trust this upstart, from second-string *cable*; because it had never been done any other way before.

"This is the first time any of us has seen this tape," Reynolds told viewers as the dramatic video, just rushed into the studio, began to roll.* The eight minutes of footage, he cautioned, were not edited and thus not as neat as it could be. That it was raw made it all the more compelling. Television had changed radically since just six years earlier, when two women in the span of weeks attempted to shoot then president Gerald Ford. TV crews then, not yet equipped to use videotape in the field, captured those incidents on film. Then, the networks had interrupted programming to inform viewers what had occurred, but, with little else to report, waited till their regular nightly newscasts to add to the story.

Now, with the emerging influence of CNN, broadcasters could not afford to fact-check and wait. Reynolds narrated the footage as he watched it for the first time himself.

This is not live, Reynolds remembered to mention as he improvised, but it is fresh tape of the shooting, which had occurred just fifteen minutes earlier. It appeared, he observed, that press secretary Jim Brady had been struck in the head. This prompted a phone call by the anchor, on-set, to a reporter. Where is the president? The president had not yet returned to the White House. He was on the way to the hospital. *Wait, the president is on the way to the hospital? Is he* on his way, *or is he being* taken *there?*

After playing the tape on the air again, Reynolds signed off for the moment. There were so many unanswered questions.

"There really is nothing more that we can tell you at this point," the ABC newsman told his audience, recapping what he knew so far. "So,

* To see ABC's bulletin, visit https://www.youtube.com/watch?v=PRTFyWb9fQU.

that's it. As soon as we get any more information on this we will come back on the air as quickly as we can."

Back to the soap opera *Edge of Night*.

At the first all-news channel, Bernard Shaw didn't have the luxury to break away and wait for the facts to click into place. This was exactly the kind of developing story made for CNN, the kind Reese had been waiting for—a golden opportunity to "capture the surfers."

Besides, CNN had nothing to break away *to*.

A producer tried to fight the edict to stay on the story.

"We don't have any information," he argued. "We don't know anything!"

"It doesn't make any difference," came the order. "Get Bernie back in the chair, and get ready to go."

Nearly twenty years earlier, during the stone ages of television news, Reese had had to watch as the networks grabbed the glory during the Kennedy assassination—with nary a frame of film of the actual shooting.

Here, now, was his chance to play alongside the networks, in their league—thanks to the invention of videotape, thanks to portable cameras and satellites, thanks to this crazed lunatic of a gunman whose name no one knew yet. Thanks, most of all, to Ted Turner.

But Reese would only be sure he'd arrived completely when he gained admission to that press pool.

To him, the clubby collusion of the networks—how the existence of their troika silenced other competition—boiled his blood and embodied all that was wrong with television.

By bizarre coincidence, this was the day he planned to fire his greatest salvo in this fight to force his way into the inner sanctum. CNN had prepared a lawsuit against the White House and the networks, charging them with antitrust and violation of the First Amendment for blocking CNN from the pool. Now, because of these bullets, the suit would have to wait.* But to prove his point, he rolled tape on that pooled video and

---

* The suit to gain access to the White House press pool was filed several months later.

ran a copy of it on his airwaves, anyway. "A pool for one was a pool for all." Let the networks sue *him* if they weren't happy.

Now it was Shaw's turn to narrate that jarring video for CNN's tiny audience, his voice competing with a cacophony of sounds—the clanking electric typewriter, bleating television monitors, agitated voices of his behind-the-scenes colleagues, working the phones, hawking the wires, in search of the latest. Details, meanwhile, dribbled in, some tiny, some large, some ultimately incorrect, all absolutely raw. *That's all we have. That's all we know. We still don't have that for you. Is that correct? I'm not sure what we're getting right. Things are in a state of confusion. Chaos around the hotel. The president is okay. Press Secretary James Brady is on the ground and may not be. A Secret Service agent and a cop have been shot, too.*

Soon it would be discovered that, despite what they'd been confidently reporting, the president was not okay. This stark fact hastened the networks back on the air, though they were still scrambling for details. Over the next hours, confusion reigned at all four newsrooms on display for viewers, echo chambers all. The unfolding drama of the news was as riveting as the shooting itself. With a blank slate of airtime to fill, video of the heinous act replayed again and again, in realtime, in slow-mo, examined, dissected, frame by frame, as reporters stitched together their facts and the confusion morphed into a complete story.

At CNN, Daniel Schorr joined Shaw on set and bantered to fill the time, sharing that he just returned from medical leave in the same hospital where the president of the United States was now being treated by the same surgeon who'd recently treated him.

Senator Howard Baker, having announced to Congress the turn of events, called his daughter Cissy, the CNN assignment editor, to deliver a grim scoop: He'd been told that Press Secretary Brady was dead. She, in turn, passed along the information to Sandy Kenyon, who quickly crafted a script for Shaw—who refused to read it. The other networks began to report the news: James Brady had succumbed to gunshot wounds. Dan Rather even called for a moment of silence in his honor.

Around the CNN newsroom, watching competition report the news, the anxious staff confronted Kenyon. *Why won't Bernie say it? We had it first.*

Since it wasn't clear how Baker had received his information, and since it seemed that he hadn't witnessed Brady's demise himself, Shaw deemed the senator's information unreliable. Despite his instincts, the anchor capitulated: CNN had learned from a "top-level congressional source," he told viewers, that James Brady had died. Quickly, he hedged his bets: "We are not sure, we have no official confirmation. This is just one report. Brady, in fact, may be alive."

Not long after came word that, in fact, he was—and the three mighty networks were in the awkward position of having to retract the story. But the mistake was less of a reminder about rushing to be first than it was one of the first post-CNN examples of how television journalism would be redefined. For "news" no longer meant reporting an event in its aftermath. Forevermore, news would mean following an endless shower of unfolding details, right before your very eyes. News, in other words, had become sports.

On this day, side by side, as newbie CNN resembled the big three networks, and the networks looked and sounded like CNN, media critics decried that the shooting of the president was evidence that television news had collectively sunk to a new low.

Who cared, syndicated columnist Nicholas Von Hoffman wrote, if a reporter had been in the same hospital as the president and attended by the same doctor? Rumor, gossip, hearsay, and tongue-wagging: "While a worried nation sought information," he lamented of the coverage, "it got incompetent, if ardent hysterics."

* * *

Every start-up organization in history, if it is lucky to survive its mewling infancy, emerges into its next phase in a series of defining, chrysalis moments—the corporate equivalent of puberty. The first such moment for CNN was that day in March.

Soon after came another milestone in its coming-of-age: the announcement of a rival. Westinghouse and ABC had partnered to create an all-news headline service, built on the premise of a wheel format similar to what Ted had wished CNN to follow. It would debut sometime in 1982, based in the non-union bastion of Connecticut. Imitation might be flattery, but to Ted this was a declaration of war. Without missing a beat, he announced a counterattack. CNN would launch a similar venture to start earlier, on January 1, 1982. Chosen as mastermind of this headline news service was the king of the fast-paced newscast, Ted Kavanau.

Helfrich's team got to work expanding the old country club, entombing the fallow vegetable garden in the old pools with a new structure to accommodate CNN2. It all happened so quickly that after proudly showing off the construction site out back live on the air, the network got busted for not pulling city permits. For its part, Westinghouse brazenly set up a recruiting operation in an Atlanta hotel room, hoping to lure overworked, underpaid CNN employees to join them. Some did.

The next chrysalis moment served a collective punch to the staff's solar plexus. Alec Nagle, age thirty-six, was found dead from a heart attack in CNN's hotel suite in New Orleans, where he'd traveled with colleagues to represent CNN at the annual meeting of the Radio Television News Directors Association. There had been a cocktail party in the room the night before.

As if discovering his body wasn't awful enough, Jane Maxwell had to convey the terrible news to a stunned Kavanau. Stricken by grief, he corralled seventy of the conference attendees for donations to hire an eight-piece jazz band for a traditional Dixieland funeral march. After convincing the morgue to let him borrow Nagle's driver's license, he managed to get the photo blown up onto poster board. Hoisting high the picture of his departed colleague, Kavanau somberly lead several hundred mourners through the streets of the Big Easy, in the traditional New Orleans style. He couldn't bear to see the remains of his dear friend travel unaccompanied back home, so he hopped a plane to ride with them.

As employees arrived for their shifts and learned what had happened, an unrelenting pall shrouded the headquarters. The newsroom computer system finally worked more reliably, and distressed employees took to their terminals to type out their messages of grief. Forced by their jobs to remain composed and soldier on, newscasters read loving on-air tributes to their departed senior producer, including words composed by Kavanau:

> Lord, you have need of a great television producer to help spread your good news to the world, so you took Alec Nagle. Lord, we loved his humor and his gentleness and his toughness and his great feel for offbeat lead stories. Lord, we commend the soul of our colleague Alec Nagle to you.[*]

Since the frenzied beginning, the pioneering reverie that had bonded the originals had been slipping away with each passing day, as originals moved on to new jobs, newcomers without the shared history arrived, and office politics and jockeying for power polluted the founding spirit. Nagle's death irretrievably swept that spirit right out behind the building, past the construction site, over the pools, and into that satellite dish farm, up into the heavens, but a memory.

* * *

Mike Boettcher had been pinching himself for a year now. Just before that, he'd been a wannabe foreign correspondent chasing stories at channel 9 around his native Oklahoma. The journalism bug had bit while he watched CBS News each night during the Vietnam War, desperately hoping to get a glimpse of his beloved older brother, a serviceman. Now, after making his way into local television from radio and print, he was living the dream, trouncing around the world as part of Ted Turner's

---

[*] Nagle's nephew posted the tributes online: https://www.youtube.com/watch?v=QmydKIliYKw.

news army. It was all a testament to fate and connections. When Reese had relented and hired Ed "No Relation" Turner, that opened a hiring pipeline for Okies. When Boettcher got the call, he didn't hesitate to load his pickup truck and hit the road, where he would be the first and for some time the only field reporter based in Atlanta.

That maiden hour of CNN had portended his fate. For $5,000 a month, the network was entitled to five days' use of an ad-hoc mobile satellite unit. The contraption was an improvement over the microwave trucks becoming common in local TV news, which could only beam a signal to the local area. For the momentous first day, Reese struggled with where to send the hulking beast. While the recent eruption of Mount St. Helens was high on the list of timely possible stories, it hadn't been clear that the crude, eighty-foot flatbed rig that lugged a five-meter dish could make it from Atlanta all the way west to Washington State.

Instead, Boettcher and crew found themselves routed south to Florida, where they reported live from a beach in Miami on a massive "freedom flotilla" of Cuban refugees landing on America's shores. The exodus was part of a political play by Fidel Castro, who'd granted dissenting citizens the green light to leave. *Marielitos*, they were called, for the harbor through which they left. Since it was impossible for producers in Atlanta to talk directly to Boettcher as he stood by to deliver his report, he put one of the fresh arrivals to work holding the nearby pay phone so he could cue him when it was time to go live.

By 1981, Boettcher had reported several times from inside Cuba, always under tightly controlled circumstances, as tensions flared between Castro and the Reagan administration. Invited to cover May Day festivities, Boettcher had been told by his omnipresent handlers that their president wished to meet his.

The president of Cuban TV wants to meet Ted Turner? the young reporter asked. No, they corrected, the president of *Cuba*.

Back at headquarters in Atlanta, Boettcher stood outside Ted's office on the third floor, holding the formal invitation he'd promised to hand-deliver from Havana. Though Ted had retired from yacht racing, he was still often away from headquarters—and yet, when he was on the premises, he frequently literally slept in the Murphy bed in his office suite. Clad in a white terrycloth bathrobe, he'd wander around in the middle of the night on the fringes of the newsroom in a fit of sleeplessness, searching for coffee and conversation, amusing the staff. They didn't want to ignore the boss's entreaty to catch him up on the news of the day, but their never-ending deadlines beckoned. Occasionally, Ted meandered with a companion. An early employee noted one night that alongside a grinning robe-clad Ted was spotted another white bathrobe, worn by actress Raquel Welch.

Fresh from Cuba, Boettcher exclaimed the news to his colorful boss. This was about as far from city council meetings back home as he could imagine.

"Ted, you're not going to believe this. Fidel Castro is inviting you to visit him." Castro—the same man US officials feared was angling inexorably toward confrontation with the United States.

Thanks to the flow of US mail, Ted's executives were clued into the fact that the signals of both channel 17 and CNN could be received beyond US borders by inventive television watchers. Orders streamed in for merchandise from as far away as Martinique. A viewer from Yukon Territory in Canada sent in his personal movie requests. Once, even, a letter had arrived from a scold in Belize who feared *Leave It to Beaver* and its ilk were ruining the minds of his fellow citizens. Didn't Ted Turner, he wondered, worry about that, too? Since both channels were transmitted unscrambled—just like much of satellite television at the time—an enterprising person who built an antenna and strung a wire through the trees could capture the signals. It wasn't only Americans who complained about not having enough to watch, it seemed.

Among the curious viewers pirating CNN was the avowed enemy of the United States—who didn't seem to hold that fact against the news channel's owner.

"I just wanted to let you know that I think CNN is the most objective source of news," Fidel's invitation read, "and if you ever want to come down to Cuba . . ."

From a master media manipulator who controlled every word of the news his citizens could read, hear, and see, this was particularly immense praise.

Conservative Ted had been taught by his capitalist father to despise communism. "The commies," Ed had told him, would invade the United States and shoot anyone who carried more than fifty dollars. For years, Ted had carried only forty-nine dollars in his wallet. Fiercely patriotic, he decried conscientious objectors who refused to serve their country. Since his military school days, he'd had an unending fascination with power, war, combat history—and Hitler. And here a modern dictator was flattering him and the new creation that had proved so vexing to launch and, once it had, proved financially vexing to sustain. In all his worldly sailing adventures, Ted had never visited a Communist country. As far as he knew, he'd never even *met* a Communist before.

Aspirations of political power still danced in Ted's brain. Some said he'd established residency in South Carolina, where he owned both a 5,000-acre plantation and a 4,600-acre private island, in order to make a bid for Senate. (Though he waffled, when he imagined serving in higher office, about the spoils of political power versus the comforts enterprise had afforded him. Combined, his own properties, he observed, were far bigger than Camp David.) His concern about the inevitable collapse of the nation and the deterioration of the world had deepened. He wished to visit every country that would let him in, meet with the leaders, and find out what they were thinking. Maybe he could help broker peace.

Castro had a long history of bamboozling the US media. Just before the Batista dictatorship fell in 1959 and the young revolutionary was being celebrated as the great hope for Cuban democracy, he stood in the dark of night in a remote location with Ed Sullivan, the most famous television personality in North America. A vision: the starched, powerful TV tastemaker, outfitted in his usual dapper businessman's suit, surrounded by machine gun–toting supporters in fatigues, right beside the towering Fidel. Sullivan deigned to ask the man if he was a Communist.

"We are all Catholics," Fidel responded coyly, pointing to the religious medal around his neck. "How would we be Communists?" Batista will be the last dictator, he assured Sullivan and fifty million rapt citizens of the United States.

Similar softball appearances with other TV royalty like Jack Paar and Edward R. Murrow preceded Fidel's "charm offensive" victory lap around the United States, orchestrated by a stateside public relations firm. Standing before the American Society of News Editors, he opined about his hope for a free press for Cuba, and at the National Press Club, he declared in broken English, "Only real public opinion is when men and women can hear, can speak, and can write." Days later, he strengthened ties with the Soviet Union. The relationship between Cuba and the United States tensed to boiling. The failed Bay of Pigs invasion gave way to the Cuban Missile Crisis and numerous attempts by the CIA to assassinate El Jefe. (Back when he was employed by CBS, none other than Daniel Schorr had revealed this.)

Most recently, a trade embargo and travel ban had been reinstated by the Reagan administration. Was Castro now trying to use Ted and his news channel to trick the nation again? Perhaps, Ted rationalized, coming face-to-face with a "commie dictator" might be somehow educational. Maybe, Reese supposed, he could even bring home an interview with the embattled leader—as long as Boettcher went along and did the quizzing, not Ted. Perhaps this invitation meant CNN could become the first American network to win accreditation for a bureau there. Ted wondered what he and CNN might have to lose in accepting. Was this an elaborate ploy to kidnap him? Maybe then, Ted joked, finally he could get some rest.

As Boettcher stood in the doorway of his office, Ted commanded, "Set it up."

* * *

And so, in February 1982, Captain Outrageous kissed his wife and children goodbye, unsure what would become of him when he arrived in

Havana. On the commercial charter jet that ferried him there, he carried gifts for his host—a Braves baseball cap and fishing gear—and a
small entourage: a cameraman, a sound man, Boettcher, and Ted's lady
friend, Liz Wickersham, who'd appeared on the cover of *Playboy* in April
1981.* After performing a successful screen test for a bug-spray commercial, she'd just joined WTBS as co-host of a new comedic spin on the
news, featuring Bill Tush. Soon, the program would be recast to high-
light what Ted felt was so lacking on the tube: good news. (Wickersham
had both brass and a sense of humor. She'd commissioned a sweatshirt
to wear to work with lettering that spelled out "The Other Woman.") In
her suitcase, she carried a Nikon FM camera, a Polaroid Instamatic, and
a leopard-print bathing suit. Castro had never seen the instant camera
before, but he appeared equally tantalized by her swimwear.

Along with an eye for beautiful women not their wives, the two
men, it turned out, had a lot more in common. Each feared Armaged-
don and felt the world was currently on the verge of catastrophe. Each
voraciously consumed the stories of famous military leaders and battles,
and each was particularly fascinated by, even obsessed with, Alexander
the Great—Fidel, so much so that he'd named three of his five sons
variations of "Alex."

Like Ted, Fidel could talk like a radio for hours, nonstop, and each
man possessed an ego as wide as the sky. And each, to varying degrees,
had airbrushed his personal life: to offset his wealth, Ted drove that
beat-up car that made him feel like Mr. Everyman, espousing family
values while being seen in the company of a parade of other women;
Fidel by concealing from his citizenry the very existence of his wife,
children, and fortune in order to keep up the fiction that he was an
ordinary comrade.

The two also reveled in the outdoors and nature—in particular,
hunting for ducks. Ted was about to embark on a priceless experience—
setting foot on his host's magnificent *Cayo Piedra* in the Bay of Pigs.

---

* Though Ted and Liz Wickersham have both publicly discussed the trips they made to
Cuba, each carefully omits mentioning that they were together.

Only a handful of outsiders had ever been permitted to see this spar-kling private island paradise, among them the ABC television journalist Barbara Walters.*

While CNN's crew would not be permitted to roll tape for most of the trip, Fidel's official photographer documented the visit—and so did the beautiful Liz. Though some of her film was confiscated one night by his team, she'd managed to safely store the best.

Snapshots: Ted and Fidel enjoying a nighttime baseball game. Ted instructing Fidel, a spear fisherman, how to work his gift of a rod and reel. Heavily armed men in flat-bottomed boats with guns guarding the men as they searched for prey. Ted gripping a twelve-gauge shotgun. (Later, he confessed to wondering what the CIA would pay to be that close to Castro with a gun.) Fidel casually dressed, barefoot, a rare sight-ing of El Comandante *sin* trademark military fatigues. The aftermath of the hunt: 153 neatly stacked fresh-killed ducks. For Ted's hunting prowess, the Cuban president awarded him with honors for deftly shooting more ducks than any other visitor.

At their feast that evening, Wickersham protested what she saw as a senseless massacre and refused to eat the fresh-killed fowl. Castro indulged her, heading back to the kitchen and personally bringing the blond beauty a steak.

That night, the two men sat together like old drinking buddies, casually discussing world affairs. Emboldened by the alcohol, Ted deigned to ask his host whether news reports that Cuba was interfer-ing in Angola and Central America were true.

Yes, Castro responded, and so are you. "What makes you think that it's okay for the US to interfere there but Cuba shouldn't?"

"Because we stand for freedom and capitalism, and you don't," said Ted, the righteous patriot.

Castro's retort: "So what makes you think you're right and we're wrong?"

---

* For a partial transcript of Walters's 1977 interview with Castro, see http://foreign policy.com/1977/09/15/an-interview-with-fidel-castro/.

Sleep that night for Ted proved fitful. He was surprised by how much he liked Fidel, that he was hardly "some horrible person." In reality, he was a "great guy." The Cuban people, like all people, loved kids, and a drink, and a good cigar. Communists didn't have horns, after all, or smoke coming out of their ears, as he half expected they might.

People at their core were not so different, after all, he concluded— the difference was their politics. Perhaps his American nationalist point of view wasn't the only way of thinking. For years, he'd believed a stronger military was essential. He began to consider that maybe he'd been wrong. Killing and the arms race—what was the point of the Charles Atlas theory of "bulking up" he'd long espoused? Dialogue and understanding seemed preferable to might.

And news, he saw, could provide the bridge to understanding. If you could see only one side of the story, how could you possibly arrive at an informed decision? His conviction that an all-news channel allowed time to present varying points of view seemed to hold sway with at least one world leader. If a "commie dictator" like Fidel loved CNN, wouldn't others? They needed to stay aware, too.

Ted began to see he had created something that mattered. Castro's approval convinced him he had an obligation to make sure the rest of the world could see CNN, too. His vision of a peaceful world might be within reach— thanks, precisely, to this creation.

* * *

Fortified by this new conviction, Ted and his entourage stopped in to say goodbye to their host. As souvenirs, they were presented with Cuban cigars, a fancy alligator purse for Liz, three expertly taxidermied ducks from their hunting expedition, and an agreement for CNN to broadcast live programming from Havana in the coming weeks.*

* CNN's *Take Two*, with married co-hosts Don Farmer and Chris Curle, aired live for a week from Havana in April 1982. Among the crew on this historic broadcast was a young CNN producer and aspiring reporter, Katie Couric.

While they said their goodbyes, Ted asked for the ultimate memento: Perhaps Fidel would agree to record a testimonial of his appreciation for CNN?

"He can say it in Spanish," Ted explained to the omnipresent translator, offering up an extemporaneous script. " *'It's very important for me to keep up with what's going on in the United States. And when there's a crisis of some sort, or news I need to see, I watch Cable News Network.'* "

Why not, Castro shrugged amiably, toking on his cigar, as CNN's midday program *Take Two* rattled on in the background from the antiquated television console.

Ted beamed a shit-eating grin that Castro had consented. He reached over and turned down the sound, adding—as if Castro needed the publicity—"And we'll put this on the television."

The Cuban leader might prohibit the free flow of news to his people. But about this new channel, he had nothing but praise. He thought for a moment and began to speak.

"We may at any time watch and listen to a program by the CNN," he said in Spanish, as his translator recited the words in English, "because the programs of the CNN stay for twenty-four hours and it's very useful for us to have these programs when we need to know about news, about what's going on in the United States and what happens in the world . . ."

Castro smiled a bit as he continued, looking back and forth from the translator to the television as he mulled what to say next—Ted's co-conspirator.

"We receive an important, a very important service, by the CNN," he said, "though we are clients, we are customers, we are not registered as such. Some has said we receive the news by smuggling them."

He stopped for a moment, as if to absolve his theft of the television signal.

"One cannot smuggle news," he said, looking straight at the camera. "Space is universal, and news is universal, too."

Ted entered the shot as the two men shook hands, a Chamber of Commerce grip-and-grin.

"For the tremendous hospitality you have shown us, and the wonderful time we have spent in your beautiful and very progressive country," Ted said, "it's a pleasure to exchange the news and friendship with you."

He was dying to show this tape back in Atlanta, and then rush this most unorthodox endorsement to air. What would the naysaying networks say about *this*?

Castro reached back over to the television and turned up the volume.

CHAPTER ELEVEN
The Little Girl in the Well, 1987

It happened in an instant on a hot October morning in a yard in Midland, Texas, as the kids played and the world pulsed with dramas great and small. Cissy McClure had stepped inside the white frame house on Tanner Drive to answer the phone. When she returned, her eighteen-month-old daughter, Jessica, had vanished. The girl's playmates gestured frantically near the opening to an eight-inch hole in the ground—the little girl had fallen into an abandoned well. "I was only gone for five minutes," the incredulous mother said. *"I was only gone for five minutes."*

In Texas oil country, mobilizing a skilled rescue operation didn't take long, but diamond-tipped pneumatic drill bits were no match for the fortress of hard rock surrounding Jessica. Digging a tunnel parallel to the well, and then across to it, would not be easy or quick, even once workmen unleashed a custom auger bit and the rathole rig they nicknamed "Green Machine." From the sheer vibration of a backhoe, the trapped girl plummeted farther, from eight feet down to twenty-two.

Local press arrived soon after. Kids didn't fall into wells every day in Midland. The television cameraman from KMID lowered a microphone into the shaft that allowed Jessica's parents to talk to their trapped child. One minute, the girl was crying. The next minute, she was sweetly singing nursery rhymes.

"How does a kitten go?" one of the rescue workers asked.

"Meow," came the response. She was alive, and they were going to get her.

Thanks to KMID's new microwave truck, the only one in town, the station had an advantage over the other locals as the ordeal dragged on: Two reporters took turns filing live updates from the scene to the Midland audience fortified only by M&M's. Soon, six satellite news-gathering trucks from bigger, better-funded television markets barreled into town. These more powerful beasts allowed reporters to trumpet news far beyond the region. The network of affiliates created by Jane Maxwell years earlier made it easy for CNN to pick up the phone and ask for the story.

As word spread across the vast, interconnected, global village, a snarl of media from everywhere descended on West Texas. Dozens of photographers perched like hawks on ladders they'd brought or borrowed from the neighbors, angling for the money shot. Surely it was just a matter of time before Jessica was plucked from beneath the earth.

Stock markets all over the globe were fumbling precipitously, and would crash just a few days later. The nation awaited a Senate vote on a polarizing conservative Supreme Court nominee. An Iranian missile struck a US tanker in Kuwait. Scandals roiled the next year's presidential election, with candidates Gary Hart and Joe Biden bowing out after, respectively, a shameful discovery and a series of gaffes. First Lady Nancy Reagan, making headlines because of a breast cancer diagnosis, delayed a biopsy so she—like the rest of an anxious world—could track the story that trumped all other concerns: the fate of baby Jessica.

In the year 1987, half of the United States was now wired for cable, with forty million sets equipped to receive CNN. Just as networks were beginning to scale back their international bureaus and rethinking the limo-and-Learjet mind-set that had long propelled them, the network formerly derided as Chicken Noodle News was expanding—from three hundred to fifteen hundred people, spread across eighteen bureaus around the world. The fact that CNN spent a third as much money to produce exponentially more hours of news was turning long-established news-gathering conventions upside down. Profits for the network had been on the rise—projected for this year to total more than $60 million.

In Atlanta, CNN needed so much more space it had traded headquarters in the former Jewish country club in midtown for a failed indoor amusement park, featuring the world's longest escalator, inside a tired high-rise hotel complex downtown. Bunky Helfrich's crew retrofit the place to the tune of $30 million. There was even a movie theater, where Ted could play his jewel in the crown, the newly acquired film, his favorite, *Gone with the Wind*.

This fortress-like building seemed more secure than the Tara on Techwood; here, Ted's office had been wired with controls to operate the network should terrorists attack. Gone, though, were the two quaintest quirks of the old space: the overhead thuds of wrestling that startled newsroom employees during the weekend matches, and the chance to run into Ted in his bathrobe in the breakroom in the middle of the night.

For anyone who didn't know that he "was cable when cable wasn't cool," Ted commissioned a twangy country music song to trumpet the message. An accompanying music video was taped late one night. Those who'd been around for his ascent remembered that the Turner empire traced its roots back to billboards, onto which he also plastered this "cool" campaign.

Ted could sing that he was cool to his heart's content, but by 1987, his baby wasn't entirely his any longer. Earlier in the year, he'd sold a 37 percent chunk of his empire to a group of cable companies in exchange for $560 million and their executives' say in how Turner Broadcasting was run. It was that, or risk sinking under the nearly $2 billion in debt he'd acquired to finance the purchase of historic movie studio MGM. That deal had been universally regarded as bonkers, with Ted selling back the studio to its wily owner, Kirk Kerkorian, months later, while holding on to the blue-chip film library that later became the basis for Turner Network Television. After years of risky moves and deals where he'd managed, improbably, to emerge triumphant, this time he'd come perilously close to being crushed.

Even when things didn't work out for Ted, oh, how far he'd traveled from the days of the baseball nose push and the Super Bad Party Ring and groveling to viewers to please lend him a couple of bucks. Now he haggled with the titans of media. He'd risen, improbably, to titan status, too. Before MGM, there'd been his failed takeover of the "whorehouse," CBS; after, a brief flirtation with the media mogul from Australia, Rupert Murdoch, who'd just planted a flag on the US television landscape with his purchase of seven independent stations and his own movie studio investment, 20th Century Fox. Gannett's Al Neuharth had designs on the Turner empire, but Ted refused to sell, especially to the dinosaur newspaper business. Later, he deflected NBC's parent company, GE, and Jack Welch.

He'd even moved on in his personal life, finally, mercifully, divorcing Janie. For a while, he took up with his thirty-year old private pilot—titans need not fly coach, as Ted had bragged for years he loved to do—and eventually attracted the affections of the ultimate symbol of success: a movie star. Jane Fonda knew a thing or two about the spoils of early technology adoption. While Ted was conquering the cable landscape, she'd been raking in a fortune, early in the VCR revolution, by peddling exercise tapes.

The win/loss column mostly balanced, even if Ted's books didn't. His Cable Music Channel failed after a month, and he sold out to MTV; not long after, he picked up Westinghouse's Satellite News Channel, the competitor that inspired him to start Headline News. The Goodwill Games, his attempt to do the Olympics one better, had lost him $26 million, but he thoroughly believed it a worthy investment that underscored his personal involvement in hastening the end of the Cold War. (It also got him an in with the Russians.) You could almost believe Ted when he insisted his motivational force was not money. Bridging the divide was. Who else could claim friendship with archconservative Senator Jesse Helms *and* communist Fidel Castro—whom he and Liz had returned to visit again in 1983?* (The promotional spot they'd taped with him back in 1982 had never made it to air, vetoed by Ted's shocked employees, who refused to buckle to his insistence it air—but the stuffed ducks were still prominently displayed in his office, a totem to his globalist transformation.)

Aside from the cast of characters and the theatrics, his most

---

* Ted made a third trip in 1990, with a different paramour, Kathy Leach. This time, he did conduct a taped, sit-down interview with Castro. It was widely criticized for being softball. You can watch it here: https://www.youtube.com/watch?v=rvnUwvnvxgw.

enduring legacy had been in upending the conventional order of the television universe and the news business.

"They are watching us in Moscow right now, in Havana, in London," Ted bragged as deal after intoxicating deal was signed to beam CNN around the globe—Canada, Australia, Japan, Mexico, China. (In more restrictive countries, of course, the channel was off-limits to all but its ruling elite, confined for the most part to their offices and tourist hotels.) "Within the next three years, virtually every leader in the world will be watching CNN with a satellite receiver."

Indeed, the same potent cocktail of satellites and cable television that had put Ted on the map was currently wreaking havoc on every corner of the planet. Governments accustomed to controlling television were yielding to commercial newcomers as well as the incursion of "cultural imperialists" like Ted. But it wasn't American culture Ted was hoping to sell. It was some vast, ineffable promise to save the world.

"I'm trying to get bigger, so I'll have more influence. It's almost like a religious fervor," he said. He still muttered, from time to time, that he should run for president.* "My main concern is to be a benefit to the world, to build up a global communications system that helps humanity come together, to control population, to stop the arms race, to preserve our environment. We're steaming at thirty knots on the *Titanic* trying to break the transatlantic record on an iceberg-strewn sea. We're out of control, we've got to get in control."

Could television help the world steady its course, to coalesce and transform? Or was it, indeed, a pernicious anesthetic, the Hitler of its

---

* Whether it would be possible for someone with Ted's long history of outrageous comments and behavior to run for president never seemed to be his concern. Perhaps the most pointed example of this was a flight he took with *Playboy* interviewer Peter Ross Range in 1983. Liz Wickersham accompanied them as they rode and talked in first class, though Range was asked not to mention that fact. When Ted became angry with Range's questioning about his television programming, he ripped the recorder out of the reporter's hand, threw it at the cockpit door, and then did the same with his bag of tapes. Next, he stood up and began stomping on them, like grapes. When Ted retreated to the bathroom, Wickersham explained that he was under tremendous pressure and that once he'd kicked her in the shins.

time, a destructive force worse than cigarettes that, Ted believed, had turned the American populace "lazy, drugs, homosexuals, sex maniacs, materialists, disrespectful?" Ted, the television magnate who despised television, couldn't seem to make peace, after all these years, that the truth was it was a bit of both.

* * *

As the rescue of baby Jessica dragged on, the weary local crew kept vigil, afraid to duck out for bathroom or meal breaks lest they miss the money shot. Even though these stations typically signed off the air each night, there was no question they'd staff the switchboard and stay on the air all night for this.

From the new news mission control in downtown Atlanta, CNN producers decided the story was big enough to merit sending their own crew to Midland, rather than continue piggybacking off affiliate feeds. CNN's Dallas bureau chief, Tony Clark, found himself knocking on doors of surrounding homes, hoping to borrow both a phone and a ladder. Though technology had progressed far enough that images from Midland could be beamed live around the world, a hardline phone was still necessary to call back to the newsroom.

A kid plus distress equaled timeless drama. Clark and many of his colleagues hadn't worked at the network back in June 1981, when Reese picked up a satellite feed from Italy, where efforts had been under way to free a two-year-old boy trapped in a well near Rome.

As for CNN's founding president, he could only view this latest human-interest circus from a distance. He'd been gone from CNN for five years now, since May 1982.

* * *

Reese's end had come swiftly, although his union with Ted had been dissolving, as is so often the case with breakups, bit by painful bit. The phone was ringing when Reese returned to his home in Atlanta from a much-needed vacation in Martinique. Ted asked him to come in—a request he'd not usually make on a weekend. There was something in the sound of his voice that Reese found unsettling.

Was it that Reese had made the unilateral decision to dump Sandi Freeman, who he'd decided was lightweight?

Was it that he replaced her with a duo from local Washington radio, Tom Braden and Pat Buchanan, on a show that would be named *Crossfire*? Ted had called them "turkeys."

Was it that without asking Ted, he'd hired talk show host Mike Douglas on a two-year contract for a decidedly non-CNN salary of a million dollars?*

Would it have made a difference if Reese had actually read the copy of Dale Carnegie's *How to Win Friends and Influence People* that Ted had handed him months earlier in response to complaints about his iron, belligerent rule?

Was Ted pissed that Reese had yanked him off the air last fall when he was testifying to Congress about sex and violence on TV?

Hadn't Reese successfully staved off the encroaching threat of a union, which could have crushed the budget?

Wasn't Ted happy to have settled the anti-trust White House pool suit with the networks, which meant CNN would now be included in this rarefied group? Ever since, the presidential press office had referred in its schedules to the *four* television networks.

Was it the whispers from other top brass who hated Reese and his brash style and wished to get their hands on this trophy?

The list was long, but the why, in the end, didn't matter. Yes, Reese had unquestionably served as Frankenstein, toiling tirelessly to build the beast. But ultimately, it was Ted who owned the monster.

---

* Reese writes in his memoir that his first choice had been Tom Snyder and his second, legendary director Orson Welles, who in his later years had written a newspaper column. Perhaps it's for the best that he didn't go to work for CNN. Several years later, when Ted acquired the MGM film library and stated his intention to colorize classic black-and-white films, Welles famously commanded before his death, "Don't let Ted Turner deface my movies with his crayons."

On his way into midtown at Ted's command, he'd stopped off and picked up his old friend and ally Burt Reinhardt for backup. But Ted wished to see Reese alone.

We're going to make some changes, he told his founding president. He was rehiring Sandi Freeman, he said, and putting her back on the air. And Reese was out. He'd be paid through the end of his contract.

Like that, in a flash, the dream was over.

* * *

As a media swarm awaited the rescue of a little girl in the fall of 1987, Reese was fully settled back in New York, angling to launch a daily syndicated show called *Crime Watch Tonight*, with ten bureaus around the world that promised to unearth stories of terrorism and espionage and violence, all conveniently fed to subscribers by satellite. As his producer on this unabashedly tabloid show, possible only in an age of new technology, he'd hired none other than the man whose sensibilities fit this project so well: Ted Kavanau.

In Midland, the rescue operation had plodded along for two nights and three days now, straight into Friday night prime time. Television viewers could choose from *I Married Dora* on ABC, about a single dad who weds his undocumented housekeeper, followed by sci-fi borg sensation *Max Headroom*. CBS aired *Beauty and the Beast*, about a man-beast and his bond with a district attorney. NBC played *Rags to Riches*, about a self-made millionaire who adopts six orphans, then the sexy crime drama *Miami Vice*.

Anchors sat at the ready in the network newsrooms in New York. When it seemed that a conclusion to the ordeal was minutes away, all three broadcast networks dumped out of the entertainment and joined in, marveling that they had a better view of the action than their reporters in the field.

On CNN, the unscripted drama of reality was, as usual, the centerpiece. Hooked up to a satellite truck provided by their affiliate from Dallas, the network had three cameras trained on the action. Tony Clark hushed the anchor: "Let the pictures speak for themselves." And at long last, weary, dirt-encrusted workers triumphantly extracted tiny Jessica and held her up like a trophy for all the world to see, to whoops and cries and wonderment.*

The drama complete, ABC, CBS and NBC resumed their entertainment programming. But on CNN, the news continued.

A symphony of horns alerted the people of Midland that one of their own was safe. But the reverie was superfluous. No one needed to go outside to know what had happened. Thanks to television, all over town and all around the planet, millions of people already knew. That night, CNN scored its highest ratings ever.

---

* CNN cameraman David Rust, who worked for the network from launch until 2019, "procured" one of the little girl's socks that fell off as she was whisked away to the hospital. It's one tiny item in his exhaustive collection of memorabilia amassed from his lifetime in the field.

AFTERWORD
June 2000

Even before he landed in Atlanta for the twentieth-anniversary party, Reese had made up his mind how he'd cast his role at the affair. The part of "bastard at the wedding" seemed apropos.

He couldn't feel less wanted. No invitation had been issued to him for the tenth anniversary, which stung. The pain was more acute eight months after that, during CNN's most celebrated moment, in 1991, when on a terrifying, triumphant night a trio of his guys—Bernie Shaw, John Holliman, and Peter Arnett—bravely narrated the launch of war from the ninth floor of a hotel in Baghdad. Reese happened to be traveling for business in Paris, and the next morning at breakfast all the other gobsmacked guests could talk about was the dramatic heroism they'd witnessed on television the night before.

He wanted to scream to these awestruck new admirers of the network, "I started CNN. CNN is my thing."

Since Ted had fired him, he'd had his hand in so many other "things." His credit as founding president served him well as he helped to launch a twenty-four-hour news channel on Long Island and, later, the Television Food Network—a particular feat for a man who'd had the kitchen removed from his apartment. He'd consulted for various blue-chip media companies on a wide variety of projects involving a wide range of subjects from international business news, medical news, and fiber optics. He'd shopped the idea of a new twenty-four-hour cable news format in conjunction with ABC and the *New York Times*. None of it, *none of it*, ever approximated the thrill of invention he'd experienced with CNN. He was a newsman, first and foremost. He longed to be back in the fray he'd created. In late 1997, he was so desperate to get back into it, he even called Ted to ask him for a job—any job.

Meetings then at the network went, not surprisingly, nowhere. His reputation preceded him. And now, here he was a few years later, lodged at a third-rate hotel in a room he had to pay for himself, across a highway from where the VIPs had been invited to stay gratis as they celebrated his baby. How many people recalled, as he did, the toil of invention, the roadblocks, the widespread doubt, the financial precariousness. There'd been weeks when it wasn't clear Ted could make payroll.

Now CNN inhabited a rarefied and admired perch, even going so far as to tout itself as the "world's most important network." The combined revenue for CNN and Headline News totaled $800 million. Ferocious competition had arrived in the form of all-news channels Fox, and then MSNBC. The constant heroin-drip rush of news now being transmitted by the Internet had obliterated what little there was left of time and space. There was no clock anymore, just an endless stream of information. Or was it noise? No one of any age could recall that quaint, long-ago past when news aired only at dinnertime and wasn't available instantly.

Reese's prediction had proven to be spot-on: The public indeed possessed a voracious appetite for news it didn't even know it had.

When he picked up his name tag at the CNN Center, just another face in the crowd, Reese felt another slap: His name was misspelled. Way back when, it was just the pronunciation Ted got wrong. He'd add another syllable: "Scho-en-field." The next blow: A commemorative book credited someone else with hiring Peter Arnett, damn it. The jealousy overwhelmed him when he spotted "his" Jane Maxwell, now senior vice president of special events, hugging Time Warner's Jerry Levin, the man for whom he'd produced a news pilot at HBO—the man who now dictated Ted's fate.*

In 1997, having sold the entirety of Turner Broadcasting to Time Warner and finding himself a multibillionaire, Ted impetuously

---

* Jane retired in 2009. Her husband, Rick, founder of the network's Satellites and Circuits desk, left CNN in 1985 and started an industry newsletter.

announced a ten-year, billion-dollar pledge to the United Nations. As a nod toward his reinvention as a philanthropist, UN Secretary-General Kofi Annan was on the agenda to speak that day.

But Ted's fortune was now on the decline. Earlier in the year, there'd been a disastrous turn of events: Time Warner's merger with AOL, eventually classified as the biggest mistake in corporate history. And *that* had been announced just days after Jane Fonda had packed up and left him. He was now all but a figurehead at the company he created.

"I'm in spiritual and mental pain," he told a reporter. "When you've worked to build a company for forty years and you know all the people there and one day it's gone, well, that's a hard transition for anyone. It's like taking your pencil away and telling you you can't write anymore."

He was sharpening the pencil now, hoping to invest in a broadcast network in Russia. Besides that virtual real estate, he was buying thousands of acres of land in the United States, focusing his energies on environmental preservation. Watchful Time-Warner PR staff swirled around him at the CNN Center to make sure reporters who'd been invited to cover the carefully orchestrated festivities didn't get too close. He was as frank and as outspoken as ever, and he was miserable.

Seated at a table yards away from the podium, Reese and his wife, Pat, listened as former president Jimmy Carter extolled the wonders of CNN in helping spread the power of peace. CNN isn't the agent of peace, Reese thought bitterly—just the *messenger boy.* Up on stage, the current CNN president, Tom Johnson, acknowledged that the founding CNN president, "Reese Scho-en-field," was in their midst. Big Mo genially rose to applause and attempted a joke, "Thank you, Tom, for throwing this party for me." But he was too far back for the joke to work. Even his booming voice couldn't carry that far.

Running into old allies like Burt Reinhardt, now the emeritus second president of CNN, Mike Boettcher, who'd become an award-winning war correspondent, and Liz Wickersham, happily married to an attorney in New York, helped soften this visit, while at the same time making it feel a bit more anthropological. For Reese was writing a book to set the record straight. All those years earlier, he'd been too numb to feel much in the aftermath of his ouster. Numbness then morphed into anger. Every chance he got, he publicly railed against the network's poor choices, poor ratings, how it had become "bloated and constipated." A book would be his chance to claim his place in history.

History was becoming the place where many of the origi-nals resided.

As for Bill Tush, Ted's first newsman and cable television's very first star, he'd gone on to serve as CNN's roving entertainment correspon-dent. Early channel 17 viewers never forgot that time he'd co-hosted the news with a German shepherd. Way back when, Ted had promised Tush he'd have a job as long as he did. And he had. He left CNN in 2002.

Daniel Schorr lasted at the network only through 1985. The year before, he'd been asked to provide political analysis alongside a for-mer governor. This outraged Schorr. A politician wasn't a political analyst! He should not be seated next to a journalist! Burt Reinhardt had refused to continue guaranteeing the clause Schorr had insisted on when he'd taken the job—the clause that said he didn't have to do or say anything he didn't want to. As if being fired wasn't bad enough, CNN had demanded its satellite dish back, too. Take it as long as you landscape the hole in the ground, he told them. They just left it.

Sandi Freeman exited around the same time. After Ted resurrected her, she'd moved her program to New York, divorced her husband, and married her agent. When, at the end of her contract, Ted got tired of negotiating with him, he called late-night radio talk show host Larry King and offered him $200,000, twice what he was currently earning, to take over the plum evening talk slot. Though he was reluctant to give up his evenings—prime time for dating—he figured the gig was worth a shot.*

---

* Larry King hosted his show on CNN for twenty-five years.

* * *

When Reese and Pat discovered that their seats for the twentieth-anniversary festivities weren't anywhere near each other, they skulked back to the third-rate hotel instead. This trip down memory lane, coming face-to-face with so many of the people whose careers Reese had launched, whose lives CNN had changed, triggered his capacity, at long last, to mourn. Unable to sleep, twenty years to the day after his greatest achievement, he sat up in the shadowy room and cried.

Celebratory fireworks were scheduled for the night CNN turned twenty, along with a party featuring a performance by Diana Ross and the Supremes—a far cry from the armed forces band that entertained guests on launch day. That tape of "Nearer My God to Thee" still sat on the hold shelf, waiting for the apocalypse.

And the apocalypse arrived, after a fashion, in 2019, a year before CNN's fortieth anniversary. That's when AT&T, deemed such a powerful monopoly that it had been smashed apart by government decree back in 1982, received government approval to proceed with its $85 billion acquisition of Time Warner. The telecommunications giant, almighty once again, announced not long after that it would sunset what was left of Ted Turner's name from the businesses he'd created. The consolation prize: The campus of the old Progressive Club, now home to myriad other Turner networks, was dedicated late in 2019 to "The Original Maverick." A soaring mural depicting a youthful Ted beside a mountain range was also revealed, a nod to his more recent work in environmental preservation.

From the front lawn where he'd stood on that June Sunday in 1980, a now-frail eighty-one-year-old Ted told the guests who gathered in his honor that the media company he created remained his greatest professional achievement. Despite his diminished state, his feisty spirit was still in evidence. "I didn't really leave [CNN] because I wanted to," he said. "But anyway . . . here I am!"

Blocks away on West Peachtree Street, the original WTCG building sits slated for demolition, as developers plan to erect two residential towers on the site. Even a majestic old tree out front that Ted once told Tush would outlive them all is red-tagged.

Despite the many changes, the name "CNN" survives. Not even the mighty phone company, recast as a modern media giant, can obliterate the spirit of exploration and singular moment in time that gave rise to the first all-news channel—and, for better or worse, the news revolution it sparked.

Timeline

March 1963	Ted Turner's father dies. Ted takes over Turner Outdoor.
1968	Ted buys radio station WAPO in Chattanooga; renames it WGOW.
1969	WGOW merges with Rice Broadcasting.
1970	WTCG debuts on January 1, 1970.
	Ted purchases WCTU in Charlotte; renames it WRET.
1972	Importation of distant signals allowed by FCC.
April 6, 1973	WTCG throws "Thank the Viewers" party.
April 20, 1973	WRET initiates all-night broadcasting on Fridays.
1973	Ted signs deal to air Atlanta Braves games on WTCG.
August 19, 1974	WTCG begins airing twenty-four hours, six days a week.
December 3, 1975	Ted has Earth station installed.
January 14, 1976	Ted purchases the Atlanta Braves.
July 20, 1976	Ted testifies before Congress on cable television oversight.
December 17, 1976	WTCG goes up on the satellite.

April 1977	WTCG goes twenty-four hours, seven days a week. Ted attempts to buy Orlando station WSWB Channel 35; later denied.
September 1977	Ted wins America's Cup.
September 1, 1978	WRET launches Action News format after winning NBC affiliation.
December 1978	Ted floats the idea for CNN to National Cable and Telecommunications Association board. Flops.
May 5, 1979	Braves GM Bill Lucas dies; Ted rekindles the CNN idea.
May 21, 1979	Ted announces CNN at NCTA show in Las Vegas with Reese Schonfeld and Daniel Schorr.
May 24, 1979	Ted buys call letters WTBS from MIT's radio station.
June 1979	Ted testifies before Congress a second time.
August 21, 1979	WTCG becomes WTBS.
December 1979	Satcom 3 goes missing.
June 1, 1980	CNN launches.
December 31, 1981	CNN2 launches.
February 10, 1982	Ted visits Cuba for the first time.
January 1982	Liz Wickersham and Bill Tush debut together on WTBS's *The Lighter Side*.
April 1982	CNN broadcasts midday show *Take Two* live from Cuba.
	CNN is allowed to join the White House press pool.
May 18, 1982	Reese Schonfeld is fired.
June 1982	Satellite News Channel launches.
February 18, 1983	Ted returns to Cuba with Liz Wickersham.
October 12, 1983	Ted buys out Satellite News Channel.
March 1985	Daniel Schorr is fired.
May 1985	Sandi Freeman is fired.
April 1985	Ted launches attempt to take over CBS.
August 1985	Ted announces he's withdrawing CBS offer and instead taking over MGM.
1986	First Goodwill Games are held in Moscow.

June 1987	Ted sells major stake to Time Warner.
July 1987	CNN begins broadcasting from the former Omni in downtown Atlanta.
June 1990	Ted returns to Cuba and conducts sit-down interview with Fidel Castro.
2000	AOL buys Time Warner.
2001	Bill Tush leaves CNN.
2006	Ted exits Time Warner's board.
2019	AT&T completes $85 billion purchase of Time Warner; Turner's name removed. Progressive Club campus named for Ted.
June 1, 2020	CNN celebrates its fortieth anniversary.

Notes

Epigraph

vii   Bob Hope, *We Could've Finished Last Without You: An Irreverent Look at the Atlanta Braves, the Losingest Team in Baseball for the Past 25 Years* (Atlanta: Longstreet Press, 1991), 143.

March 2001

3   "If I had come to college": "Ted Turner: The Goldsmith Awards Ceremony," Joan Shorenstein Center on the Press, Politics and Public Policy, Institute of Politics, Harvard Kennedy School, March 13, 2001, accessed at https://iop.harvard.edu/forum/ted -turner-goldsmith-awards-ceremony.

Chapter One: The Little Girl in the Well, 1949

5   That late Friday afternoon: William Deverell, Haynes Foundation Lecture, "Little Girl Lost: The Kathy Fiscus Tragedy," Huntington Library, San Marino, CA, March 30, 2009; Alta Podcast, Episode 16, "The Original Girl in the Well," January 29, 2019.

7   "cultural development that promises . . .": *Television in Germany,* official pamphlet of the XI Olympic games, Berlin, Germany, 1936, cited in Evelyn De Wolfe and George Lewis, *Line of Sight: Klaus Landsberg—His Life and Vision* (Hollywood, CA: The Ashlin Press, 2016), 14.

7   When the film studio Paramount: De Wolfe and Lewis, *Line of Sight,* 39.

8   "The word 'cannot' simply did not": Ibid., 40.

9   Fewer than twenty thousand: Evelyn De Wolfe, "The Day Live TV News Coverage Was Born," *Los Angeles Times,* October 17, 1987.

10   "Pretend it's a sporting event": William Deverell, "A Little Girl, a Deep Well, and a Big Story," *Alta,* January 28, 2019, https://altaonline.com/a-little-girl-a-deep-well-and-a-big-story.

10   emotion was precisely what made this: Paul Henninger, "Landsberg: TV's Dynamic Pioneer," *Los Angeles Times,* September 16, 1966.

11   "I hope you don't mind": Associated Press, "All World, Except Red Orbit, Worries About Little Kathy," *The Morning News,* Wilmington, Delaware, April 11, 1949, 8.

11   The state news agency of Czechoslovakia: "Czech Press Cold to Kathy's Fate." *The Sun,* April 11, 1949.

11   apologizing to viewers for his failure: Stan Chambers with Lynn Price, *KTLA's News at 10: 60 Years with Stan Chambers* (Lake Forest, CA: Behler Publications, 2008), 31.

12   "Until that night": Stan Chambers, "The Kathy Fiscus Story: Turning Point in TV News," *Los Angeles Times,* April 8, 1989.

12   It hadn't been broadcast: Patt Morrison, "The Little Girl Who Changed Television Forever," *Los Angeles Times Magazine,* January 31, 1999.

Chapter Two: The Lunatic Fringe

13   He was so much more comfortable: Bill Tush, interview by Karen Herman, Television Academy Foundation: "The Interviews,"

June 14, 2010, https://interviews.televisionacademy.com /interviews/bill-tush.

14 Lucky neighborhood kids: Tommy Hicks, " 'SuperStation's' Growth Didn't Surprise Bill Tush," *The Montgomery Advertiser*, August 27, 1982.

17 "I'd like to apply for a job": Bill Tush, interview with author, January 8, 2018.

17 "Brilliance Is a Heavy Burden": Jim Auchmutey, "Masterpieces of Bad Taste," *Atlanta Constitution*, January 29, 1978.

18 the UHF (ultra high-frequency): For an exhaustive look at UHF, please see http://www.uhftelevision.com.

18 "plot to bankrupt Jewish dentists": "Down in the Mouth over UHF," *Broadcasting*, March 6, 1972, 34.

19 a photo in the next day's paper: Paul Jones, "Channel 17 Joins Atlanta's TV Scene Today," *Atlanta Constitution*, September 1, 1967.

19 If every one of the 107 million: "Is Pay-TV Worth Paying For?," http://www.uhftelevision.com/documents/PayTV_1963.pdf.

19 Pay television seemed: *The Public Television Act of 1967: Hearings, Ninetieth Congress, First Session, on S. 1160,* 90th Cong. 24 (October 9–16, 1967) (statement of W. Robert McKinsey, General Manager of WJRJ-TV, Atlanta).

20 to "gouge the American people": Matt Messina, News Around the Dials, *New York Daily News*, October 3, 1967, 31c.

21 "A few fleas are good for": *Talking with David Frost.* Season 1, episode 8, "Ted Turner." Aired October 25, 1991, on PBS.

21 Where he became a hell-raising "show-off": Ted Turner with Bill Burke, *Call Me Ted* (New York: Grand Central Publishing, 2008), 11.

21 "skinny little shrimp": Peter Ross Range, "*Playboy* Interview: Ted Turner," *Playboy*, August 1978.

21 Ted piped up, "Edison, T., sir": Randy Schultz, "Turner, R.: Still Trying Hard, Sir," *Palm Beach Post*, May 18, 1980.

21 "When basic characteristics": Ted Turner and Gary Jobson, *The Racing Edge* (New York: Simon & Schuster, 2008), 13.

22 he adopted his father's mistrust: Daniel Schorr, *Staying Tuned: A Life in Journalism* (New York: Washington Square Press, 2001), 306.

22 A womanizer who bragged: Roger Vaughan, *The Grand Gesture: Ted Turner, Mariner and the America's Cup* (Boston: Little, Brown and Company, 1975), 92.

22 Once the staff helped him: Robert Goldberg and Gerald Jay Goldberg, *Citizen Turner: The Wild Rise of an American Tycoon* (New York: Harcourt, Brace, 1995).

23 But the God that: Curry Kirkpatrick, "Going Real Strawwng," *Sports Illustrated*, August 21, 1978.

23 When his daily prayers: Patricia Sellers, "Ted Turner Is a Worried Man," *Fortune*, May 26, 2003.

23 "It probably wouldn't have been much fun": Vaughan, *The Grand Gesture*, 29.

23 "WARNINGS FROM THE KKK": Ibid., 92.

24 "his basic racist tendencies": Ibid.

24 But when his father refused: Kirkpatrick, "Going Real Strawwng"; Christian Williams, *Lead, Follow or Get Out of the Way: The Story of Ted Turner* (New York: Times Books, 1981), 89, attributes Ted's fall off the wagon to his parents' divorce and his screed against his choice of major.

24 "Well, what do you think": Vaughan, *The Grand Gesture*, 26.

25 It was the first time: Ibid., 30.

25 "being a bum": Williams, *Lead, Follow or Get Out of the Way*, 34.

25 Though the captain found his dedication: Ibid., 366.

26 The tenacity and strategic sensibility: Vaughan, *The Grand Gesture*, 100.

27 "I'm not Ed Turner": Ibid., 100; *Talking with David Frost*, "Ted Turner."

28 He was a fighter: Vaughan, *The Grand Gesture*, 101.

29 "unsightly man-made obstructions": Frances Lewine, "Highway Beauty Measure Signed," Associated Press, *The Greenville News*, October 23, 1965, 10.

30 Acrimony ruled the roost: Goldberg and Goldberg, *Citizen Turner*, 108.

30 "F. Scott Fitzturner": Roger Vaughan, *Ted Turner: The Man Behind the Mouth* (Boston: Sail Books, Inc., 1978), 45.

30 "My impulse was to run": Williams, *Lead, Follow or Get Out of the Way*, 49.

31 He also wasn't ashamed: Ibid., 65.

33 Fortunately, said Dr. Twisdale: "Local TV-Radio & Syndication: Two-Year-Old Charlotte UHF Goes into Receivership; Lost $600,000 but Owner Twisdale Building Two Others," *Variety*, October 1, 1969, 38.

33 Who else likened billboard painters: Williams, *Lead, Follow or Get Out of the Way*, 53.

33 the Frank Sinatra song "*My Way*": *Super Ted* film, Sid Pike Collection, University of Georgia, Walter J. Brown Media Archives and Peabody Awards Collection, Athens, GA. This film, which satirizes Ted, was made by the staff of WTCG in 1978 for his fortieth birthday.

34 The general managers at the other stations: Letter to Mr. John Gilbert from George Hagar, June 11, 1970, Sid Pike Papers.

35 "Hang on to my coattails": Interview with Turner executive Jim Roddey, Gerald Jay Goldberg Papers, UCLA Special Collections. In Williams, *Lead, Follow or Get Out of the Way*, 89, production manager R. T. Williams tells the story of his climbing, while Ted stayed on the ground. He says it took him nine hours to get down from the top.

Chapter Three: Girdle 'Round the Earth

36 To be born: Reese Schonfeld, interview by Brian Lamb, *C-SPAN Booknotes*, February 23, 2001.

36 Early on, Reese: Reese Schonfeld, interview by Karen Herman, Television Academy Foundation: "The Interviews," November 9 and 11, 2005, https://interviews.televisionacademy.com/interviews/reese-schonfeld.

36 "more influence on America's reaction": Robert Landry, "Edward R. Murrow," *Scribner's Magazine*, December 1938.

37 It wasn't politics so much: Reese Schonfeld, interview by Karen Herman.

37 He'd sold subscriptions to the: Reese Schonfeld, video memoir, Box 1, November 11, 1996, Steven H. Scheuer Television History Interviews, Special Collection Research Center, Syracuse University, Syracuse, NY.

37 In 1956, a campus employment office: Ibid.

38 Library use plummeted: Erik Barnouw, *Tube of Plenty: The Evolution of American Television* (New York: Oxford University Press, 1975), 114.

39 "Two and a half words a second": Reese Schonfeld, *Me and Ted Against the World: The Unauthorized Story of the Founding of CNN* (New York: Cliff Street, 2001), 23.

40 On index cards: Ibid., 22.

40 "You will watch": Ibid., 3.

41 The system wasn't explicitly: For a closer look at the technology of the so-called Long-Lines, please visit http://www.long-lines .net and watch "AT&T Archives: Stepping Along with Television," https://www.youtube.com/watch?v=6jYm2SVZIPk.

41 The key to success: Reese Schonfeld, video memoir.

43 In 1945, the futurist: Arthur C. Clarke, "Extra-Terrestrial Relays," *Wireless World*, February 1945, http://lakdiva.org/clarke/1945ww.

44 A CBS executive calculated that: Interview with Sig Mickelson, executive director, San Diego State University Center for Communications, and Distinguished Visiting Professor of Journalism, 1979–81, from 1979, "Raising Our Voices: The History of San Diego State and San Diego in Sound," San Diego State University, San Diego, CA.

44 This included renting: Interview with Sig Mickelson, "Raising Our Voices"; Reuven Frank, "The Great Coronation War," *American Heritage* 44, no. 8 (December 1993).

45 After a battery of tweaks and tests: "AT&T Archives: Telstar!,"

uploaded September 14, 2011, https://www.youtube.com/watch ?v=uKH-GijnAGk.

47   "not so much what they saw": "Lull in the Streets' During First Telstar Broadcast," NBC News Web Exclusive, July 24, 1962, http:// www.nbclearn.com/portal/site/k-12/flatview?cuecard=59642.

48   "This is another indication": Sid Smith, interview by Karen Herman, Television Academy Foundation, November 12, 1997, https:// interviews.televisionacademy.com/interviews/sid-smith.

50   "If that fucking Lawrence": Reese Schonfeld, oral history interview by Stephen Fagin, The Sixth Floor Museum at Dealey Plaza, August 15, 2011.

50   The state-of-the-art cameras: "JFK coverage 12:30pm–1:40pm 11/22/63," uploaded November 18, 2013, https://www.youtube .com/watch?v=pDOojsg62Oo.

51   "I'm going upstairs, I'm going to bed": Schonfeld, *Me and Ted Against the World*, 35.

52   "Burt, we got a lady here": Reese Schonfeld, oral history interview by Stephen Fagin.

53   This grand communications exchange: "How Satellites Are Changing Your Life Now," *American Legion Magazine*, September 1964.

53   More than fifty cameras: Richard F. Shepard, "TV Pools Camera Coverage," *New York Times*, November 26, 1963.

53   He felt it disrespectful: Colin McEnroe, "A Page from History," *Hartford Courant*, March 25, 1998.

55   With these and several dozen: Dean Gysel, "Look at Fourth TV Network," *Des Moines Register*, October 30, 1966; Lawrence Laurent, "Fourth Network Serious Business," *Arizona Republic*, July 24, 1966.

55   "but one blue chip": Lawrence Laurent, "New Network to Go All Out," *Los Angeles Times*, August 1, 1966.

56   Coors was rich enough: Schonfeld, *Me and Ted Against the World*, 40.

56   Though the service was losing money: "Old Tricks," *New York*,

January 24, 2014, http://nymag.com/news/frank-rich/roger-ailes -tvn-2014-2.

56 Ailes boasted that: Gabriel Sherman, *The Loudest Voice in the Room: How the Brilliant, Bombastic Roger Ailes Built Fox News— and Divided a Country* (New York: Random House, 2014).

57 At long last, the first private: Victor K. McElheny, "Westar Opens Drive to Cut U.S. Communications Costs," *New York Times*, April 15, 1974.

57 "chance to break the AT&T leash": "TVN Also Sees Satellite Use by Program Syndicators," *Broadcasting*, January 27, 1975.

58 $12 million of Coors "beer money": Schonfeld, *Me and Ted Against the World*, 40.

58 another of his potential customers: Sidney Topol, interview by E. Stratford Smith, Penn State Collection, The Cable Center, July 24, 1990, https://www.cablecenter.org/media-room/index.php ?option=com_content&view=article&id=447.

60 "Can you imagine": Sid Topol, interview with author, August 12, 2018; Reese Schonfeld interview, August 3, 1992, Gerald Jay Goldberg Papers (Collection 1666), Department of Special Collections, Charles E. Young Research Library, UCLA, Los Angeles, CA.

Chapter Four: Watch This Channel Grow!

61 some gal in promotions: Ted Turner in *Cable Television Regulation Oversight*. 94th Congress, 1st session, House of Representatives. July 20, 1976.

62 Had the competition lasted: Sidney Pike, *We Changed the World: Memoirs of a CNN Satellite Pioneer* (St. Paul, MN: Paragon House, 2005), 33.

62 "Tell me about your family": Gerry Hogan interview, July 22, 1992, Box 27, Folder 20, Gerald Jay Goldberg Papers (Collection 1666), Department of Special Collections, Charles E. Young Research Library, UCLA, Los Angeles, CA.

63 Irate about this possible incursion: Pike, *We Changed the World*, 33.

63 "Why do we go off the air" Paul Jones, "TV Independents Make Changes," *Atlanta Constitution*, August 26, 1974.

64 as a boat hand in Annapolis: Christian Williams, *Lead, Follow or Get Out of the Way: The Story of Ted Turner* (New York: Times Books, 1981), 117.

64 The daily prayer break: Charlie Hanna, "Thanks to Begathon, Religious Tone, WRET Dialing off Red," *Charlotte Observer*, May 16, 1973.

64 "I pledge to you": Pike, *We Changed the World*, 42.

65 The $26,000 collected: "Viewers Helping WRET-TV," Associated Press, February 14, 1972.

65 "asleep at the switch": Sam Hopkins, "Turner Makes Ch. 17 Work with Sports," *Atlanta Constitution*, December 25, 1972.

65 Now he could also brag: Ibid.

66 dogs most viewers hadn't seen: Paul Jones, "Ch. 17 Builds Major Film Library," *Atlanta Constitution*, July 22, 1977.

66 "Jerry Lewis's Wacky Professor": Gerry Hogan interview, July 22, 1992, Gerald Jay Goldberg Papers (Collection 1666), Department of Special Collections, Charles E. Young Research Library, UCLA, Los Angeles, CA.

66 No decision he made: "Atlanta Tape at Turner a Hot Spot in S.E," *Backstage*, May 14, 1976; Turner, *Call Me Ted*, 128.

67 The simulated stones: WTCG employees Greg Gunn and Ron Kirk, interviews with the author, February 19, 2019, and February 20, 2019; "Super Bad Party Ring Commercial," WTCG Channel 17 Atlanta, edited version, https://www.youtube.com/watch?v=PHxZ_s_pyuI.

69 An engineer cut out: Stephen Banker, "The Cable News Network Sets Sail," *Panorama*, April 1980.

69 every citizen was obligated: Ted Turner, interview by Phil Donahue, *Donahue*, April 1, 1981.

71 "I don't think it makes": Craig M. Allen, *News Is People: The Rise of Local TV News and the Fall of News from New York* (Ames: Iowa State University Press, 2001), 19.

71 The station had been working: Paul Farhi, "Going Live," *American*

Journalism Review 24, no. 9 (November 2002): 28–33, https://ajrarchive.org/article.asp?id=2685&id=2685.

72 "happy talk": Edward Bliss, Jr., *Now the News: The Story of Broadcast Journalism*, New York: Columbia University Press, 1991, 459.

72 "I don't think people will accept": Nick Thimmesch, "ABC Five-Million Dollar Woman Raises Some Questions About News Business," *South Bend* (Indiana) *Tribune*, May 3, 1976.

72 With her smooth blend: James Doussard, "If You Like Cosell, You'll Love Warner Wolf," *The Courier-Jounal* (Louisville), August 5, 1975.

72 Channel 17, he gloated: Roger Vaughan, *The Grand Gesture: Ted Turner, Mariner and the America's Cup* (Boston: Little, Brown and Company, 1975), 11.

73 By the end of the day: Ron Buchwald, phone interview with author, July 30, 2018.

73 Tush felt a bit guilty: Bill Tush, phone interview by Karen Herman, Television Academy Foundation, June 14, 2010, https://interviews.televisionacademy.com/interviews/bill-tush.

73 "You're doing a good job": Bert Roughton, "Mr. Emcee," *Atlanta Journal-Constitution*, October 19, 2013.

74 feared he'd wind up—"anonymity-ville": Steven Vinnacombe, "Tush Making Great Time," *Buckhead Atlanta*, February 29, 1980.

75 "Hey, I saw that 'Dull News'": Richard Zoglin, "A Tush for All Seasons," *Atlanta Journal-Constitution*, November 1, 1981.

75 to the shock and admiration of friends: Roger Vaughan, *Ted Turner: The Man Behind the Mouth* (Boston: Sail Books, 1978), 220–21.

75 "What's wrong with that?": Nick Taylor, "The American Hero as Media Mogul," *Atlanta* magazine, March 1982.

75 "I tell them to look": Vaughan, *Ted Turner: The Man Behind the Mouth*, 34.

75 Once, he subjected his most trusted: Williams, *Lead, Follow or Get Out of the Way*, 59.

75 his very presence seemed to inspire: Gerry Hogan interview, Gerald Jay Goldberg Papers, UCLA, Los Angeles, CA.

76 "you strike me as": Ron Kirk, WTCG employee, phone interview with author, February 19, 2019.

76 "So, you're the one": Greg Gunn, interview with author, February 20, 2019.

77 Dressed in black robes: Bill Tush, interview with author, July 9, 2019.

77 "This morning, the thoughts of": Gayle White, "Some Pyrite from the Lips of Brother Gold," *Atlanta Constitution*, October 3, 1978; Bill Tush, e-mail to author, July 9, 2019; David Bell, personal collection.

79 "We can't do the news like that": Tush, interview by Karen Herman.

79 deciding a onetime $300 cash bonus: Pike, *We Changed the World*, 43.

79 The fan mail that streamed into: Paul Jones, "Bill Tush's Fan Club Grows Nationwide," *Atlanta Constitution*, July 25, 1977.

80 "an opaque cloud of": Williams, *Lead, Follow or Get Out of the Way*, 92.

81 While other broadcasters feared: Thomas Southwick, *Distant Signals: How Cable TV Changed the World of Telecommunications* (Overland Park, KS: Primedia, 1998), 126.

81 seventy-three cable systems across five states: Gordon W. Chaplin, "Cable TV Zeroes in on the Cities," *Baltimore Sun*, July 4, 1972.

81 Now it was a full-on: Williams, *Lead, Follow or Get Out of the Way*, 89.

81 hundreds of pieces of mail: Former channel 17 head of research Bob Sieber, e-mail to author, September 20, 2019.

82 Every penny helped: Turner, *Call Me Ted*, 138.

83 "ABC will shrink down": Williams, *Lead, Follow, or Get Out of the Way*, 85.

Chapter Five: Captain Outrageous

85 "It is a peculiar trait": Wayne Minshew, " 'Damn Braves': Turner Purchase Blow to Carpetbaggers," *Atlanta Constitution*, January 8, 1976.

86 "No other team": Bob Hope, *We Could've Finished Last Without You: An Irreverent Look at the Atlanta Braves, the Losingest Team in Baseball for the Past 25 Years* (Atlanta: Longstreet Press, 1991), 1.

86 "Atlanta is my home": Robert Ashley Fields, *Take Me Out to the Crowd: Ted Turner and the Atlanta Braves* (Huntsville, Alabama: The Strode Publishers, Inc.,1977), 29.

87 When the owners had revealed: Christian Williams, *Lead, Follow or Get Out of the Way: The Story of Ted Turner* (New York: Times Books, 1981), 94.

87 Patrons donned their finest: Jim Minter, "Old Friends Say 'Farewell' to Glennon," *Atlanta Journal-Constitution*, September 15, 1968.

88 "ball from a balk": Fields, *Take Me Out to the Crowd*, 87.

88 "We may lose it all on this deal": Fields, *Take Me Out to the Crowd*, 39.

89 "like switching from Mozart to Lynyrd Skynard": Furman Bisher quoted in ibid., 41.

89 He planned to run buses: Hope, *We Could've Finished Last Without You*, 82.

89 "Please do not be too lengthy": Ad, *Atlanta Journal-Constitution*, February 1, 1979.

89 "Hope, I want this team to be": Hope, *We Could've Finished Last Without You*, 81.

91 If he knew they cost $150: Roger Vaughan, *The Grand Gesture: Ted Turner, Mariner and the America's Cup* (Boston: Little, Brown and Company, 1975), 41.

91 Though the weather was bitter cold: Hope, *We Could've Finished Last Without You*, 82.

91 The fans needed to know: Ibid., 70.

91 "It will mean more money": Tony Lang, "The Rhett Butler of Baseball," *The Enquirer Magazine* (Cincinnati), June 13, 1976.

91 A screening of a film: Hope, *We Could've Finished Last Without You*, 84–85.

92 "Lord, it would blow his mind": Curry Kirkpatrick, "Going Real Strawwng," *Sports Illustrated*, August 21, 1978.

92   The gentility quickly devolved: Hope, *We Could've Finished Last Without You*, 86.

93   "The Civil War was a boon": Lang, "The Rhett Butler of Baseball."

93   After the very first game: Larry Guest, "Is It a Bird? A Plane? No! It's Ted Turner!," *Orlando Sentinel*, May 6, 1976.

94   baseball was for "little people": Ron Hudspeth, "Ted's 'Little People' Philosophy Dissected," *Atlanta Journal-Constitution*, May 6, 1978.

94   "My wife and I are unable": Guest, "It's a Bird? It's a Plane? No! It's Ted Turner!"

94   an allegedly profligate man: Frank Hyland, "Little Guy Gone: Braves Fire Davidson . . . and an Era Ends," *Atlanta Journal and Constitution*, April 25, 1976.

94   The spurned employee's wife: Hope, *We Could've Finished Last Without You*, 32.

94   "Ted Turner has money": Fields, *Take Me Out to the Crowd*, 88.

95   "a package of dynamite": Roger Vaughan, quoted in *Courageous: Ted Turner and the 1977 America's Cup*, NBC, June 17, 2017.

95   "would make coffee nervous": Hope, *We Could've Finished Last Without You*, 92.

95   "I call people that": Ibid., 142.

95   Pitcher Dick Ruthven: Maralyn Lois Polak, "Ruthven: Balking When the Owner Advanced His Wife," *Today: The Inquirer Magazine* (Philadelphia), August 20, 1978.

95   For his part: Bob Carter, "Ted Turner: He Only Talks Like One of the Little Guys," *The Morning News* (Wilmington, DE), May 16, 1979.

96   "Ted's French whore": Hope, *We Could've Finished Last Without You*, 93.

96   "Excuse me, I have to call": Jonathan Black, "Bluebloods Must Learn to Live with Yachting Bad Boy's Name on the Cup," *Miami News*, September 20, 1977.

96   "Every pig in the southeast": DeWitt Rogers and Wayne Minshew, "Atlanta's Super Promoter: Madcap Gimmicks Helping Give Braves Turnout Quite a Hype," *Atlanta Constitution*, August 27, 1977.

97   He'd almost backed out: Hope, *We Could've Finished Last Without You*, 113.

97   "I may look like a clown": Peter Ross Range, "*Playboy* Interview: Ted Turner," *Playboy*, August 1978.

97   "Now everybody knows me": Williams, *Lead, Follow or Get Out of the Way*, 142.

98   "If all charges and kidding": Wayne Minshew, "Turner Hearing Is Due Jan. 18," *Atlanta Constitution*, January 4, 1977.

99   "People might suddenly realize": Hope, *We Could've Finished Last Without You*, 148.

99   "I double locked my door": "Turner Complains about Harassment," Associated Press, December 8, 1978.

99   At the hotel restaurant: Hope, *We Could've Finished Last Without You*, 150.

99   "Ted, there's a fine line": Ibid.

101   "Steal this Signal": Longtime Turner executive Terence McGuirk, phone interview with author, March 20, 2019.

101   From the ladies in the brothels: Williams, *Lead, Follow or Get Out of the Way*, 102.

101   The surge of calls: Hope, *We Could've Finished Last Without You*, 169.

101   "How many people in Alaska": Bob Mayes, "Instant Replay: Not Avid Fan, Cameraman Follows Blue-Gray Closely," *Alabama Journal*, December 28, 1976.

101   the city of Valdez: Bert Roughton, "Mr. Emcee," *Atlanta Journal-Constitution*, October 19, 2013.

102   "Hitler was more likely": Hope writes on page 177 of his book, *We Could've Finished Last Without You*, that the purchase of the Hawks was another part of a complex scheme in the house of Turner. He feared the FCC prohibiting a station in a market the size of Atlanta from continuing to distribute its signal over the cable and satellite. If that were to happen, he'd then have to shift operations to his Charlotte station, which was not in the top 20. Ted needed to own the Hawks in order to move them, if need be, to North Carolina. Some games were even played there as a test.

102   He planned to supply up to sixteen: "Turner Sets Sports Net," *Atlanta Constitution*, February 3, 1977.

102   Jimmy, Rosalynn, and Amy: Frank Hyland, "Braves at Plains: A Real Happening," *Atlanta Journal-Constitution*, January 16, 1977.

103   Wouldn't the media love to see: Peter Ross Range, "*Playboy* Interview: Ted Turner," *Playboy*, August 1978.

103   And on the way back home: Curry Kirkpatrick, "Going Real Straw-wng," *Sports Illustrated*, August 21, 1978.

104   The alibi she gave: Taylor Branch and Eugene M. Propper, *Labyrinth: The Sensational Story of International Intrigue in the Search for the Assassins of Orlando Letelier* (New York: Penguin Books, 1983), 391–96.

104   "I want to keep a low profile": Red Smith, "Maverick Ted: Turner Shakes up Writers' Party," *New York Times*, April 6, 1977.

104   "You should have some reason": Red Smith, "Maverick of the Breakfast Table," *New York Times*, April 6, 1977.

104   In a letter to the local: Letters to the Editor, "Ted Turner Employees 'Take Exception," *Southern Israelite* (Augusta, GA), April 15, 1977.

105   Observers looked on with amusement: Phil Pepe, *Talkin' Baseball: An Oral History of Baseball in the 1970s* (New York: Ballantine Books, 1998), 271.

106   "If you want to beat the Mouth": Vaughan, *The Man Behind the Mouth*, 102.

106   "Show me your titties": Ibid., 203.

107   "There are times you'd like to bash": Dick Sadler, quoted in *Courageous*.

107   "This has to be a dream": Al Thomy, "Turner Defends U.S. Honor," *Atlanta Constitution*, September 13, 1977.

107   "floating Times Square on New Year's Eve": Vaughan, *The Man Behind the Mouth*, 204.

108   "Pike, give me that": Williams, *Lead, Follow or Get Out of the Way*, 152.

108   "I'm happy to be alive": Ted Turner appearing in Enersen, *The Best Defense*.

108   "Shoot, Pike," Williams said: Williams, *Lead, Follow or Get Out of the Way*, 153.

Chapter Six: "No News Is Good News"

110   This was his best salvo: Reese Schonfeld, *Me and Ted Against the World: The Unauthorized Story of the Founding of CNN* (New York: Cliff Street, 2001), 65.

110   Ted had not budged: Don Kowet, "Why Are They Watching a Georgia Station in Nebraska?," *TV Guide*, July 16, 1977.

110   "I hate the news": Reese Schonfeld, interview by Karen Herman, Television Academy Foundation, November 9 and 11, 2005, https://interviews.televisionacademy.com/interviews/reese -schonfeld.

111   One of them was: Ted Kavanau, phone interview with author, March 11 and 12, 2018.

113   "We'd chase people": Ted Kavanau, phone interview, March 12, 2018.

113   "Ted's idea of continuity": Jeff Greenfield, "The 10 O'Clock News: It's Not Pretty, but It's Good," *New York* magazine, October 24, 1977.

115   "don't know anything": Ted Kavanau, "TV Newsmen Are Superficial," *Variety*, November 3, 1971, 32.

116   Abend was rabidly: "Kavanau Goes Round 'Abend,'" *Variety*, August 14, 1974, 30.

116   There was a liberal bias: Dorothy Rabinowitz, "The Bitter Prescriptions of Dr. Feelbad," *New York* magazine, May 7, 1973.

116   The day he did: "Kavanau Goes Around 'Abend.'" Bill Greeley, "Morale of WNEW-TV News Staff in Tailspin Over Editorial Immunity for Abend's 'Angled' Commentary," *Variety*, January 14, 1970.

118   SUGGEST YOU TAKE THE OTHER OFFER: Daniel Schorr, interview by Don Carleton, Television Academy Foundation, "The Interviews: An Oral History of Television," May 22, 2001, https://interviews .televisionacademy.com/interviews/daniel-schorr.

118   "immigrant from the world of words": Daniel Schorr, *Clearing the Air* (Boston: Houghton Mifflin, 1977) .

118   America's "giant classroom": Ibid., 92.

118   Tipped off in the middle: Av Westin, *Newswatch: How TV Decides the News* (New York: Simon & Schuster, 1982), 20.

119   "I chafed at the straightjacket": Schorr, *Clearing the Air*, 93.

120   He even ranked a crossword-puzzle clue: Ibid., 232.

120   "brash little appendage": Ibid., 289.

120   "Hey, didn't you used to be": Ibid., 321.

121   "The postmarks tell the tale": Christian Williams, *Lead, Follow or Get Out of the Way: The Story of Ted Turner* (New York: Times Books, 1981), 100.

122   "Who had the devious and cunning mind": Roger Vaughan, *Ted Turner: The Man Behind the Mouth* (Boston: Sail Books, 1978), 120.

123   "only horny people shoot": Peter Ross Range, "Playboy Interview: Ted Turner," *Playboy*, August 1978.

123   Might they have to blow up: Hank Whittemore, *CNN: The Inside Story: How a Band of Mavericks Changed the Face of Television News* (Boston: Little, Brown, 1990), 236.

124   a "born-again journalist": Stephen Banker, "The Cable News Network Sets Sail," *Panorama*, April 1980, 46.

124   Tantalized by the unfurling: Gerald Levin, telephone interview with author, July 10, 2019.

124   When the phone rang: ITNA and CNN employee Gerry Harrington, telephone interview with author, April 8, 2019.

125   he knew "diddley-squat": Ted Turner, interview by Michael Rosen, Television Academy Foundation, June 12 and December 6, 1999, https://interviews.televisionacademy.com/interviews/ted-turner.

127   "Well"—Ted shrugged: Reese Schonfeld, *Me and Ted Against the World: The Unauthorized Story of the Founding of CNN* (New York: Cliff Street, 2001), 16.

127   And great companies were: Ted Turner, interview by Michael Rosen.

127   "With film you needed": Paul Farhi, "Going Live," *American Journalism Review* 24, no. 9 (November 2002): 28–33, https://ajrarchive.org/article.asp?id=2685&id=2685.

129 "The cable industry doubts": Banker, "The Cable News Network Sets Sail."

129 "Attila the Hun": Ibid.

129 "Seeing such a young, vibrant guy": Ted Turner with Bill Burke, *Call Me Ted* (New York: Grand Central Publishing), 124.

130 "big baseball league in the sky": Bob Hope, *We Could've Finished Last Without You: An Irreverent Look at the Atlanta Braves, the Losingest Team in Baseball for the Past 25 Years* (Atlanta: Longstreet Press, 1991), 192.

130 "This is gonna make me": Schonfeld, *Me and Ted Against the World*, 5.

131 an invitation to sail: Williams, *Lead, Follow or Get Out of the Way*, 254.

132 "that make-believe world": Schorr, *Clearing the Air*, 284.

132 a "drunk" who "sailed ships": Schorr, interview by Don Carleton.

132 Lending his name: Roxinne Ervasti, "Daniel Schorr Joins Turner's New Network," Associated Press, November 10, 1979.

133 "Live, live, live": Schonfeld, *Me and Ted Against the World*, 5.

133 They would not and could not last: "HBO History Makers Series: A Conversation with Ted Turner," Council on Foreign Relations, May 13, 2010, https://www.cfr.org/event/hbo-history-makers-series -conversation-ted-turner.

134 "No demand will be made": Daniel Schorr Papers, Box 22, Library of Congress Manuscript Division, Washington, D.C.

135 The energy in the small hotel conference room: "Turner Says He'll Have His Cable News Network On in a Year's Time," *Broadcasting*, May 28, 1979; trade reporter Howard Polskin, who was present at the time, e-mail exchange with author, August 13, 2019.

135 "the greatest achievement": CNN promotional film, also as quoted by Williams, *Lead, Follow or Get Out of the Way*, 252.

Chapter Seven: Every Drop of Blood

136 going to be necessary—effective immediately: Robert Bianco, "Former Pittsburgher a Fixture at TBS," *Pittsburgh Press*, March 10, 1990.

136 Ted had promised: Steven Vinnacombe, "Tush Making Great Time," *Buckhead Atlanta*, February 29, 1980.

136 Making him act like: Bill Tush, interview by Karen Herman, Television Academy Foundation, June 14, 2010, https://interviews .televisionacademy.com/interviews/bill-tush.

136 purple wizard's hat: Ibid.

137 When he said CNN was a "crusade": "Rebel with a Cause," *Broadcasting*, May 19, 1980.

137 "Nothing, dummy," Ted responded: Christian Williams, *Lead, Follow or Get Out of the Way: The Story of Ted Turner* (New York: Times Books, 1981), 248.

137 "Somebody forced to make a public": Williams, *Lead, Follow or Get Out of the Way*, 247.

138 "some little company": Hank Whittemore, *CNN: The Inside Story: How a Band of Mavericks Changed the Face of Television News* (Boston: Little, Brown, 1990), 30.

138 "Turner Be Sure": Jeff Denberg, "Visionary Ted Turner Sets Sails for New Challenge in Cable TV," *Atlanta Journal-Constitution*, February 24, 1980.

138 His query to the original WTBS: Trustee of WMBR Todd Glickman, interview with author, March 5, 2019.

140 An earlier potential buyer: Frederick Allen, " 'Cursed' Building Is Vacant Again," *Atlanta Constitution*, May 26, 1977.

141 From that moment on: Information about the activities at the Progressive Club can be found in Box 2, Files 4, 5, 6, in Mss 6, Jewish Progressive Club Papers, The Cuba Family Archives for Southern Jewish History, The William Breman Jewish Heritage Museum, Atlanta, Georgia.

142 It would take an equal sum: George Rodrigue, "Turner Gets Approval on Bonds," *Atlanta Constitution*, July 13, 1979.

143 or "snakes fucking": Reese Schonfeld, *Me and Ted Against the World: The Unauthorized Story of the Founding of CNN* (New York: Cliff Street, 2001), 56.

143 "I think I'd rather be broke": Whittemore, *CNN: The Inside Story*, 66.

143   especially after Sid Pike assured him: Sidney Pike, *We Changed the World: Memoirs of a CNN Satellite Pioneer* (St. Paul, MN: Paragon House, 2005), 96.

143   The space, as he imagined it: Reese Schonfeld, interview by Karen Herman, Television Academy Foundation, November 9 and 11, 2005, https://interviews.televisionacademy.com/interviews/reese-schonfeld.

143   "The idea was to demystify news": Reese Schonfeld, as quoted in unpublished Chris Chase manuscript, Tape 3, Side A, October 27, 1999.

144   what CNN absolutely could in no way: Keith Graham, "Cable News Is Ready for Action in 'Progressive' Home," *Atlanta Constitution*, May 22, 1980.

146   The trip got off to: Williams, *Lead, Follow or Get Out of the Way*, 194. Journalist Christian Williams crewed on *Tenacious* during Fastnet and writes in detail about the experience.

146   As the day dawned: *Ted Turner's Greatest Race*, ESPN Films: 30 for 30 Shorts, dir. Gary Jobson, June 3, 2015, http://www.espn.com/30for30/film?page=tedturnersgreatestrace. Also, "The Fastnet Yacht Race Tragedy of 1979," https://www.youtube.com/watch?v=GHTKMGOoYYw.

147   The first time he'd raced: Peter Ross Range, "*Playboy* Interview: Ted Turner," *Playboy*, August 1978.

147   The seasickness among the men: Williams, *Lead, Follow or Get Out of the Way*, 214.

147   Frantic, crackling radio calls: *Ted Turner's Greatest Race*.

148   Once during a competition: Ted Turner and Gary Jobson, *The Racing Edge* (New York: Rutledge Books, 1979), 40.

148   "It's no use crying": Christian Williams, "Disaster at Sea: 'My God . . . Not Like a Race," *Asbury Park Press*, August 17, 1979.

149   "The public is manipulated": Daniel Schorr, *Staying Tuned: A Life in Journalism* (New York: Washington Square Press, 2001), 304.

150   "I'm not going to say it": Williams, *Lead, Follow or Get Out of the Way*, 16.

151   There had to be a backup: Turner, interview by Michael Rosen,

"The Interviews: An Oral History of Television," June 12 and December 6, 1999; Turner, *Call Me Ted*, 79.

151 "We are searching the heavens": Whittemore, *CNN: The Inside Story*, 78.

152 "Keep watching the skies!": Tom Shales, "Cable TV's Bye-Bye Birdie," *Washington Post*, December 12, 1979.

152 Ted quipped to an audience: "CTAM Prologue to Western Cable Show," *Broadcasting*, December 17, 1979.

152 "Who the heck will watch": Edward Valenti and Barry Becher, *The Wisdom of Ginsu: Carve Yourself a Piece of the American Dream* (Franklin Lakes, NJ: Career Press, 2005), 124–26; Ed Valenti, telephone interview with author, July 8, 2019.

152 "I can't do that": Schonfeld, *Me and Ted Against the World*, 93.

152 eager for the latest: Archie T. Miller, *Birds in Hand: RCA and a Communications Revolution* (Manchester, NJ: ATM Consulting, 2011), 19.

153 He was sure they were: Schonfeld, *Me and Ted Against the World*, 115.

153 new National Christian Network: Miller, *Birds in Hand*, 23.

154 an uncontrollable rage: RCA attorney Carl Cangelosi, telephone interview with author, June 29, 2019.

154 "Rasputin Mad Monk" routine: Terry McGuirk, telephone interview with author, March 20, 2019.

154 have a hysterectomy: Andy Inglis, RCA Americom president, recounted this story in a taped interview, Box 27, Folder 24, Gerald Jay Goldberg Papers, Department of Special Collections, Charles E. Young Research Library, UCLA.

154 "I'm a small company": Schonfeld, *Me and Ted Against the World*, 115; RCA's Inglis and Cangelosi, Box 27, Folder 24, Gerald Jay Goldberg Papers, Department of Special Collections, Charles E. Young Research Library, UCLA.

155 As the station's fortunes: Ron Alridge, "WRET Plans to Pay Back Viewer Loans," *Charlotte Observer*, February 5, 1976.

155 a black woman hired: Former WRET employee Curtis O. Peters, telephone interview with author, March 11, 2019.

155 Westinghouse threatened to scrub: Vanessa Gallman, "Rights Deal Will Permit WRET Sale," *Charlotte Observer*, May 1, 1980.

155 Ted had secured: "FCC Clears Way for Turner Sale," *Broadcasting*, May 5, 1980.

155 Now, he lamented: Williams, *Lead, Follow or Get Out of the Way*, 257.

155 Reese felt as if he'd been: Schonfeld, *Me and Ted Against the World*, 58.

156 "You gotta let me sell this": Turner, *Call Me Ted*, 189.

156 It was a worthy chunk: Gallman, "Rights Deal Will Permit WRET Sale."

157 "Unless television changes a lot": "FCC Clears Way for Turner Sale," *Broadcasting*, May 5, 1980.

157 forty million viewers on thirty stations: "Still Another New News Group," *Broadcasting*, May 5, 1980.

159 "do that whole process": Jon Nordheimer, e-mail to author, April 17, 2018. This diatribe is not verbatim, but it mirrors what Ted said to Dan Schorr on the day he hired him.

159 "But in reality, aren't you": Schonfeld, *Me and Ted Against the World*, 127.

160 "Barring satellite problems": Richard Zoglin, "Turner Network Assured Space on RCA Satellite by Court Rule," *Atlanta Constitution*, March 5, 1980.

160 The *Independent Network News*: "John Corporon and the Independent Network News," Associated Press, June 15, 1980.

Chapter Eight: Reese's Pieces

162 In the winter of 1979: The description of how Jane Maxwell and Rick Brown arrived at CNN was generously shared by them during my visit to their home on May 22, 2018, and in subsequent telephone conversations and email exchanges.

163 "Bangladesh bazaar" style of news: Reese Schonfeld, as quoted in unpublished Chris Chase manuscript, chapter 24.

165 pungent aroma of vagrancy: Reese Schonfeld, *Me and Ted Against*

the World: The Unauthorized Story of the Founding of CNN (New York: Cliff Street, 2001), 84–85.

166 "I don't even know what you guys do": Hank Whittemore, *CNN: The Inside Story: How a Band of Mavericks Changed the Face of Television News* (Boston: Little, Brown, 1990), 85.

168 Back of the stall in the restroom: Email exchange with CNN original Rick Brown, June 11, 2019.

169 "the lifeblood of citizenship": David Colker, "Sam Zelman Dies at 100; Pioneer of Local TV News Helped Start CNN," *Los Angeles Times*, June 2, 2015.

170 because of a drinking problem: Drew Jubera, "Ed Turner, Commanding the Troops at CNN," *Atlanta Constitution*, February 26, 1991. Over the years, Ed Turner helped other staffers conquer their alcoholism.

170 would be a mitzvah: Schonfeld, *Me and Ted Against the World*, 73.

170 Deputy did not equal secretary: Whittemore, *CNN: The Inside Story*, 116.

171 "Any similarity between Alec": See the obituary printed on the Dartmouth Class of 1967 website: http://1967.dartmouth.org /s/1353/images/gid319/editor_documents/obituaries/nagle.pdf.

171 "Kavanau would say": Schonfeld, as quoted in unpublished Chris Chase manuscript, chapter 38.

172 "Go around with your Geiger": Reese Schonfeld, transcript of interview for unpublished manuscript co-authored with Chris Chase, Tape 14, November 15, 1999.

173 "A bank interest rate": Alec Nagle and Peter Vesey, *Inside CNN* manual, 1980, from the personal collection of CNN original Scott Leon.

173 "It soon became clear": Whittemore, *CNN: The Inside Story*, 100.

173 "Let's say a plane goes down": CNN original Randy Harber, telephone interview with author, July 27, 2018.

174 "How do you start": Whittemore, *CNN: The Inside Story*, 118.

174 Too many in the avalanche: John Baker, *Chicken Noodle News: A CNN Whodunit* (Pinole, CA: Dailey Swan Publishing, 2009), 23.

174 "An anchor is an anchor": Whittemore, *CNN: The Inside Story*, 220.

175 "Women are attracted to cable": Priscilla Tucker, "Cable: Boomtown for Women," New York *Daily News*, January 19, 1982.

175 "if red fire ants had bit him": Mary Alice Williams interview, September 24, 1992, Box 29, Folder 74, Gerald Jay Goldberg Papers (collection 1666), Department of Special Collections, Charles E. Young Research Library, UCLA.

177 His wife convinced him: Howard Kurtz, "Bernard Shaw, Under Siege," *Washington Post*, January 22, 1991.

177 "I don't view it": Carla Hall, "Turner's Talent Hunt: Cable News Raids the Broadcast Ranks," *Washington Post*, April 28, 1980.

177 "Cable Nepotism Network" Ted Turner, *Call Me Ted*, 186. Ted's son Teddy became a cameraman at the network and later worked on the Goodwill Games.

177 One early employee: Chris Turner, son of CNN original Ed Turner, hired as a copyboy in June 1980, wrote a tribute on Facebook, December 3, 2018, to the late copy editor Mark Dulmage, who once roared at him for being a "nepit."

177 "Dee," Ted shouted: Baker, *Chicken Noodle News*, 24–25.

178 "a mynah bird with an adenoid problem": Larry Wright, "On the Air Everywhere," *Atlanta Weekly*, July 6, 1980.

178 "Do you realize that": Baker, *Chicken Noodle News*, 31.

179 "the most exciting opportunity": Richard Zoglin, "The All-News Mastermind," *Atlanta Constitution*, August 13, 1979.

179 In the hopes of: Schonfeld, *Me and Ted Against the World*, 151.

180 dull, dull, dull: Ibid., 119.

180 He didn't want critics: Ibid., 122.

180 Sandi Freeman of WLS-TV's: Ibid., 122.

180 After watching her reel: Howard Polskin, "Nothing Stops Sandi Freeman for Long," *TV Guide*, June 25, 1983.

180 Unlike Bunnies at the nearby: Ibid.

180 Mostly, she appeared in: Angela Rocco DeCarlo, "It's All in a Day's Work for Sandi Freeman," *TV Week*, June 19, 1977.

181 As second banana: Cheryl Lavin, "Good Morning, Sandi Freeman!," *Chicago Tribune Magazine*, February 25, 1979.

181 "Her job was to look": Fred Rothenberg, "Paducah Sandi Freeman

Has Come Far Since Being Just TV Window Dressing," Associated Press, January 7, 1985.

181 NBC confirmed that: Diane Marimbas, "Today on TV," *The Daily Herald*, Arlington Heights, IL, May 21, 1979.

182 "Pleasant looking blonde": Jules Witcover, *Washington Evening Star*, January 23, 1981.

182 "It was very difficult to pick up": Marilynn Preston, "Freeman Airs Her Enthusiasm for Cable News Network Role," *Chicago Tribune*, May 29, 1980, section 2, 12.

183 The sink-or-swim school: Peter Arnett, *Live from the Battlefield: From Vietnam to Baghdad, 35 Years in the World's War Zones* (New York: Simon & Schuster, 1994), 327. Various people claim credit for inventing the title "video journalist."

184 "next rock star of Earth": Fred Cowgill, phone interview with author, January 7, 2019.

184 Like John Towriss: John Towriss, phone interview with author, January 8, 2019.

186 They loved and relied on her: Reese Schonfeld, interview by Karen Herman, "The Interviews: An Oral History of Television," Television Academy Foundation, November 9 and 11, 2005, https://interviews.televisionacademy.com/interviews/reese-schonfeld; Reese Schonfeld, interview by Brian Lamb, *C-SPAN Booknotes*, February 23, 2001.

186 Everyone, all together: Ron Taylor, "An Institution, a Bar That Chafes Under a Single Label," *Atlanta Constitution*, January 20, 1980.

187 "I just hope we can avoid": Larry Wright, "On the Air Everywhere," *Atlanta Weekly*, July 6, 1980.

187 In six weeks: Iain Johnstone, *The Man from Atlanta—Ted Turner*, BBC Television, 1982. Accessed online https://www.youtube.com/watch?v=q-uGoKQ7phs. Ted aired the special on WTBS in 1983.

188 Even more vexing: Gary Sherman, interview by Lela Cocoros, Cable Center Oral History Program, July 31, 2019, https://www.cablecenter.org/media-room/press-releases-2016/51-the-oral-history-project/s-listings.html.

188 "Make our newscasts so good": Nagle and Vesey, *Inside CNN*.

189   custom-designed microprocessor: Steve Miller, "NAB Brings Out Newsroom Computers," *Broadcast Management/Engineering*, July 1980.

190   "I don't know a thing about": Randy Schultz, "All-News TV First in Independent Programming," *Palm Beach Post*, May 18, 1980.

191   "that can't take a joke": Baker, *Chicken Noodle News*, 48.

191   "got off the ground": CNN original Tom Gaut, telephone interview with author, January 7, 2019.

191   became known as the "CNN Salute": CNN original Randy Harber, telephone interview with author, July 27, 2018.

191   "That's all we have": Baker, *Chicken Noodle News*, 45.

191   All the dazzled Reese would confess to: Schultz, "All-News TV First in Independent Programming."

192   "I've been hearing that some of you": Ted Kavanau, telephone interview with author, March 17, 2018.

Chapter Nine: Until the End of the World

195   A headline in the *Sarasota Herald-Tribune*: Jack Gurney, "America, Not America's Cup, on Turner's Mind," *Sarasota Herald-Tribune*, January 26, 1980. Also Jeff Denberg, "The World According to Turner," *Atlanta Constitution*, February 24, 1980.

195   "Ted Turner for President": John Ahern, "Committee Says Goodby, Ted," *Boston Globe*, August 26, 1980, 37.

195   That day's band, standing tall: Ted Turner, *Call Me Ted*, 189.

196   Microphone in hand: *CNN: Birth of a Network*, from the personal collection of David Bell.

197   Sensing that she needed something: Interview with Reese Schonfeld, Gerald Jay Goldberg Papers, UCLA, Los Angeles, CA.

198   Imagine, he had said: "News: Why We Do It the Way We Do," C-SPAN, February 8, 1985, https://www.c-span.org/video/?125307-1/news.

198   To Lamb, the arrival of CNN: Brian Lamb, interview by Jim Keller, The Cable Center, August 26, 1998, https://www.cablecenter.org/media-room/index.php?option=com_content&view=article&id=140.

199 "great step forward": Larry Wright, "On the Air Everywhere," *Atlanta Weekly*, July 6, 1980.

200 "an awful lot of people": Tony Schwartz, "The TV News, Starring Ted Turner," *New York Times*, May 25, 1980.

200 "Any establishment doesn't": Randy Schultz, "All-News TV First in Independent Programming," *Palm Beach Post*, May 18, 1980.

200 From this day forward: Reese Schonfeld, *Me and Ted Against the World: The Unauthorized Story of the Founding of CNN* (New York: Cliff Street, 2001), 156.

201 "We hope that the Cable News Network": *CNN: Birth of a Network.*

201 "Let us pray," said Reverend Borders: Phil Garner, "In Atlanta, the Dream and the Drive," *Washington Post*, June 2, 1980.

202 The husband-and-wife anchor team: Brandon Lisy, "CNN's First Anchors on the Birth of 24-Hour Cable News," *Bloomberg*, December 3, 2014, https://www.youtube.com/watch?v=NhY4FP6crHI.

203 "I'm so happy I could die": Christian Williams, *Lead, Follow or Get Out of the Way: The Story of Ted Turner* (New York: Times Books, 1981), 239.

204 "How do you like the way": Ibid., 242.

205 "You realize," he declared: John Baker, *Chicken Noodle News: A CNN Whodunit* (Pinole, CA: Dailey Swan Publishing, 2009), 50.

206 "Goodbye, Walter Cronkite": Jonathan Miller, "Ted Turner's 24-Hour Cable Network: New News Is Good News," *Washington Post*, July 6, 1980.

206 "A new day dawned at dusk": Tom Shales, "CNN Sets Sail," *Washington Post*, June 2, 1980.

206 "The question 'Will Turner pull it off?'": Dick Williams, "The Faces of Cable News Network," *TV Week, the Television Magazine of the Atlanta Journal and the Atlanta Constitution*, June 1, 1980.

Chapter Ten: Duck Hunting with Fidel

207 An internship at a local television: Reese Schonfeld, *Me and Ted Against the World: The Unauthorized Story of the Founding of CNN* (New York: Cliff Street, 2001), 110.

207 She found herself daydreaming: Hank Whittemore, *CNN: The Inside Story: How a Band of Mavericks Changed the Face of Television News* (Boston: Little, Brown, 1990), 189.

208 who some called "the dictator": Peter Arnett, *Live from the Battlefield: From Vietnam to Baghdad, 35 Years in the World's War Zones* (New York: Simon & Schuster, 1994), 325.

209 The bush-league errors: "This Was CNN," *Atlanta* magazine, June 2005.

210 But when a tape operator: CNN original Rick Brown, e-mail interview with author, August 8, 2018.

210 struggling to make payroll: Richard Zoglin, "Network in Red, but Deficit Shrinking," *Atlanta Constitution*, January 23, 1981.

210 "I SUPPORT CNN": Claudia Cohen, "Turner's Bold Scheme to Save TV Network," New York *Daily News*, January 7, 1981.

211 "Several $100 bills": Howard Rosenberg, "Cable News Network Survives First Year," *Los Angeles Times*, June 3, 1981.

211 "greedy bunch of jerks": Christian Williams, *Lead, Follow or Get Out of the Way: The Story of Ted Turner* (New York: Times Books, 1981), 12.

211 CBS President Bill Small: Harry F. Waters, "Ted Turner's Empire: A Sports King Tackles TV News," *Newsweek*, June 16, 1980.

212 "Someday, I'm going to own": Bill Leonard, *In the Storm of the Eye: A Lifetime at CBS* (New York: G. P. Putnam's Sons, 1987), 221–22.

212 "I'm concerned about the journalism": Richard Zoglin, "CNN Success a Bit Fuzzy," *Atlanta Constitution*, January 23, 1981.

213 his nickname at CBS had been "Jukebox": Reese Schonfeld, as quoted in unpublished Chris Chase manuscript, chapter 38.

215 economy into a tailspin: Shaw said this later in the broadcast as he bantered with Daniel Schorr.

215 he sat at Shaw's feet: Kenyon in "A Fond Farewell to Bernie Shaw," *Larry King Live*, March 8, 2001, http://transcripts.cnn.com/TRANSCRIPTS/0103/08/lkl.00.html.

217 "We don't have any information": Whittemore, *CNN: The Inside Story*, 191.

217 the suit would have to wait: Reese Schonfeld, *Me and Ted Against the World: The Unauthorized Story of the Founding of CNN* (New York: Cliff Street, 2001), 218; Seth Kantor, "Ted Turner Sues Reagan, Networks," *Atlanta Constitution*, May 12, 1981.

219 "While a worried nation sought information": Nicholas Von Hoffman, "Networks Bottom out on Top Story, *Ithaca Journal*, April 10, 1981.

222 ad-hoc mobile satellite unit: Schonfeld, *Me and Ted Against the World*, 159.

223 An early employee noted: John Baker, *Chicken Noodle News*, 175.

223 A viewer from Yukon Territory: Sidney Pike, *We Changed the World: Memoirs of a CNN Satellite Pioneer* (St. Paul, MN: Paragon House, 2005), 63.

223 Once, even, a letter: Former WTCG employee Bob Sieber, e-mail to author, May 27, 2019.

223 "I just wanted to let you know": Robert Goldberg and Gerald Jay Goldberg, *Citizen Turner: The Wild Rise of an American Tycoon* (New York: Harcourt, Brace, 1995), 283.

224 Conservative Ted had been taught: Ted Turner, *Call Me Ted*, 207.

224 "The Commies," Ed had told him: Ibid., 8.

224 Some said he'd established: Peter Ross Range, "*Playboy* Interview: Ted Turner," *Playboy*, August 1983.

224 He wished to visit every country: Christian Williams, *Lead, Follow or Get Out of the Way: The Story of Ted Turner* (New York: Times Books, 1981), 272.

224 in a remote location with Ed Sullivan: "Fidel Castro Interview on *Ed Sullivan*—1959," https://www.youtube.com/watch?v=kjpnf DwWd7Y.

225 "How would we be Communists?": Jerry Bowles, "A Thousand Sundays: *The Ed Sullivan Show*," *Windsor Star*, October 11, 1980.

225 "Only real public opinion": Gil Klein, "National Press Club in History: What Fidel Told the Club," The National Press Club,

August 21, 2018, https://www.press.org/news-multimedia/news /national-press-club-history-what-fidel-castro-told-club.

226 "The Other Woman": John Aldock, oral history interview by Judith S. Feigin, Historical Society of the District of Columbia Circuit, May 11, 2010, https://dcchs.org/sb_pdf/complete-oral -history-aldock.

226 In her suitcase: Gary Perilloux, "Liz Wickersham Recalls Visit with Fidel Castro, Who Turns 78 Today," *Port Arthur News*, August 13, 2004; Liz Wickersham, telephone interview with author, July 30, 2019.

226 tantalized by her swimwear: Perilloux, "Liz Wickersham Recalls Visit with Fidel Castro, Who Turns 78 Today." Castro asked Wickersham on her second visit to Cuba why she hadn't brought along the swimsuit.

227 Only a handful of outsiders: Juan Reinaldo Sánchez, *The Double Life of Fidel: My 17 Years as Personal Bodyguard to El Líder Máximo* (New York: St. Martin's Press, 2015), 12.

227 some of her film was: Liz Wickersham, e-mail to author, August 2, 2019.

227 bringing the blond beauty a steak: Perilloux, "Liz Wickersham Recalls Visit with Fidel Castro."

227 "What makes you think": Turner, *Call Me Ted*, 209.

228 Communists didn't have horns: Ted Turner, interview by Michael Rosen, Television Academy Foundation, June 12 and December 6, 1999, https://interviews.televisionacademy.com/interviews /ted-turner.

228 People at their core: Gary Smith, "What Makes Ted Run?," *Sports Illustrated*, June 22, 1986.

229 "He can say it in Spanish": "Meeting with Fidel Castro," raw footage, February 1982, DVD copy provided by Ted Turner.

229 "We receive an important": *New York Times* News Service, "Castro to Go Cable to Plug U.S. News," *Miami News*, February 22, 1982. Ted shocked his executives when he showed this promotion and wished to air it. He even had the tape recut after they refused to run it, but they still refused.

Chapter Eleven: The Little Girl in the Well, 1987

231 Kids didn't fall into wells every day: Ray Richmond, "How TV Covered Jessica's Ordeal," *Orange County Register*, May 21, 1989. Also based on my conversations with KMID's DeAnn Holcomb and CNN's Tony Clark.

233 This fortress-like building: Turner Director of Interior Planning Marty Harrell, e-mail to author, August 22, 2019.

233 For anyone who didn't know: The Turnstyles, "He Was Cable When Cable Wasn't Cool," https://www.youtube.com/watch?v=9KoJ12Wohcw.

235 "Within the next three years": Michael Schrage and David A. Vise, "Murdoch, Turner Launch Era of Global Television," *Washington Post*, August 31, 1986.

235 "I'm trying to get bigger": Stratford P. Sherman, "Back from the Brink," *Fortune*, July 7, 1986.

235 "My main concern is to be a benefit": Gary Smith, "What Makes Ted Run?," *Sports Illustrated*, July 23, 1986.

236 "lazy, drugs, homosexuals, sex maniacs": Nick Taylor, "American Hero as Media Mogul," *Atlanta* magazine, September 1982.

237 Would it have made a difference: Reese Schonfeld, *Me and Ted Against the World: The Unauthorized Story of the Founding of CNN* (New York: Cliff Street, 2001), 285–92.

238 *Crime Watch Tonight*: James Verini, "Reese's Pieces: Mr. Schonfeld, Forgotten Founder of CNN, Is a Man of Many Projects," *New York Observer*, January 29, 2001.

Afterword: June 2000

241 "bastard at the wedding": Reese Schonfeld, *Me and Ted Against the World: The Unauthorized Story of the Founding of CNN* (New York: Cliff Street, 2001), xiv, 362.

241 "CNN is my thing": Schonfeld, *Me and Ted Against the World*, 330.

241 He'd shopped: Schonfeld, *Me and Ted*, 342–47.

243 "I'm in spiritual and mental": Paul Farhi, "Nothing Left but

Billions: Put Out to Pasture, Ted Turner Looks for Grass That's Greener," *Washington Post*, April 4, 2001.

243 CNN isn't the agent of peace: Schonfeld, *Me and Ted Against the World*, 329–30.

244 Numbness then morphed into: Schonfeld, *Me and Ted Against the World*, 362.

244 Take it as long as you: Daniel Schorr, *Staying Tuned: A Life in Journalism* (New York: Washington Square Press, 2001), 319.

245 That tape of "Nearer My God": The CNN Doomsday video can be seen at https://jalopnik.com/this-is-the-video-cnn-will-play-when-the-world-ends-1677511538.

Bibliography

To tell the origin story of CNN required many thousands of hours of research and reading, as well as the generous assistance of many people. As this book was not authorized by CNN, I had no access to corporate archives, nor was there one single repository for information.

I am ever grateful to archivists and archives, librarians and libraries, and to individuals who archive or record their personal histories in some form or fashion, then make them publicly available. My research was also enriched by the work of authors who have tackled this story, or other aspects of broadcast history, from other perspectives.

Of particular help was the audio source materials associated with the Goldberg and Goldberg biography of Ted Turner, which they generously left to UCLA, and the Television Academy Foundation's "The Interviews."

Allen, Craig M. *News Is People: The Rise of Local TV News and the Fall of News from New York*. Ames: Iowa State University Press, 2001.

Arnett, Peter. *Live from the Battlefield: From Vietnam to Baghdad, 35 Years in the World's War Zones*. New York: Simon & Schuster, 1994.

Arroyo, Raymond. *Mother Anjelica: The Remarkable Story of a Nun, Her Nerve, and a Network of Miracles*. New York: Doubleday, 2005.

Baker, John. *Chicken Noodle News: A CNN Whodunit*. Pinole, CA: Dailey Swan Publishing, 2009.

Bliss, Edward, Jr. *Now the News: The Story of Broadcast Journalism*. New York: Columbia University Press, 1991.

Branch, Taylor, and Eugene M. Propper. *Labyrinth: The Sensational Story of International Intrigue in the Search for the Assassins of Orlando Letelier*. New York: Penguin Books, 1983.

Bravo, Estela. *Fidel: The Untold Story*. New York: First-Run Features, 2001.

Brown, Les. *Television: The Business Behind the Box*. New York: Harcourt, 1971.

Byron, Christopher. *The Fanciest Dive: What Happened When the Media Empire of Time-Life Leaped Without Looking into the Age of High-Tech*. New York: W. W. Norton, 1986.

Chambers, Stan. *KTLA's News at 10: 60 Years with Stan Chambers*. Santa Barbara, CA: Capra Press, 1994.

Chinoy, Mike. *Assignment: China—as the Doors Opened (1970s)*. 2014.

———. *China Live: People Power and the Television Revolution*. Lanham, MA: Rowman & Littlefield, 1997.

Courageous: Ted Turner and the 1977 America's Cup. NBC. June 17, 2017.

De Wolfe, Evelyn, and George Lewis. *Line of Sight: Klaus Landsberg—His Life and Vision*. Hollywood, CA: The Ashlin Press, 2016.

Enersen, Dick. *The Best Defense*. San Rafael, CA: Offshore Productions, 1977.

Farmer, Don, and Skip Caray. *Roomies: Tales from the Worlds of TV News and Sports*. Atlanta: Longstreet Press, 1994.

Fields, Robert Ashley. *Take Me Out to the Crowd: Ted Turner and the Atlanta Braves*. Huntsville, Alabama: The Strode Publishers, Inc., 1977.

Frank, Reuven. *Out of Thin Air: The Brief Wonderful Life of Network News*. New York: Simon & Schuster, 1991.

Frantzich, Stephen, and John Sullivan. *The C-SPAN Revolution*. Norman: University of Oklahoma Press, 1996.

Goldberg, Robert, and Gerald Jay Goldberg. *Citizen Turner: The Wild Rise of an American Tycoon*. New York: Harcourt, Brace, 1995.

Halberstam, David. *The Powers That Be.* New York: Alfred A. Knopf, 1979.

Hochfelder, David. *The Telegraph in America 1832–1920.* Baltimore: Johns Hopkins University Press, 2016.

Hope, Bob. *We Could've Finished Last Without You: An Irreverent Look at the Atlanta Braves, the Losingest Team in Baseball for the Past 25 Years.* Atlanta: Longstreet Press, 1991.

Jobson, Gary. *Gary Jobson: An American Sailing Story.* White River Junction, VT: Nomad Press, 2011.

Johnstone, Iain. *Ted Turner: The Man from Atlanta—Ted Turner.* BBC Television. 1982.

King, Larry. *My Remarkable Journey.* New York: Weinstein Books, 2009.

Klein, Edward. *Katie: The Real Story,* New York: Crown, 2007.

Leonard, Bill. *In the Storm of the Eye: A Lifetime at CBS.* New York: G. P. Putnam's Sons, 1987.

Lipscomb, James. "Enterprise—Ted Turner and the News War—1984." WGBH Productions. 1984. https://www.youtube.com/watch?v=la ZbCckAME8.

Mesce, Bill, Jr. *Inside the Rise of HBO: A Personal History of the Company That Transformed Television.* Jefferson, NC: McFarland & Company, 2015.

Mickelson, Sig. *The Decade That Shaped Television News: CBS in the 1950s.* Westport, CT: Praeger, 1998.

Miller, Archie T. *Birds in Hand: RCA and a Communications Revolution.* Manchester, NJ: ATM Consulting, 2011.

Miller, James Andrew, and Tom Shales. *Those Guys Have All the Fun: Inside the World of ESPN.* New York: Little, Brown and Company, 2011.

Munk, Nina. *Fools Rush In: Steve Case, Jerry Levin, and the Unmaking of AOL Time Warner.* New York: HarperCollins, 2004.

Parsons, Patrick R. *Blue Skies: A History of Cable Television.* Philadelphia: Temple University Press, 2008.

Pepe, Phil. *Talkin' Baseball: An Oral History of Baseball in the 1970s.* New York: Ballantine Books, 1998.

Pike, Sidney. *We Changed the World: Memoirs of a CNN Satellite Pioneer.* St. Paul, MN: Paragon House, 2005.

Ponce de Leon, Charles L. *That's the Way It Is: A History of Television News in America.* Chicago: University of Chicago Press, 2011.

Rasmussen, Bill. *Sports Junkies Rejoice! The Birth of ESPN:* Q. V. Pub, 1983.

Sánchez, Juan Reinaldo. *The Double Life of Fidel Castro: My 17 Years as Personal Bodyguard to El Líder Máximo.* New York: St. Martin's Press, 2015.

Schechter, Danny. *The More You Watch, The Less You Know: News Wars, (Sub)merged Hopes, Media Adventures.* New York: Seven Stories Press, 1997.

Schonfeld, Reese. *Me and Ted Against the World: The Unauthorized Story of the Founding of CNN.* New York: Cliff Street, 2001.

Schorr, Daniel. *Clearing the Air.* Boston: Houghton Mifflin, 1977.

———. *Staying Tuned: A Life in Journalism.* New York: Washington Square Press, 2001.

Sherman, Gabriel. *The Loudest Voice in the Room: How the Brilliant, Bombastic Roger Ailes Built Fox News—and Divided a Country.* New York: Random House, 2014.

Smith, Ralph Lee. *The Wired Nation: Cable TV, the Electronic Communications Highway.* New York: Harper, 1972.

Southwick, Thomas. *Distant Signals: How Cable TV Changed the World of Telecommunications.* Overland Park, KS: Primedia, 1998.

Tartell, Genie, and Ted Kavanau. *Get Fit in Bed: Tone Your Body and Calm Your Mind from the Comfort of Your Bed.* Williamsville, VT: Echo Point Books, 2011.

Tator, Joel. *Los Angeles Television.* Charleston, SC: Arcadia Publishing, 2014.

Turner, Ted, with Bill Burke. *Call Me Ted.* New York: Grand Central Publishing, 2008.

Turner, Ted, and Gary Jobson. *The Racing Edge.* New York: Simon & Schuster, 1979.

Valenti, Edward, and Barry Becher. *The Wisdom of Ginsu: Carve Yourself a Piece of the American Dream.* Franklin Lakes, NJ: Career Press, 2005.

Vaughan, Roger. *The Grand Gesture: Ted Turner, Mariner and the America's Cup.* Boston: Little, Brown and Company, 1975.

———. *Ted Turner: The Man Behind the Mouth*. Boston: Sail Books, 1978.

Weinraub, Judith. Interview with Reese Schonfeld. "Voices from the Food Revolution: People Who Changed the Way Americans Eat." August 18, 2009. http://dlib.nyu.edu/beard/content/reese-schonfeld.

Weller, Sheila. *The News Sorority: Diane Sawyer, Katie Couric, Christiane Amanpour—and the (Ongoing, Imperfect, Complicated) Triumph of Women in TV News*. New York: Penguin Press, 2014.

Westin, Av. *Newswatch: How TV Decides the News*. New York: Simon & Schuster, 1982.

Wheeler, Tom. *Mr. Lincoln's T-Mails: How Abraham Lincoln Used the Telegraph to Win the Civil War*. New York: Collins, 2006.

Whittemore, Hank. *CNN: The Inside Story: How a Band of Mavericks Changed the Face of Television News*. Boston: Little, Brown and Co., 1990.

Wiener, Robert. *Live from Baghdad: Gathering News at Ground Zero*. New York: Doubleday, 1992.

Wilkinson, Todd, and Ted Turner. *Last Stand: Ted Turner's Quest to Save a Troubled Planet*. Guilford, CT: Lyons Press, 2013.

Williams, Christian. *Lead, Follow or Get Out of the Way: The Story of Ted Turner*. New York: Times Books, 1981.

Archives and Research Libraries

Cotton Alston photographs, VIS 247, Kenan Research Center at the Atlanta History Center

David Bell, Personal Archive Collection

Edwin Diamond Political Audiovisual Collection and Steven H. Scheuer Television History Interviews, Special Collections Research Center, Syracuse University Libraries, Syracuse, NY

Gerald Jay Goldberg papers (Collection 1666). Department of Special Collections, Charles E. Young Research Library, UCLA

Bruce Herschensohn papers, Collection no. 0006, Special Collections and University Archives, University Libraries, Pepperdine University, Malibu, CA

Jewish Progressive Club Papers, the Cuba Family Archives for Southern

Jewish History, the William Breman Jewish Heritage Museum, Atlanta, GA

Sig Mickelson Oral History, San Diego State University, https://library.sdsu .edu/scua/raising-our-voices/sdsu-history/faculty/sig-mickelson

Sid Pike Collection, University of Georgia, Walter J. Brown Media Archives and Peabody Award Collection, Athens, GA

Sid Pike Papers, ms 3767. Hargrett Rare Book and Manuscript Library, the University of Georgia Libraries

Harry Reasoner papers, Dolph Briscoe Center for American History, the University of Texas at Austin

Daniel Schorr Papers. Library of Congress, Washington, D.C.

The Sixth Floor Museum at Dealey Plaza, Dallas, Texas

Ted Turner Personal Archives

George Watson Papers, 1955–2017, Dolph Briscoe Center for American History, the University of Texas at Austin

Additional Libraries That Offered Invaluable Assistance

Atlanta-Fulton Public Library

Americanradiohistory.com

Brown University Archives, Providence, RI

The Cable Center, Denver, CO

Los Angeles Public Library

New York Public Library

The Paley Center, New York and Beverly Hills

Ronald Reagan Presidential Library, Simi Valley, CA

Sarasota County Libraries

Television Academy Foundation, North Hollywood, CA/*The Interviews: An Oral History of Television*

Vanderbilt Television News Archive, Nashville, TN

Robert W. Woodruff Library, Emory University, Druid Hills, GA

Congressional Appearances Involving Channel 17 and Ted Turner

Cable Television Regulation Oversight. 94th Congress, 1st session, House of Representatives. July 20, 1976. Ted Turner's testimony begins at https://babel.hathitrust.org/cgi/pt?id=uiug.30112104109845; view=1up;seq=468.

Amendments to the Communications Act of 1934, part 3. 96th Congress. Senate. Committee on Commerce, Science. May 10, 11, and 16 and June 5–7, 1979. Ted Turner's testimony begins at https://babel .hathitrust.org/cgi/pt?id=uc1.b5176504;view=1up;seq=1345.

Subscription Television. 90th Congress, 1st session. October 16, 1967. Statement of W. Robert McKinsey, president of WJRJ-TV, Atlanta at https://babel.hathitrust.org/cgi/pt?id=uc1.$b654511;view=1up; seq=664.

Acknowledgments

I've often wondered what direction my life would have taken had I not run into my Midwood High School classmate Peter Brackman on the Newkirk Plaza subway platform on a sweltering summer day in 1981.

I was seventeen, on my first summer home from college, en route to a video store near the United Nations, where I was working as a clerk. The future wasn't my concern as much as helping defray my enormous tuition bill.

Peter was in a three-piece suit on his way to 1 World Trade Center, where he had a summer internship in finance. Each day, he couldn't help but pass the fishbowl newsroom of the just-over-a-year-old CNN. Brooklyn wasn't yet wired for cable, and though my father brought home a stack of newspapers every night, I'm not sure I was aware of its existence.

Peter glowed about the ability to peer into the inner workings of a television operation and recalled my involvement in the school newspaper. Print was where I wanted to be, but—already in the early eighties, even before the information cataclysm caused by the World Wide Web—newspapers were said to be dying.

When I got to the store, I furtively used the phone to dial directory assistance in pursuit of CNN's phone number. (A decided no-no, since that incurred an extra charge.) Then I snuck in another call. A gruff man answered. "Newsroom. Roth."

Assignment desk editor Richard Roth, today one of the last remaining CNN originals, told me to report for duty the next day. There was no formal internship program. He just put this warm body to work.

After three summers in the CNN New York and D.C. bureaus, there was one logical place to hit up for a real job when I graduated from Hampshire College in the winter of 1984. My last supervisor, the late and great writer and media critic Chris Chase, contacted Burt Reinhardt on my behalf and arranged for me to head to Atlanta to work for CNN Headline News. I booked a one-way plane ticket, and off I was to "Tara on Techwood." (The dark personal reason why I moved on from Atlanta after several years involves an incident I've discussed briefly in my first book, *Radio Shangri-La*.)

Over the years since, many of the jobs I've had trace back to that very first one, which offered this young woman from humble means incredible connections and experiences. In particular, I would like to thank former CNN supervising producer Mark Benerofe for introducing me to the Internet at a seminal time for the new medium, and long ago nurturing my goal to become a writer of something other than broadcast copy. Thanks to him, I was able to make the transition and to become immersed in another thrilling period in media history, the run-up of the dot-com era.

My dear friend Sid Leader, whom I met in the CNN Headline News newsroom on practically the first day I arrived in Atlanta, suggested I write this book after he read my last one, about the founding of another iconic American company (McDonald's) run by a larger-than-life character (Ray Kroc) almost as intriguing as Ted Turner. After surveying what had previously been written about the launch of CNN, I decided the time was right to tell the CNN origin story. I had no idea how complex my self-assigned task would be.

I'm grateful for the people who worked at channel 17, as well as the CNN originals, who generously gave their time, dug deep into their memory banks, and sleuthed through storage in search of documents to assist me.

In particular, I can never adequately thank those who I leaned on the most: Reese Schonfeld, Bill Tush, Ted Kavanau, Jane Maxwell and Rick Brown (who also invited this complete stranger to stay as a guest in their home), Bob Sieber, Mike Boettcher, Melanie Goux (whose late husband, Jay Antzakas, had the foresight to digitize and post many channel 17 videos), Jim Schoonmaker, Tom Gaut, Glen Olsheim, Scott Leon, and David Bell, self-appointed keeper of a formidable and indispensable private archive. CNN original Jeff Jeffares stepped forward with incredible photographs he took that very first day, which are being published here for the very first time.

Among the many, many others who have helped:

Danielle Amos, whose late husband, Paul, was a CNN original and mentor (and later my employer at a variety of post-CNN ventures). Cotten Alston. Gary Arlen. Bailey Barash. Bob Cramer. Myron Kandel. Renée Edelman. Judy Milestone. Gail Evans.

Randy Harber; Ken England; Verna Gates; Ken Gwinner; Dini Diskin and Bill Zimmerman; Lois Walker and Dave Hart; Peter Fox; Dave Rust; Jon Nordheimer; Sid Topol; Mark Goldsmith; Bob Berkowitz; Mark Walton; Peter Ross Range; Nick Taylor; Gerry Levin; J. C. Burns; Jiggs McDonald; Larry Sprinkle; Curtis O. Peters; Ed Valenti; Tony Clark; Greg Gunn; Marty Harrell; DeAnn Holcomb; Bob Hope; Steve Korn; Will Sanders; Denise LeClair Cobb; Derwin Johnson; Kymberleigh Richards; Roger Strauss; John Towriss; Diane Durham; Mary Alice Williams; Sandra Bevins; Terry McGuirk; Merrill Brown; Bill Lance; Glenn Hubbard; Arthur Sando; Tom Wheeler; Gerry Goldberg; Bev Haut; Brian Kenny of the Cable Center; Peter Kiley at C-SPAN; Andrew Schwartzman; Gerry Harrington; Rip Pauley; Adam Clayton Powell III; Liz Wickersham; Carl Cangelosi; John Corporon; Rick Davis; Dick Enerson; Toni Shifalo; Howard Polskin; Ron Kirk; Greg Daugherty; Rafael Ortiz-Guzman; Faye DeHoff; Kenny Reff; John Hillis; Tex Walters; Debbie Masterson and her colleagues in Ted Turner's office. Thanks, too, to all who patiently responded to my queries on social media.

And then there was the eleventh-hour surprise that lead me to veteran CNN cameraman Bill Langley, a confluence of events courtesy of performance art on display at Track 16 in DTLA, an elevator ride, Sally Granieri, and Ted (Habte-Gabr), to whom this book is dedicated.

In addition to my agent and friend Dan Conaway and his assistant, Lauren Carsley, I am deeply grateful to Genevieve Gagne-Hawes, who helped us get the proposal for this book to the stage where it convinced Jamison Stoltz at Abrams Press that the project had merit. Thanks to the entire team there for their enthusiastic support—including assistant Sarah Robbins, senior publicist Maya Bradford, marketing manager Kim Lew, social media and digital marketing manager Mamie Van Langen and senior managing editor Lisa Silverman. Andrea Monagle painstakingly copyedited this book, though any errors remaining are my own. A special thanks, too, to Jane Cavolina, the footnote goddess.

Lucy Stille's enthusiasm in bringing this to the attention of Hollywood, in particular to Danny Strong and Blumhouse Productions, has been the super-fudge buttercream icing on the cake.

I am fortunate to have an army of wonderful friends and family who, as always, offered tremendous encouragement and support, even when it hasn't been entirely clear what I've been up to.

Aside from brief but lovely stints at the far-flung homes of dear and generous friends Barbara Rybka, Matthew Mirapaul, Katherine Weaver, and Susan Stern, this book was written largely in the high-rise on Bunker Hill in downtown Los Angeles that I've called home for too many years now (in between laps in the swimming pool and only temporarily jolted by two earthquakes that shook the building as I was working) as well as at my beloved mother Jane's home in Florida, where the memory of my father, Vincent, who would have loved seeing this project reach fruition, looms large.

Index

Aaron, Hank
  Atlanta Braves and, 85, 86, 88, 90, 90, 103, 156
  Carter, Jimmy, and, 103
  legacy, 85
  Turner, Ted, and, 86, 88, 90, 90, 156
ABC, 151, 241
  affiliates, 18, 173
  programming on, 238, 239
  Telstar and, 45–46
ABC News
  early years, 40–41
  Kennedy, John, assassination and, 50
  with Reagan, Ronald, shooting of, 215–17
  Shaw and, 176–77
  Walters and, 72
  Westinghouse and, 220
Abdullah the Butcher, 196
Abend, Martin, 112, 116
Abrams, Roz, 176
Academy Award Theater (television show), 68
Academy of Television Arts and Sciences, 157
The Adventures of Ozzie and Harriet (television show), 38
advertisements
  CNN, 207, 207
  commercials, 8, 64, 66–68, 152
  revenue, 29, 50, 152
  sponsors, 119, 121, 152
  WTCG, 61, 61, 63, 66–68, 152

affiliates, network, 18, 65, 155, 173
AFL-CIO, 213
African Americans
  civil rights movement and, 85
  racism against, 116, 155, 156, 205
  women newscasters, 155, 176, 204, 204
Agnew, Spiro, 70
Ailes, Roger, 56–57
Akron Beacon-Journal (newspaper), 47
Albuquerque Journal (newspaper), 10–11
Alexander the Great
  Castro and, 226
  Hitler and, 89
  Turner, Ted, and, 23, 28, 89, 226
Ali, Muhammad, 90
All-Channel Receiver Bill, 55
American Eagle, 146
American Society of News Editors, 225
America Online (AOL), 2, 243
America's Cup, 122, 126, 142
  defending, 107–8
  failed bid for, 92, 98
  history of, 98–99
  popularity of, 106
  preliminary trials, 194–95
Amos, Paul, 191
Anderson, John, 209–10
Andersson, Donald, 101, 120
Andrea Doria, SS, 41
The Andy Griffith Show (television show), 65
Annan, Kofi, 243

Anti-Defamation League, 104
anti-Semitism, 6, 18, 23, 104, 118, 164
AOL. *See* America Online
AP. *See* Associated Press
arms race, 228, 235
Arnett, Peter, 241, 242
Associated Press (AP), 49, 162–63, 194
Association of Independent Television
    Stations, 110
astrologers, 131
Atlanta Braves
    Aaron and, 85, 86, 88, 90, 90, 103, 156
    club history, 85, 86
    critics and, 94–95
    dedication to, 86–87
    Hope and, 86–90, 95–97, 99–100, 102
    Lucas and, 99, 129–30, 156
    pep rally, 87–89
    promotional tour, 89–91, 102
    with promotions for fans, 89–90, 95
    publicity stunts with, 91, 97, 98
    purchase of, 85–87
    revenue, 210
    with scoreboard technology, 93
    stats, 86, 88, 96, 104–5, 105
    support for, 85–86, 98
    suspension from, 98–101, 105–8
    team members, 88, 91–96, 98, 102–3
    team staff, 93–94
    wages for, 92, 96
    World Series and, 86, 87, 103
    WTCG and, 87
Atlanta Chamber of Commerce, 89
Atlanta Constitution (newspaper), 19, 61, 61,
    94, 206
Atlanta Flames, 65, 98
Atlanta Hawks, 65, 101–2
Atlanta Journal (newspaper), 94
Atlas, Charles, 195, 228
AT&T, 43, 84
    breakup of, 245
    competition from, 57
    with networks paying transmission bills,
        41, 55, 56
    television production and, 7
awards
    sailing, 26, 26, 195
    of Turner, Ted, 1–4

back-timing, 189
Baird, Bill, 78
Baker, Cissy, 207, 213, 218
Baker, Howard, 214, 218, 219
Baker, John, 184–85, 188, 191

Baker, Lisa, 19
Bakker, Jim, 66
Bakker, Tammy Faye, 66
Baltimore Sun (newspaper), 11
Barker, Bob, 13
Barrett, Rona, 114
Bartholomay, Bill, 86
basketball, 65, 101–2
Basys Newsfury computer system, 189
Bathtubs Are Coming, The (industrial
    musical), 181
Batista, Fulgencio, 224, 225
Bauman, Steve, 113–14
BBC. *See* British Broadcasting Corporation
beg-a-thon, at WRET, 64–65, 79, 155
Bell, Jack, 49
Biden, Joe, 232
Bigfoot, 114
Big Mo, 42
Bisher, Furman, 89
"blame game drill-down," 208
Boettcher, Mike, 221–23, 225–26, 243
Bogart, Humphrey, 197
bomb threat, 67
Borders, William, 199, 201–2
boxing, 65
Braden, Tom, 237
Brady, Jim, 216, 218
The Bride Wore Boots (television show), 66
Brinkley, David, 47
Bristol, Dave, 104
Bristol-Myers, 152
British Broadcasting Corporation (BBC),
    44, 153
Broadcasting (trade magazine), 184
Brothers, Joyce, 131, 199
Brown, James, 66
Brown, Jimmy, 28, 156
Brown, Rick, 162–69, 177, 242
Brown University, 3, 23
Buchanan, Pat, 237
Bumble Bee Seafoods, 119

Cable Music Channel (CMC), 234
Cable News Network. *See* CNN
cable operators, FCC decision on, 81
Cable-Satellite Public Affairs Network. *See*
    C-SPAN
cable television
    growth of, 232
    TNT, 233
cable television news, growth of, 232
Cain, Bob, 214–15
Camel, 8

Campbell, Glen, 94
Captain Outrageous, 128, 134, 142, 165,
    225–26, 235. *See also* Turner, Ted
Caray, Skip, 101
Carnegie, Andrew, 157
Carnegie, Dale, 237
Carter, Amy, 102
Carter, Billy, 102, 103
Carter, Jimmy, 78
    Aaron and, 103
    on CNN, 243
    interview, 206
    Jordan and, 205
    as president-elect, 102–3
    presidential debates and, 209–10
Carter, Lillian, 103
Carter, Rosalynn, 102
Castro, Fidel
    Alexander the Great and, 226
    CIA and, 225
    on CNN, 229–30
    interview with, 224–25, 234
    Reagan, Ronald, and, 222, 225
    Turner, Ted, and, 222–30
CATV. *See* Community Antenna Television
CBS, 151
    affiliates, 17–18
    failed takeover of, 233
    Morning Show, 78
    programming on, 238, 239
    Telstar and, 45–46
CBS News
    with CNN purchase, 211–12
    Cronkite and, 46, 50–51, 70, 70, 131
    early years, 9, 40–41
    with Elizabeth II, coronation of, 44
    with expanded hours, 169
    Kennedy, John, assassination and, 53
    Murrow and, 117–18, 119
    Rather and, 126–27, 131, 218
    Schonfeld, Pat, at, 164
    Schorr and, 117–20, 134
CBS radio, 117
Central Intelligence Agency (CIA)
    Castro and, 225
    with illegal activities, 119
Chambers, Stan, 9–10, 11
Chaney, Darrel, 92
Channel 17. *See* WTCG
CHAN-TV, Vancouver, 147, 148
Charlemagne (lion puppet), 78
Charlotte Coalition, 155
Chayefsky, Paddy, 131
Chicago Cubs, 47

Christian Science Monitor (newspaper), 117
CIA. *See* Central Intelligence Agency
Cincinnati Reds, 98
civil rights movement, 85
Clark, Tony, 236, 238–39
Clarke, Arthur C., 43, 45
Clearing the Air (Schorr), 120
CMC. *See* Cable Music Channel
CNN (Cable News Network)
    advertisements, 207, 207
    beginnings, 124–35
    Brown, Rick, and, 162–69, 177, 242
    Carter, Jimmy, on, 243
    Castro on, 229–30
    CBS News with purchase of, 211–12
    control room, 203, 203
    crew, 182–87
    critics of, 137–38, 200–201, 212
    early years, 140–61
    entry-level jobs and, 183–86
    farm report, 193–94
    finances, 155
    Freeman and, 180–82, 244
    gardens at, 193–94, 220
    Grass Valley 1600 switcher with, 145,
        145
    growth of, 235
    headquarters, 233–34
    with hires, new, 162–88, 207, 221–22
    with *Inside CNN* manual, 188–89
    Kavanau and, 165, 168, 170–74, 183–84,
        186–87, 191–94, 203, 208, 220–21
    launch of, 193–206, 196
    Maxwell and, 162–71, 177, 205, 220
    Nagle and, 171–75, 178, 190, 191, 203,
        205, 220–21
    newscasters and, 174–78
    newsroom design, 143–46, 144, 145
    on-air talent, 174–82
    power shift at, 3, 233
    with presidential debates, 209–10
    profits, 232
    programming, 137, 160, 179, 208, 228
    Progressive Club and, 140–42, 141, 165,
        189, 193, 245
    ratings, 239
    with Reagan, Ronald, shooting of,
        213–19
    retyping pool and, 192
    revenue, 210–11, 242
    salutes, 191, 209
    satellites, 193, 193, 202, 209, 222
    Schonfeld, Pat, and, 164, 167, 177, 179,
        186, 199, 243, 245

CNN (cont.)
Schonfeld, "Reese," and, 124–27, 129–35, 137, 144, 148, 152–53, 155, 157, 159, 162–67, 170–72, 174–80, 183, 186–87, 191, 194, 197–99, 200–201, 204, 204, 208–10, 212, 217, 222, 225
Schorr, Daniel, and, 137–38, 148–50, 170, 176, 176, 210, 213, 218, 225
staff turnover at, 212, 220
Take Two, 228–29
twentieth-anniversary party, 241–43, 245
twofer hiring at, 177
video journalists and, 183, 186–88, 190, 190, 197
viewer numbers, 1, 138, 160, 208–9, 223, 232
WTBS and, 196, 210
CNN2, 220
CNN College, 187–88, 190, 190
CNN: The Birth of a Network, 196
Coast Guard, US, 24, 25, 76
Cold War, 234
Cole, Nat King, 198
Colombo, Joe, 115
color television, 55
commercials. See also advertisements
with direct marketing business, 66–68, 152
playback, 188
sponsors, 8, 64
Community Antenna Television (CATV), 80
Concepcion, Dave, 88
Congress, U.S., 209
Coors, Joseph, 58, 120, 125
on Turner, Ted, 60
TVN and, 56–57, 109, 162
Courageous, 98–99, 107–8, 189
Couric, Katie, 228
Cowgill, Fred, 183–84
Crane, Bob, 55
Crawford, Joan, 19
Crime Watch Tonight (television show), 238
Cronkite, Walter
with Charlemagne, 78
comparisons to, 76, 136, 206
influence of, 74
Kennedy, John, assassination and, 50–51
sailing and, 126, 131
on Telstar, 46
as trusted source, 70, 70

Crossfire (current events debate show), 237
C-SPAN (Cable-Satellite Public Affairs Network)
birth of, 150–51, 198
Gore and, 199
Cuba. See Castro, Fidel
Cuban Missile Crisis, 170, 225
Cuban refugees (Marielitos), 222
Cugat, Xavier, 142
Curle, Chris, 228
Czechoslovakia, 11

Dallas (television show), 208
Dallas News (newspaper), 10
Dead Ernest, 64
Deep Valley (television show), 66
Dimbleby, Richard, 46
direct marketing business, commercials with, 66–68, 152
Dixon, Jeane, 131
Donahue, Dan, 86
Donahue, Phil, 179
Donnelly, William, 200
Dorsey, Tommy, 142
Douglas, Mike, 237
Dr. Ehrlich's Magic Bullet (television show), 66
Dr. Feelgood, 67
DuMont network, 55
Dunphy, Jerry, 169

earth stations
FCC and, 100
installation of, 87, 135
limitations, 87, 153–54
primed and ready, 97
role of, 84, 105–6
Scientific Atlanta with, 58, 83
Edison, Thomas, 157
E-gor's Chamber of TV Horror Show Hosts, 64
Eisenhower, Dwight D., 49–50
Elizabeth II (Queen of England), 44–45
Ellerbee, Linda, 180
entry-level jobs
CNN and, 183–86
wages, 184
Epstein, Harry, 141
ESPN, 150
Evans, Rowland, 131

Fairbanks, Mary, 157
"family concept," 72

fans
   Atlanta Braves promotions for, 89–90, 95
   Tush with mail from, 81–82
Farmer, Don, 228
farm report, CNN, 193–94
Farnsworth, Philo T., 7
Fastnet
   competitors, 147
   surviving, 146–50, 152
   "Yachtsman of the Year" at, 194–95
Federal Bureau of Investigation (FBI)
   with illegal activities, 119
   surveillance, 103–4
Federal Communications Commission
   (FCC)
   with cable operators, decision on, 81
   with earth stations, 100
   HBO and, 58
   lobbyists and, 122
   news and, 79
   UHF channels and, 18, 55
   WRET and, 155
Feeney, Chub, 96
First Amendment, 115, 217–18
Fiscus, Kathy, 5–6, 8, 9–11
FitzGerald, Edward, 23
Flair, Ric "Nature Boy," 142
Fonda, Jane, 2, 3, 234, 243
Ford, Gerald, 216
Forum of Public Affairs at Harvard
   University, 1–4
Fox News, 242
Freeman, Sandi
   CNN and, 180–82, 244
   firing of, 237
   rehiring of, 238
The Freeman Report, 182
Friday Night Frights (television show), 64
Friendly, Fred, 72
Fromme, Squeaky, 110
Frost, David, 180
Future Shock (television show), 66

Gameboree, Eddie Glennon, 88
Gannett, 234
gardens, at CNN, 193–94, 220
Garroway, Dave, 44
Gaut, Tom, 208
General Electric (GE), 234
General Outdoor, 27
George Washington Hospital, 214
Georgia Championship Wrestling (television
   show), 65, 110

Ginsu Knife, 66, 152
Gold Diggers of 1933 (television show), 66
Goldsmith Career Award for Excellence in
   Journalism, 1
Goldwater, Barry, 30
Gone with the Wind (film), 30, 233
Goodwill Games, 234
Gore, Albert, 199
Grass Valley 1600 switcher, 145, *145*
Greig, Joan, 208
Gulf War, 241
Gunn, Greg, 67

ham radio operators, 90
Handy-Looky, 71
Harp, Clyde, 10
Hart, Gary, 232
Hart, Lois, 177, 203–4, 206
Harvard University, 1–4, 23, 37
HBO. *See* Home Box Office
Headline News, 234, 242
Hearst, Patty, 71, 110
Heater, Gabriel, 36
Hecht, Ben, 115
Helfrich, Bunky, 142, 146, 147–48, 194, 232
Helms, Jesse, 234
Hillis, John, 173
Hitler, Adolf, 99, 235
   Alexander the Great and, 89
   at Olympic Games (1936), 6–7
   rise of, 36
   Turner, Ted, and, 24, 33, 89, 102, 104,
     224
hockey, 65, 98
Hogan, Gerry, 138–39
Hogan's Heroes (television show), 66, 72
Holliman, John
   with CNN farm report, 193–94
   Gulf War and, 241
Home Box Office (HBO), 242
   critics of, 84
   early years, 2, 82, 121, 123
   FCC and, 58
   growth of, 124, 128, 153
home videotape recorder, 122
The Honeymooners (television show), 38
Hope, Bob
   Atlanta Braves and, 86–90, 95–97,
     99–100, 102
   on club stats, 86
   with promotions for fans, 89–90, 95
   Turner, Ted, and, 89–90, 95, 99–100,
     102

Horner, Bob, 129
Howitt, Robert, 200
How to Win Friends and Influence People
    (Carnegie), 237
Hrabosky, Al, 96
Hudspeth, Ron, 94
Hughes, Howard, 178
Humphrey, Robinson, 31
Huntley-Brinkley Report, The, 170
Hyland, Frank, 94

I Love Lucy (television show), 38, 66, 110,
    119, 138, 152, 188
Independent Network News (television show),
    157, 160–61
Independent Television News Association
    (ITNA)
    with *Independent Network News*, 157,
        160–61
    member stations, 110, 143
    Schonfeld, "Reese," and, 109–11, 117,
        120, 129, 130–32, 142–43, 146,
        160–61, 162
"industrial music" circuit, 180–81
Inside CNN manual, 188–89
Internet news, 242
Israel Day parade, 206
ITNA. *See* Independent Television News
    Association
Ivicek, John, 181
Ivy Five, 181

Jackson, Maynard, 98
Japan, 53, 71, 235
Jews, 111, 125, 143
    anti-Semitism and, 6, 18, 23, 104, 118,
        164
    Orthodox, 113–14
    at Progressive Club, 140, 141, 232
    Russian, 140
    WNEW and "The Jew Crew," 112–13
    in World War II, 36
J. Fred Muggs, 44, 78
Jobson, Gary, 106
Johnson, Lyndon, 29
Johnson, Tom, 243
Jordan, Vernon, 205
Jorgensen, Bill, 113, 116

Kaltenborn, H. V., 36
Kandel, Myron, 131
Kapstein, Jerry, 104, 125
Kaufman, Monica, 72

Kavanau, Ted "Mad Dog"
    career, 111–17, 120, 131, 143
    CNN₂ and, 220
    CNN and, 165, 168, 170–74, 183–84,
        186–87, 191–94, 203, 208, 220–21
    at CNN launch, 193–94, 203
    gardens at CNN and, 193
    with "The Jew Crew," 112–13
    Nagle and, 171–74, 203, 220–21
    with news production, philosophy on, 173
    Reinhardt and, 191–92
    reputation, 111, 113
    Schonfeld, "Reese," and, 238
    video journalists and, 183–84, 186
    WNEW Channel 5 and, 111–16, 157
    work ethic, 115, 172
Kennedy, Caroline, 53
Kennedy, Joan, 182
Kennedy, John F., 47–53, 170, 206, 215, 217
Kennedy, Ted, 180, 181–82
Kenyon, Sandy, 215, 218–19
Kerkorian, Kirk, 233
Kessler, Edward, 202
Killer Khan, 196
King, Alan, 55
King, Larry, 244
Kirk, Ron, 75–76
Kitchell, Jim, 169–70, 183, 212
Klensch, Elsa, 131
KMID, 231
Knott, Thomas Joseph, 185–86
KNXT, 71
Koppel, Ted, 1
Kritsick, Steve, 131
Kroc, Ray, 91
Krugerrands, 211
KTLA, 6, 8, 11
KTVU, 110
KTXL, 110
Kubasik, Ben, 157, 158
Kuhn, Bowie, 98, 99, 101, 104

Lamb, Brian, 198–99
Landsberg, Evelyn, 7–8
Landsberg, Klaus, 6–11
LaserPhoto, 162
Laurent, Lawrence, 55
Leach, Kathy, 234
Lee, Robert E., 18
Leonard, Bill, 200–201, 211–12
Levin, Gerald, 2, 58
Levin, Jerry, 124, 242
Lewis, Jerry, 66

Life (magazine), 51–52
lobbyists, FCC and, 122
locker rooms, at Progressive Club, 165
Los Angeles Times (newspaper), 211
Lucas, Bill
    Atlanta Braves and, 99, 129–30, 156
    on Turner, Ted, 95
Lundy, Ron, 14
Lurie, Bob, 98

MacArthur, Douglas, 51
Major League Baseball (MLB). *See also*
    Atlanta Braves
    expansion of, 85
    on UHF, 65
    wages for players, 92, 96
    World Series and, 86, 87, 97–98, 103
Marielitos (Cuban refugees), 222
Masked Superstar, 142
Massachusetts Institute of Technology
    (MIT), 139
Matthews, Gary, 98
Maxwell, Jane, 242
    CNN and, 162–71, 177, 205, 220
    legacy, 232
McClure, Cissy, 231
McClure, Jessica, 231–32, 236, 238–39
McClurkin, Lee, 31
McGuirk, Terry, 149, 154
McRae, Gordon, 198
Messersmith, Andy, 96
MGM, purchase of, 233
MGM film library, 79, 233, 237
Miller, Jonathan, 206
Minshew, Wayne, 85–86
"Miracle Painter," 66
Miss America beauty pageant, 47
MIT. *See* Massachusetts Institute of
    Technology
MLB. *See* Major League Baseball
Monroe, Marilyn, 42
Monsky, Mark, 157
Mormon Tabernacle Choir, 47
Morning Show (television show), 78
"Mouth of the South," 1, 88, 98, 104, 158.
    See also Turner, Ted
Movietone, 37–39, 40–42, 51
MSNBC, 242
MTV, 234
Muchmore, Marie, 52, 53
Mufax wire machine, 44
Murdoch, Rupert, 233–34
Murrow, Edward R., 36, 54, 117–18, 119, 225

Muse, Reynelda, 176, 204, *204*
"*My Way*," 33

Naegele, Bob, 27, 28–29
Nagle, Alexander Cooper III
    CNN and, 171–75, 178, 190, 191, 203, 205,
      220–21
    death of, 220–21
    Kavanau and, 171–74, 203, 220–21
    as mentor, 173–74, 190
    with news production, philosophy on, 173
    with staff hires at CNN, 175
    on Turner, Ted, 178
National Basketball Association (NBA),
    101–2
National Christian Network, 153
National League (NL), 96
National Press Club, 209, 225
National Public Radio (NPR), 120
National Sportscasters and Sportswriters
    Association, 104
Nazis, 6–7, 42, 211
NBA. *See* National Basketball Association
NBC
    affiliates, 18, 65, 155
    commercial sponsors on, 8
    programming on, 238, 239
    Telstar and, 45–46, 47
NBC News
    early years, 40–41
    with Elizabeth II, coronation of, 44
    Kennedy, John, assassination and, 50
    Today and, 44, 54, 78, 181
"Nearer My God to Thee," 160, 195, 196,
    196, 245
Netherlands, the, rescue missions in, 117
Network (film), 131
networks. *See also specific networks*
    affiliates, 18, 65, 155, 173
    with AT&T transmission bill, 41, 55, 56
    dominance of, 110
    failed, 55–56
    with news, 70, 70–71, 167, 218–19
    power of, 40–41, 42, 70, 83–84, 211
Neuharth, Al, 234
Newhart, Bob, 55
news. *See also* television news
    American Society of News Editors, 225
    FCC and, 79
    Internet, 242
    networks with, 70, 70–71, 167, 218–19
    Radio Television News Directors
      Association, 220

news (cont.)
  violence in, 113, 205–6
  WTCG, 68–70, 70, 72–79, 77
newscasters. *See also* reporters
  CNN and, 174–78
  wages for, 72, 76, 127, 132, 174
  women, 71–72, 155, 175–76, 204, 204
  WTCG, 68–70, 70, 72–79, 77
newspapers, 158–59. *See also specific news
    outlets*
newsreels, 37–42
Newsweek magazine, 137–38
New York *Daily News* (newspaper), 109
New York Mets, 92
New York Stock Exchange, 179
New York Times (newspaper), 3, 40, 120, 241
  speech at, 156–57, 158
New York Yacht Club, 92, 104
New York Yankees, 98
Nickelodeon, 135
Nix, Orville, 53
Nixon, Richard, 71, 119, 132, 170
NL. *See* National League
Novak, Robert, 131, 199
The Now Explosion (television show), 32
NPR. *See* National Public Radio
nuclear war, 195, 228, 235
Nye, Judy Gale, 25, 27, 30

Ochs, Adolph, 3
O'Gorman, Pat. *See* Schonfeld, Pat
Olympic Games (1936), 6–7
O.N. *See* Overmyer Network
Onyx C8000, 189
Orthodox Jews, 113–14
ostrich race, 97
Oswald, Lee Harvey, 53
Overmyer, Daniel, 54–56
Overmyer Network (O.N.), 55–56

Paar, Jack, 225
Paley, William, 149
Paramount Pictures, 7, 143
Party Ring, 67
Pauley, Jane, 181
pay television, 19–20, 31, 80
PBS, 210
People (magazine), 91
Pepper, Guy, 187, 202
Philadelphia Phillies, 47
philanthropy
  Fonda and, 3
  Turner, Ted, and, 3
Pickford, Mary, 157

Pike, Sid, 143
  WTCG and, 64, 66, 78–79, 104, 108
Pittsburgh Post-Gazette (newspaper), 10
Planet Hope, 33, 61, 84
Playgirl magazine, 197
popular culture
  television and, 38, 70
  televisions and, 10, 11–12
pornography, 103, 116, 147
Povich, Maury, 180
presidential bid, 103, 106, 195, 235
presidential debates, 209–10
Presley, Elvis, 3
press corps, 6, 48–49, 86, 213
Pressman, Gabe, 116, 157
Prime Time, 153
Progressive Club, 245
  CNN launch at, 193–206, 196
  under construction, 189
  Jews at, 140, 141, 232
  locker rooms at, 144, 165
  purchase price, 141, 141, 142
  YMCA at, 141
promotions, for Atlanta Braves fans,
    89–90, 95
publicity stunts, for Atlanta Braves, 91,
    97, 98

racism, 67
  against African Americans, 116, 155, 156,
    205
  anti-Semitism, 6, 18, 23, 104, 118, 164
  civil rights movement and, 85
  at Olympic Games (1936), 6–7
  Turner, Ted, and, 24, 156, 164
radiotelephone, 49
Radio Television News Directors
    Association, 220
Range, Peter Ross, 122, 235
Rather, Dan, 126–27, 131, 218
RCA, 150–56
Reagan, Nancy, 214, 232
Reagan, Ronald
  Castro and, 222, 225
  presidential debates and, 209–10
  at Republic convention, 212
  shooting of, 213–19
  unions and, 213
reality, television and, 120
Reinhardt, Burt
  Kavanau and, 191–92
  Kennedy, John, assassination and, 51–52,
    53
  at Paramount Pictures, 143

Schonfeld, "Reese," and, 238, 243
Schorr and, 244
with staff hires at CNN, 166, 174
in World War II as still photographer, 51
reporters
with employment clause, 134, 244
newscasters, 71–79, 77, 127, 174, 175–76
press corps, 6, 48–49, 86, 213
with source confidentiality, 119–20
video journalists and, 183, 186–88, 190,
190, 197
wages for, 120, 166
in White House Press Pool, 205, 216,
217–18
Republican convention, 212
rescue missions, in the Netherlands, 117
retyping pool, 192
Rex the Wonder Dog, 78
Reynolds, Frank, 215–17
Rhodes, Dusty, 142, 196
Rice, Jack M., Jr., 18–20, 31, 140
Rice Broadcasting, 19
Rivera, Geraldo, 180
Rockwell, George Lincoln, 42
Roddey, Jim, 33, 34
roller derby, 65
Rooney, Florence, 20–21, 22
Rose, Charlie, 180, 181
Rose, Pete, 88, 127
Rosenberg, Howard, 211
Ross, Diana, 245
Rothenberg, Fred, 181
The Rubaiyat of Omar Khayyam
(FitzGerald), 23
Ruby, Jack, 52–53
Russian Jews, 140
Rust, David, 239
Ruth, Babe, 85
Ruthven, Dick, 95

Sadler, Dick, 107
sailing, 30, 66, 105, 175
achievements, 29–30, 87
America's Cup and, 92, 98–99, 106,
107–8, 122, 126, 142, 194–95
awards, 26, 26, 195
Courageous and, 98–99, 107–8, 189
Cronkite and, 126, 131
Fastnet and, 146–50, 152, 194–95
salutes, CNN, 191, 209
Sanders, Will, 154–55
San Francisco Giants, 98
Sarasota Herald-Tribune (newspaper), 195
Satcom 3, 150–54, 159–60

Satellite News Channel, 234
satellites, 43
CNN, 193, 193, 202, 209, 222
C-SPAN, 150–51, 198–99
democratization of, 57–60
earth stations and, 58, 83–84, 87, 97, 100,
105–6, 135, 153–54
Japan and, 53
Satcom 3, 150–54, 159–60
Skylab, 78
Telstar, 45–48, 57
WTCG, 83–84
Sawyer, Forrest, 180
Schlafly, Phyllis, 199
Schonfeld, Maurice Wolfe "Reese"
career, early years, 39–42, 51, 54,
56–60, 82
CNN and, 124–27, 129–35, 137, 144, 148,
152–53, 155, 157, 159, 162–67, 170–72,
174–80, 183, 186–87, 191, 200–201,
204, 204, 208–10, 212, 217, 222, 225
at CNN launch, 194, 197–99
early years, 36–37
firing of, 236–38
ITNA and, 109–11, 117, 120, 129, 130–32,
142–43, 146, 160–61, 162
Kavanau and, 238
Kennedy, John, assassination and, 49, 51
legacy, 241
management style of, 208, 209
Reinhardt and, 238, 243
with satellites, democratization of, 57–60
at twentieth-anniversary party, 241–45
Schonfeld, Pat (O'Gorman, Pat)
at CBS News, 164
CNN and, 164, 167, 177, 179, 186, 199,
243, 245
as mentor, 186–87
Schlafly and, 199
at twentieth-anniversary party, 245
Schoonmaker, Jim, 187
Schorr, Daniel
with anti-Semitism, 118
career, 117–20, 131–35, 213
CBS News and, 117–20, 134
CNN and, 137–38, 148–50, 170, 176, 176,
210, 213, 218, 225
as diplomatic correspondence, 118–20
with employment clause, 134, 244
hiring of, 133–35
Netherlands rescue missions and, 117
reputation, 131–32, 137–38
satellites and, 209
Scientific Atlanta, 58, 83

Scorpio, 130
Seven Days Leave (television show), 66
Shakespeare, William, 42–43
Shales, Tom, 152, 206
Shaw, Bernard
  ABC News and, 176–77
  Gulf War and, 241
  with Reagan, Ronald, shooting of,
    213–16, 217, 218–19
  with Republican convention, 212
Shippy, Dick, 47
Shortal, Robert, 151–52
Showtime, 135, 153
Sieber, Bob, 194
Silver Chalice, The (television show), 66
Sinatra, Frank, 33
skits, with television news, 113–14
Skylab, 78
Smith, Howard K., 131
Smith, Jane Shirley, 30, 91, 96, 107, 197, 234
Smith, Merriman, 49
Smith, Sid, 47
Snyder, Tom, 149, 237
source confidentiality, 119–20
sponsors, commercials, 8, 64
sports. See also Atlanta Braves; sailing
  basketball, 65, 101–2
  boxing, 65
  hockey, 65, 98
  roller derby, 65
Stahl, Lesley, 1
Star Trek (television show), 72, 194
Stevenson, Adlai, 49
Sullivan, Ed, 224–25
Sullivan, Kathleen, 175
SuperStation, 141, 141–42
Swayze, John Cameron, 8
Symbionese Liberation Army, 71

"Take Me Out to the Ballgame," 93
Take Two (daily news program), 228–29
Taylor, Elizabeth, 181
technology
  Atlanta Braves with scoreboard, 93
  Basys Newsfury computer system, 189
  Handy-Looky, 71
  new, 43, 45–48, 80, 122
"Teddy Baseball," 93–94, 99. See also
  Turner, Ted
telegraph, 43
television. See also cable television
  CATV, 80
  color, 55
  pay, 19–20, 31, 80

popular culture and, 10, 11–12, 38, 70
power of, 195
production by AT&T, 7
Radio Television News Directors
  Association, 220
reality and, 120
with round-the-clock broadcasting,
  63–64
with technology, new, 43, 45–48
UHF, 18, 31, 32, 34, 54, 55, 56, 62–63, 65
VHF, 18
Television Factbook, 163
Television Food Network, 241
television news. See also cable television
  news
  AT&T and, 41
  early years, 7–11, 38–41
  historic, 50–51, 71
  Kennedy, John, assassination and, 49–53
  production, 7–11, 38–41, 71, 112–14, 118,
    127–28, 187–90, 190
  production, philosophy on, 173
  sensational, 11
  skits with, 113–14
  Telstar and, 45–48
  women in, 71–72, 155, 170–71, 175–76
  writing for, 39
Television News (TVN), Coors and, 56–57,
  109, 162
television sales, 9, 10, 11, 12, 80
Telstar, 45–48, 57
Tenacious, 146, 147–48, 150
Time, Inc., 58
Time-Life service, 153
Times Mirror Company, 9
Time Warner, 1, 2, 242, 243, 245
Titanic, 195, 235
TNT. See Turner Network Television
Today (morning news show), 44, 54, 78, 181
Topol, Sid, 58, 82, 83
Towriss, John, 184–86
transmission bills, AT&T, 41, 55, 56
Truman, Harry, 51
Turner, Ed "No Relation," 170, 222
Turner, Florence, 197–98
Turner, Mary Jean, 22–23, 25
Turner, Rhett, 30
Turner, Robert E., III, 20–21, 22, 24, 25–28,
  92, 224
Turner, Ted. See also Atlanta Braves
  Aaron and, 86, 88, 90, 90, 156
  Alexander the Great and, 23, 28, 89, 226
  anti-Semitism and, 104
  awards, 1–4, 26, 26

with baseball game loss, 105, *105*
as Captain Outrageous, 128, 134, 142, 165, 225–26, 235
Castro and, 222–30
childhood, 21–23
at CNN launch, 196, *196*, 200–202, 205–6
Coors on, 60
critics and, 94–95
education, 3, 23–25
frugality of, 76, 91, 94
Hitler and, 24, 33, 89, 102, 104, 224
Hope and, 89–90, 95, 99–100, 102
as leader, 178
as "Mouth of the South," 1, 88, 98, 104, 158
Nagle on, 178
personality and temperament, 24, 33, 63, 75, 93–94, 122, 148, 150, 154, 157, 235
philanthropy and, 3
racism and, 24, 156, 164
satellites and, 59–60, 105–6
support for, 85–86, 98
as "Teddy Baseball," 93–94, 99
with women, 75, 95–96, 106–7, 122, 133, 223, 226, 235
Turner Broadcasting System. *See* WTBS
Turner Network Television (TNT), 233
Turner Outdoor, 21, 25, 27–29, 33
Tush, Bill, 246
    as *Academy Award Theater* host, 68
    career, 13–17, 68, 244
    at CNN launch, 196–99
    fan mail for, 81–82
    as newscaster, 68–70, *70*, 73–79, 77
    WTBS and, 196, 226
    WTCG and, 16–17, 68–69, 70, 73–79, 77, 81–82, 101, 121, 136–38, 143
TV Guide, 121
TVN. *See* Television News
20th Century Fox, 6, 234
Twisdale, Harold, 33
twofer hiring, at CNN, 177

UFOs, 73, 90
Uggams, Leslie, 198
UHF, 18, 31, 32, 54
    audience, 34, 56
    FCC and, 18, 55
    MLB on, 65
    stations, 62–63
unions, 127, 175, 183, 213, 216
United Nations, 201, 243
United Press, 52

United Press International, 215
United Press–Movietone News, 37–39, 40–42
United States (US)
    Coast Guard, 24, 25, 76
    Congress, 209
the Unknown Newsman, 77, 137
UPI Newsfilm, 42, 49, 51, 54, 55–56
US. *See* United States

Variety, 206
Vaughan, Roger, 95
veejays. *See* video journalists
VHF, 18
video journalists (veejays), 197
    CNN College for, 187–ᵒ8, 190, *190*
    housing for, 186
    Kavanau and, 183–84, 186
    wages for, 183
video porta-paks, 189
Vietnam War, 69, 115, 119, 221
violence, in news, 113, 205–6
Von Hoffman, Nicholas, 219

WAGA, 17–18
wages
    for entry-level jobs, 184
    for MLB players, 92, 96
    for newscasters, 72, 76, 127, 132, 174
    for reporters, 120, 166
    for video journalists, 183
Walker, Dave, 177, 203–4
Wallace, Mike, 1
Waller, Jesse, 77–78
Walters, Barbara, 1, 72, 180, 227
Washington Post (newspaper), 40, 55, 152, 206
Waters, Lou, 187
WATL
    debut, 32
    sale of, 62–63
Watson, George, 212
WCTU, 33
Welch, Jack, 234
Welch, Raquel, 223
Welk, Lawrence, 7
Welles, Orson, 237
Welsh, Bill, 9–10, 11
Western Cable Show, 128, 150–51
Westin, Av, 118
Westinghouse, 154–55, 220, 234
Whirlpool Is the One (industrial musical), 181
White House, 209

White House Correspondents Association, 205

White House Press Pool, 205, 216, 217–18

Wickersham, Liz, 133, 226–27, 234, 235, 243

Williams, Beverly, 176

Williams, Christian, 34, 80–81

Williams, Dick, 206

Williams, Mary Alice, 175–76

Williams, R. T., 17, 34, 108

Winfrey, Oprah, 180

Witcover, Jules, 180, 182

Withers, John, 122

WJRJ, 18, 19–20, 31–32

WKLY, 184

WMBR (college radio station), 139

WNEW Channel 5, 112–16, 157

women
"family concept" and, 72
newscasters, 71–72, 155, 175–76, 204, 204
pornography and, 103, 116, 147
in television news, 71–72, 155, 170–71, 175–76, 204, 204
Turner, Ted, with, 75, 95–96, 106–7, 122, 133, 223, 226–27, 235

Woods, Dolores Roberts "Dee," 177–78

WOR, 153

World News Tonight, 177

World Series, 97–98
Atlanta Braves and, 86, 87, 103

World's Fair, 7, 46

World War II, 69
Jews in, 36
Reinhardt as still photographer in, 51

World Wide Web, 2

Woy, Bucky, 129, 130

WPIX, 109

wrestling, 65, 110

WRET, 69, 129
beg-a-thon at, 64–65, 79, 155
FCC and, 155
sale of, 135, 154–55, 156

Wrigley Field, Chicago, 47

writing
with Basys Newsfury computer system, 189
with "blame game drill-down," 208
for television news, 39

WSB, 65, 72

WTBS (college radio station), 139

WTBS (Turner Broadcasting System), 169, 202, 212
call letters, purchase of, 139
CNN and, 196, 210
critics of, 128
early years, 32, 139
with RCA lawsuit, 154
sale of, 1, 233, 242
as SuperStation, 141, 141–42
Tush and, 196, 226–27
as WTCG and name change, 139–40

WTCG Channel 17, 245–46. See also WTBS
advertisements, 61, 61, 63, 66–68, 152
Atlanta Braves and, 85, 87, 96
early years, 32–33, 61–68, 72–84
earth stations and, 83–84
FCC and, 81–82
growth of, 120–24, 136–40
news, 68–70, 70, 72–79, 77
Pike and, 64, 66, 78–79
programming, 65–66, 71–73, 110, 122–24
with round-the-clock broadcasting, 63–64
Tush and, 16–17, 68–69, 70, 73–79, 77, 81–82, 101, 121, 136–38, 143
viewer numbers, 100

"Yachtsman of the Year," at Fastnet, 194–95

Young Men's Christian Association (YMCA), 141

Zapruder, Abraham, 51–52

Zelman, Sam, 169–70, 172, 174–75, 180, 203, 212